proficiency

Gold

coursebook

Jacky Newbrook   Judith Wilson

D0318425

Contents

Exam information

Overview

The Cambridge Certificate of Proficiency in English consists of five papers:

Paper 1 **Reading Comprehension** (1 hour)
Paper 2 **Composition** (2 hours)
Paper 3 **Use of English** (2 hours)
Paper 4 **Listening Comprehension** (approx. 40 minutes)
Paper 5 **Interview** (approx. 15 minutes)

Each paper tests a different area of your ability in English. The overall grade is based on the total score in all five papers. There are three pass grades (ABC) and two fail grades (DE). Typically, grade C corresponds to 60% of the total marks.

Paper 1 Reading

The paper is divided into two sections:

Section A has 25 multiple-choice questions, which test specific areas of language, including collocations, fixed expressions, phrasal verbs and linking words. (See Exam Focus Unit 5, p. 73.)

Section B contains three texts, with a total of 15 multiple-choice questions that focus on understanding the main points and details of the text. Each text is authentic and is followed by four to six multiple-choice questions. One text is usually taken from a literary work or novel and the questions test understanding of character interaction as well as plot and narrative sequence. The other two texts are more factual or discursive and the questions may focus on theme, overall purpose of the text and the writer's attitude, as well as detailed comprehension. (See Exam Focus Unit 7, p. 94.)

Paper 2 Writing

In this paper you complete two writing tasks from a choice of five. No question is compulsory and each answer carries equal marks. You can choose from:

- a **description** (See examples in Writing sections of Units 1, 2 and 9 on pp. 17, 31 and 131.)
- a **discursive** composition (See examples in Writing sections of Units 7 and 11 on pp. 103 and 159.)
- a **narrative** (See examples in Writing sections of Units 3 and 8 on pp. 44 and 117.)
- a **task-directed** composition, which may be:
  - a **formal letter** (See examples in Writing sections of Units 4 and 5 on pp. 59 and 74.)
  - a **report** (See examples in Writing sections of Units 6 and 10 on pp. 89 and 144.)
  - an **article** (See examples in Writing sections of Units 12 and 13 on pp. 173 and 187.)

There is also a question on the optional set text. (See example in Writing section of Unit 14, on p. 198.)

You normally have to write about 350 words, although the task-directed composition is usually only 300 words.

Paper 3 Use of English

This paper is in two sections: **Section A** contains four separate exercises, and **Section B** contains a longer text with comprehension questions and a summary.

Section A
Question 1: This is an open cloze text. It consists of a text with 20 gaps which you must fill in with **one** appropriate word. The focus is primarily on grammatical patterns and collocations. You are penalised for incorrect spelling. (See Exam Focus Unit 1, p. 14.)

Question 2: This consists of eight separate sentence transformations. You are required to rewrite a given sentence so that your answer is as similar as possible in meaning to the original sentence. The focus is on grammar, but common expressions may also be tested. You may be penalised for incorrect spelling. (See Exam Focus Unit 11, p. 158.)

Question 3: This comprises six separate gapped sentences which you must complete with an appropriate word or phrase. The emphasis is on whole phrases rather than individual words. You may be penalised for incorrect spelling. (See Exam Focus Unit 12, p. 172.)

Question 4: This consists of eight separate 'key' word transformations. You must rewrite the sentence using a given word, without changing its form, so that your answer is similar in meaning to the original sentence. The focus is on grammatical and lexical patterns, and you need to be aware of synonymous and parallel expressions. You may be penalised for incorrect spelling. (See Exam Focus Unit 4, p. 52.)

Section B, Comprehension and summary

This task is based on a text of 550–650 words. It involves answering detailed comprehension questions and writing a paragraph to summarise specific information in a specified number of words.

The **comprehension questions** involve interpreting meaning and identifying the function of specific language in the text. Grammatical errors are not penalised unless they make your answer impossible to understand. (See Exam Focus Unit 10, p. 134.)

The **summary task** tests your ability to choose relevant information from a text and to present it clearly and coherently in a paragraph of a specified length. The summary should not be in note form and should be in a formal or neutral style. (See Exam Focus Unit 3, p. 28 and Unit 8, p. 114.)

Paper 4 Listening

This paper contains three or four parts, each with a recorded text. There are approximately 25–30 questions in total. The texts may be taken from announcements, radio broadcasts, public speeches, interviews, talks, lectures or meetings, and you may hear a variety of accents.

There is no standard format for the paper but certain task types occur regularly. These include:

- **Note-taking:** You have to note down specified points of information using a single word or phrase. Spelling must be correct. (See Exam Focus Unit 3, p. 40.)

- **Sentence completion**: You have to complete gaps in sentences with information from the text. These sentences may focus on abstract ideas or feelings as well as factual details. Most answers are short and must fit grammatically into the sentence. Spelling must be correct. (See Exam Focus Unit 9, p. 124.)

- **Multiple-choice questions:** This task may test your understanding of attitudes or opinions and feelings expressed by the speakers, as well as factual detail. (See Exam Focus Unit 6, p. 78.)

- **Three-way choice:** You hear a conversation between two or three speakers. You then have to answer questions which may involve deciding which of a series of statements reflects the views of which speaker, or which of two speakers holds a certain opinion and whether they agree. In these tasks you need to listen for the attitude of the speakers, which may be given through intonation or choice of expression. (See Unit 5, p. 68 and Unit 11, p. 154.)

Paper 5 The Interview

This paper consists of three parts. You will have a conversation with the examiner on different aspects of a theme. You are assessed throughout the interview on your fluency, grammatical accuracy, pronunciation, interactive communication and vocabulary. If you take the test in a pair or group of three, there will be two examiners, an interlocutor and an assessor.

Part 1: After a brief introduction, you are given one or more photographs and asked to talk about them. Approximate timings: 1 candidate, 5 minutes; 2 candidates, 7 minutes; 3 candidates, 10 minutes.

Part 2: You are given a short passage and asked where you think it comes from and how it relates to the theme of the discussion. Approximate timings: 1 candidate, 2 minutes; 2 candidates, 3 minutes; 3 candidates, 3 minutes.

Part 3: You are asked to take part in a communicative activity related to the theme, which may involve problem-solving, ranking, simulation, decision-making or discussion. Approximate timings: 1 candidate, 5 minutes; 2 candidates, 8 minutes; 3 candidates, 12 minutes.

(For help with all sections of the Interview, see Exam Focus Unit 13, p. 184.)

A friend in need

Speaking

1 Look at the photos. They show scenes from an extremely popular American TV programme, *Friends*.

1 Describe the situation in each picture. Which aspect of friendship do you think each picture shows?

- sharing problems
- sharing good times
- learning together
- reaching compromises

2 Why do you think programmes like this are so popular?

2 What do you think makes a good friend? Think of three qualities or characteristics that are especially important to you.

3 Which of the following statements about friends do you agree with? Explain why you don't agree with the other statements, and modify them until you can agree with them.

1 It's more important for friends to have similar characters than similar interests.
2 Frequent arguments are a bad sign in a friendship.
3 Friends will only stay friends if they meet frequently.
4 In many ways, friends are more important than family.
5 It's only possible to have one or two real friends.
6 A friend should be trustworthy – and that means they'll always tell you the truth.

4 Do you think that the nature of friendship remains the same throughout a person's life or does it change? Think about your own friendships now and in the past.

Listening: multiple-choice questions

1 You will hear a psychologist being interviewed about friendship. Before you listen, read through the statements and the options **A–C** below. Discuss which option you think is true for each statement and underline it.

1 From 3 to 5 years old, children
  A are happy to play alone.
  B prefer to be with their family.
  C have rather selfish relationships.

2 From age 5 to 8 or 10, children
  A change their friends more often.
  B decide who they want to be friends with.
  C admire people who don't keep to rules.

3 Between 8 and 10, children
  A develop a give-and-take relationship with friends.
  B want a wider variety of relationships.
  C begin to learn how to behave with older people.

4 Adolescents aged from 12 to 18
  A develop an interest in friends of the opposite sex.
  B choose friends with similar personalities to themselves.
  C want friends who are dependable.

5 Young adults
  A continue to have a circle of intimate friends.
  B find that shared interests are the main source of new friends.
  C find that the number of close friends declines.

6 Young married people
  A focus on their children.
  B lose touch with their friends.
  C make close friends less easily.

7 In middle age people generally prefer
  A to stay in touch with old friends.
  B to see younger friends more often.
  C to have friends who live nearby.

8 How do people regard their friends after retirement?
  A They do not want to be too responsible for their friends.
  B They tend to have closer relationships with family members than with friends.
  C They do not want to be too dependent on their friends.

2 Now listen to the recording and circle the most appropriate option, **A**, **B** or **C**, according to the information given by the psychologist. How far did your opinions match the psychologist's description?

3 **Vocabulary:** phrasal verbs
1 Read the following summary of the Listening text. Replace the verbs in italics with the phrasal verbs used by the speaker from the box below.

build up	carry on	fall off	give up
keep to	keep up	take on	turn to

Between the ages of 3 and 5, a child is unlikely to (1) *sacrifice* anything for a friend. After the age of 5 children co-operate more but they expect their friends to (2) *follow* certain rules. This stage will usually (3) *continue* until the child is aged between 8 and 10.

In adolescence, friendships with the same sex (4) *acquire* great importance. Young adults may initially (5) *maintain* close relationships with their friends. Later on, the number of friendships begins to (6) *decline*. In middle age, people (7) *develop* new friendships less easily. After retirement, people may begin to (8) *ask* their children for help.

2 What is the effect of using phrasal verbs instead of one-word verbs? Are phrasal verbs more likely to be used in spoken or written English?

> **Study Tip**
>
> A good knowledge of phrasal verbs and their neutral or more formal one-word equivalents is important, as they may be tested in the Proficiency exam. When you record new phrasal verbs in your vocabulary notebook, look up their equivalents in the dictionary and record those too. For example:
>
> *get together = meet*
> *Let's get together for coffee some time soon.*
> *I get together with my old schoolfriends once a month.*
>
> Can you think of your own examples?

Reading: newspaper article

In Section B of the Reading paper, questions may test your understanding of:

- stated information and details
- implication: unstated ideas
- the writer's purpose
- text structure.

The exercises in this section focus on these aspects of the text.

1 You are going to read a newspaper article about a woman called Gunilla Gerland. First, look at this extract from the cover of her autobiography and discuss the questions below.

> ' Unable to function like other people, she struggled in vain to fit in, to be recognised, despite her differences, as "a real person". No one seemed able to realise that she could not help being the way she was. '

1 What does 'to fit in' mean here?
2 What kind of things may prevent someone from fitting in as a child and as an adult?

2 Now read the article quickly to find answers to these questions.

1 What was the cause of Gunilla's problems?
2 When and how did she find out?
3 What effect did her discovery have on her?

3 Read the text again carefully and answer the following questions.

1 Autism is a medical condition in which a person fails to develop social skills. An autistic person appears to live in his or her own world and may display the following symptoms.

- severely limited physical abilities
- difficulty in coping with new experiences
- lack of outward response to people and actions
- difficulty in forming relationships with others

Underline any evidence you can find in the text for these symptoms.

2 How did Gunilla try to cope with her problems as a child?

Plight of the

1   Gunilla Gerland is 34 and has always brushed her teeth twice a day. But every time, she has to think about what she's doing. It has never become automatic – every contact with the toothbrush is like her first.

2   Gunilla is autistic, although this is hard to imagine when one starts talking to her. She writes, lectures, travels and has good friends. But her problems are there. "Skills that others take for granted, like brushing your teeth, will never come naturally to me. I would never be able to drive a car – I wouldn't even try to learn. And if I am speaking on the phone I find it very hard to understand the person if there is any noise in the background," she says.

3   She has many professional friends from the field of autism but relationships don't come easily either: "I need to feel appreciated and useful, though I'm not sure that I can distinguish between that and being loved. I don't think I need to actually feel loved."

4   It was only at the age of 29 that she was diagnosed. "I read a book in the library about autism and recognised myself in the descriptions. I contacted the professor of child psychiatry who had written the book and after tests, evaluations and looking back through my old school records I was diagnosed. In a way, it was a huge relief to me after all those years of knowing I was different without knowing why. I had always been labelled 'naughty', 'wayward' or 'difficult' and now it was as if my reputation was cleared. But the diagnosis also made me sad, because I spent my childhood desperately wanting to be the same as others and now I knew for sure that I wasn't."

5   Gunilla could not have been an easy child to cope with. She had a deep fear of new foods, which stopped her chewing anything. She

4 Find evidence in the text to support or disprove these statements.

1 Adults thought Gunilla's bad behaviour was deliberate.
2 As a child, Gunilla felt she was unfairly treated.
3 Today she is reconciled to her condition and accepts her limitations.

outsider

was thrown into panic by sudden noises. She had no memory for people, even familiar ones; when her father left home and later returned, she thought it was a new father. Starting playgroup, and later school, were terrifying experiences for her. She had no way of understanding that her mother would pick her up at the end of the day. She developed rituals and found small, enclosed hiding places to help her contain her panic.

She was bullied and exploited throughout her youth because of being different and also because of her inability to react to pain and misery in any outward way. At school, a group of older boys used to hit her every day. She never told anyone or reacted to the blows. Indeed, such was her need for routine that she would seek out the boys if a day went by and they forgot to hit her. She thought this was the way things had to be.

Her mother tried to console her when she was panicky or distraught, but she had no idea of the depths of Gunilla's despair: "It was like being consoled for having a graze on my nose when I had in fact broken both my legs."

Gunilla eventually left home at 16 and had a succession of lost jobs and failed relationships. Then, while she was randomly picking out books in the public library, she came across the description of autism that was eventually to answer the question of why she had always felt different. She now believes that autism is a biological condition, and has written a moving autobiographical account of her experiences that she hopes will help others. She doesn't want sympathy or any talk of her condition being "devastating". Instead, she wants what most people with a disability want: tolerance and some understanding of what makes her different. "I want to feel good about myself, that's all."

5   Do you think Gunilla wrote her autobiography

A   to gain sympathy for her plight?
B   to promote understanding of autistic people?
C   to promote understanding of all disabled people?

Find evidence in the text to support your view.

6   Why do you think the article you've just read was published?

7   The article gives an account of events in Gunilla's life, but they are not in chronological order. Look at the chart below and discuss the questions.

1   Decide what stage of Gunilla's life is described in each paragraph of the article. Then write the paragraph numbers 1–8 on the appropriate line A–E in the chart to show the order of the events described in the article. Some lines may have two or three paragraph numbers.

Gunilla's life:

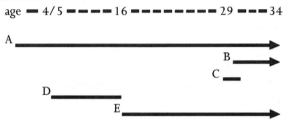

2   Why do you think the article has been organised in this way? Think about the target reader.

8   Discuss the following questions.

1   Which of Gunilla's qualities do you think are the most admirable?
2   Read the information about Gloria Estefan below. Can you think of anyone else – either a famous person, or someone you know personally – who has overcome difficulties and made a success of their lives? Explain how they have done this and what they have achieved.

When the singer Gloria Estefan broke her back in a tour-bus accident, many people feared her career was over. However, after a long and painful period of recuperation, she began a new world tour which was highly successful. Since then she has gone from strength to strength.

Grammar check: past tenses

1

1 Match the underlined verb forms in the following sentences to these tenses.

- Past simple
- Past perfect simple
- Past continuous
- Past perfect continuous

1 "I <u>had</u> always <u>been labelled</u> 'naughty', ... and now it was as if my reputation was cleared." (text, para. 4)

2 She <u>was bullied</u> and <u>exploited</u> throughout her youth ... (text, para. 6)

3 It was like being consoled for having a graze on my nose when I <u>had</u> in fact <u>broken</u> both my legs. (text, para. 7)

4 Then, while she <u>was</u> randomly <u>picking out</u> books in the library, she <u>came across</u> the description of autism ... (text, para. 8)

5 She <u>had been living</u> a life of quiet desperation until she found out why she was different.

2 Now decide which tense use is being defined in a)–e) below.

a) a completed single action at a specified time in the past

b) states, habitual and repeated actions in the past

c) an activity in progress when another past event happened

d) an activity completed before a specified time in the past

e) a continuing activity or series of activities during a period of time before an event in the past – emphasis is on the activity rather than on completion

3 Find two alternative ways of expressing habitual actions in the past in paragraph 6 of the text on page 9. Write the sentences here.

.... + infinitive, e.g.: ....

.... + infinitive, e.g.: ....

▶ Grammar reference p. 204

2 Some autistic people display great creative powers. The following text recounts an interview with the teacher of an autistic child called Stephen, who was an exceptionally gifted artist. Working with a partner, read the text and decide if the numbered verbs are in an appropriate tense or not. If not, correct them. Discuss and justify your decisions.

When Chris Marris, a young teacher, (1) *had come* to Queensmill in 1982, he (2) *was astonished* by Stephen's drawings. Marris (3) *was teaching* disabled children for nine years, but nothing he (4) *had ever seen* (5) *prepared* him for Stephen.

'I was amazed by this little boy, who (6) *was sitting* on his own in a corner of the room, drawing,' Chris told me. 'Stephen (7) *used to draw* and draw and draw; the school (8) *was calling* him "the drawer". And they were the most unchildlike drawings, like St Paul's and Tower Bridge, in tremendous detail, when other children his age (9) *drew* stick figures. It (10) *had been* the sophistication of his drawings, their mastery of line and perspective, that (11) *amazed* me – and these (12) *would be* all there when he was seven.'

S is for St Paul's Cathedral

T is for Tower Bridge

Stephen's London Alphabet, drawn when he was 10.

3

1 Divide into two groups. Students from **Group A** should complete the text on page 218 by filling in the gaps with the correct past tense form of the verbs given. Students from **Group B** should complete the text on page 222.

2 Now get together with a student from the other group and tell your completed story from memory.

Grammar check:
present perfect tenses

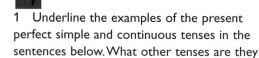

1 Underline the examples of the present perfect simple and continuous tenses in the sentences below. What other tenses are they combined with?

1 Gunilla Gerland is 34 and has always brushed her teeth twice a day.
2 She ... has written a moving autobiographical account of her experiences that she hopes will help others.
3 This is the first time I have heard of this illness.
4 I've never met anyone yet who I have admired more than my first teacher.
5 The new owners have made a lot of improvements since they have been here.
6 Ever since I heard about her, I've been trying to find her autobiography.
7 She's been living abroad since she got that job.

2 Now explain when we use the present perfect tenses.

3 Read the examples and answer the questions. Tick the correct sentence.

1 Which sentence refers to the past?
  a) I have been staying here for a week.
  b) I am staying here for a week.
2 Which activity is probably not completed?
  a) I've written a letter to the school this morning.
  b) I've been writing this letter since I got up this morning.
3 Your friend arrives an hour late. What do you say?
  a) I've been waiting for a whole hour!
  b) I've waited for a whole hour!
4 Your arm is in a sling. What does your friend ask you?
  a) What have you been doing to your arm?
  b) What have you done to your arm?

► Grammar reference p. 204

2 Read the following text. Then fill in the gaps with the correct form of the verbs in brackets.

Stephen King (1) .... (write) horror stories since he was seven years old but in his early years he (2) .... (have) little success. Throughout his twenties he (3) .... (work) as an English teacher during the day and (4) .... (spend) his free time writing. One day, in despair at receiving yet another publisher's rejection slip, he (5) .... (throw) away the manuscript of his latest novel. However, his wife (6) .... (retrieve) it from the rubbish and soon afterwards it (7) .... (finally publish). The book (8) .... (call) *Carrie*. It (9) .... (since sell) over 2.5 million copies and the film (10) .... (terrify) viewers ever since its release in 1976.

The undisputed king of literary and film horror, King (11) .... (make) a fortune through his writing but still (12) .... (live) simply with his family in the small American town where many of his novels (13) .... (set).

3 **Use of English:** sentence transformations
Finish each sentence so that it is as similar in meaning as possible to the one printed before it.

1 I started learning English when I was eight.
  I have ....
2 We last went to the theatre two years ago.
  We haven't ....
3 We haven't seen each other for a very long time.
  It's been ....
4 I have never seen her look this happy.
  This is ....
5 Stephen is the most amazing person I have ever met.
  I have ....
6 It's been two years since I stopped doing competitive sport.
  I gave ....
7 I got to know him ten years ago and I have never yet seen him get angry.
  In all ....
8 After doing that course, I started to feel much more self-confident.
  Since I ....

4 Practise using the tenses to find out about another student.

1 Complete these questions in your own way.

1 When was the first time you .... ?
2 How long has it been since you .... ?
3 When did you last .... ?
4 Who is the most .... person you have ever .... ?
5 What is the most .... thing that has ever happened to you?

2 Now ask another student your questions. Try to find out as many details as possible.

Vocabulary: multiple-choice questions

In Section A of the Reading paper you have to choose a word or phrase from a choice of four to fill in a gap in a sentence. The exercises in this section will help you to become aware of the types of vocabulary tested.
You will have more opportunities for practice in later units of this book.

Note: These areas may also be tested in other parts of the exam such as Paper 3, Questions 1-4.

1 Collocations and fixed expressions

This is one of the most important areas of vocabulary tested. Read the information, then do the exercise that follows.

> Collocations are words which are frequently found together. Words that don't collocate are rarely or never found together. For example:
>
> *The students **sat/took/did** their examination.* ✓
> *The students **revised for/passed/failed** their examination.* ✓
> *The students ~~made/followed/tried~~ their examination.* ✗
>
> Collocations may consist of
> verb + noun   e.g. take an exam
> adjective + noun   e.g. a huge relief
> verb + adverb   e.g. admire enormously
> adverb + adjective   e.g. highly successful
> noun + noun   e.g. management trainee
>
> In 'open' collocations, we can choose from a restricted set of words that mean the same thing, as in Example 1 above. In 'fixed' collocations (fixed expressions), particular words always go together and the combination has a special meaning. Other words cannot be substituted. For example:
>
> *People were walking **to and back** across the square.* ✗
> *People were walking **to and fro** across the square.* ✓
>
> **Idioms** are a type of fixed expression in which the meaning of the whole expression cannot be worked out from the meanings of each separate word. For example:
>
> *I was really lucky – the exam was **a piece of cake!*** ✓

Choose the word or phrase which best completes each sentence. Then decide which type of collocation each combination is.

1 I'm going to .... a big party for Ella's birthday this summer.
   A make   **B** do   **C** throw   **D** run

2 The two men were having a .... argument.
   A heated   **B** strong   **C** grave   **D** heavy

3 I managed to pass my driving test first time, but it was a .... thing.
   A thin   **B** close   **C** fine   **D** narrow

4 You're just .... your head against a brick wall – you might as well give up now.
   A putting   **B** hitting   **C** breaking   **D** banging

2 Words with similar meanings or forms

Here, you have to think about very precise distinctions in meaning. Read the following information, then do the exercise below.

> Many words that have the same general meaning cannot be used interchangeably, either because they don't mean exactly the same thing, they don't have the same connotation (associations) or they belong to a different register. For example, *stride, stroll, trudge* and *shuffle* all mean WALK, but they have slightly different meanings. Which word would you use in these sentences?
> 1 Tom .... along the street at a leisurely pace.
> 2 I .... up the hill, laden down by my bags of shopping.
> 3 James turned on his heel and .... off angrily.

Choose the word or phrase which best completes each sentence.

1 The doctor gave her some tablets to .... the pain.
   A erode   **B** mitigate   **C** alleviate   **D** dilute

2 Local residents have complained about the music constantly .... from the disco.
   A blaring   **B** roaring   **C** booming   **D** thundering

3 The different uses of this structure .... so that it's sometimes difficult to distinguish them.
   A overlay   **B** overlap   **C** override   **D** overflow

4 The vase I wanted was not .... so the shop assistant had to fetch it from the store room.
   A in view   **B** on sight   **C** in appearance   **D** on display

3   Words with special grammatical patterns

This group contains words which must be used with a particular structure or preposition.

Choose the word or phrase which best completes each sentence, using the hints to help you.

1   I've always been very .... of my grandmother.
A close   B fond   C affectionate   D attached
(HINT: *Which preposition - of, to, towards - follows each adjective?*)

2   His comments about our project ....
me thinking.
A made   B began   C got   D encouraged
(HINT: *Which of the four words A-D fits which of the following patterns?*)
1 .... me think   3 .... to make me think
2 .... me to think   4 .... me thinking

4   Connectors and adverbial phrases

You are more likely to be tested on phrases than on single words. Read the following information, then do the exercise below.

'Connectors' are linking expressions that signal meaning relations between sentences or clauses in written or spoken English. For example:

Time sequence: when, while, as soon as, just as; then, after that
Cause and result: because, as; as a result, therefore, thereby, accordingly
Contrast/concession: although, while; nevertheless, by contrast, instead
Explaining/reformulating: for example/instance, namely, in other words, that's to say

Another type of adverbial phrase may be used to indicate the attitude of the writer or speaker to what he/she is saying. For example:

Manner of speaking: personally, honestly
Commenting on likelihood: clearly, surely, in fact
Indicating own reaction: annoyingly, surprisingly, oddly enough etc.

▶ Writing reference p. 216

Choose the word or phrase which best completes each sentence.

1   He became a citizen recently, ... gaining the right to vote.
A as to   B so as   C thereby   D whereby

2   She said that .... she usually enjoyed skiing, she didn't feel fit enough to go that year.
A despite   B notwithstanding   C however   D while

3   He said I was definitely the best candidate for the post – .... , I've got the job!
A in other words   B namely   C for example   D further

4   I don't think there's much chance of her winning the match, ... , although she's trained hard.
A literally   B frankly   C doubtless   D indeed

5   Phrasal verbs

You may have to choose the correct phrasal verb for a particular context, or select either the correct verb or particle.

Choose the word or phrase which best completes each sentence below.

1   The girl managed to .... a conversation while doing her homework.
A carry out   B keep up   C make out   D go on

2   The bedspread was .... up of hundreds of small squares of material sewn together.
A formed   B done   C taken   D made

3   After the walk I finished .... with aching feet and a streaming cold.
A off   B out   C up   D in

6   Now try this exercise, which tests all five areas of vocabulary. The correct answers are all words and expressions you have heard or read in this unit.

Choose the word or phrase which best completes each sentence.

1   I would like to .... a warm welcome to our special guest.
A dedicate   B make   C extend   D present

2   Children become more .... of the needs of others as they grow older.
A aware   B sensitive   C open   D recognising

3   The results were generally positive; .... , many people said they had benefited from taking part.
A interestingly   B interested   C in interest   D for interest

4   The children all .... on the project.
A united   B collaborated   C integrated   D merged

5   That day I'd really been in the .... of despair, but then I heard some wonderful news.
A pits   B abysses   C valleys   D depths

6   Tom and Peter were always falling .... when they were younger but now they're good friends.
A through   B off   C to   D out

Exam Focus

Paper 3 Use of English (cloze)

In Question 1 of Paper 3 you read a text with 20 gaps. **One** word is needed to fill each gap. The main emphasis is on structure. You need to think about:

- **word combinations** such as collocations, fixed phrases and phrasal verbs
- **structural items** such as auxiliary verbs, prepositions, pronouns and articles
- **conjunctions and link words** such as *despite/unless/but*.

Some gaps may require a **vocabulary** item where the choice depends only on meaning, with no grammatical clues supplied. In this case, think about the meaning of the passage as a whole, and look for clues to meaning such as opposites, examples and synonyms.

1 To do a cloze successfully, it's essential to understand what it's about. Read through the whole of the text opposite, ignoring the gaps for the moment, and choose the best summary.

A Parents and adolescents argue mainly over everyday matters, and these arguments seem to change very little.

B Parents and adolescents have always argued over small things, but now these arguments are becoming more serious.

2 In the first paragraph the words tested have been supplied. To help you identify what is being tested, match each of the following hints to one of the words 1–10 in the text.

a) part of a phrasal verb ....*10*.....
b) part of an expression used to introduce an example ....
c) a preposition which follows an adjective ....
d) a preposition meaning *about* ....
e) a negative ....
f) a form of the verb often used in the expression *to ... a discovery* ....
g) vocabulary – a noun which is central to the topic ....
h) a conjunction meaning *taking the circumstances into account* ....
i) an auxiliary verb ....
j) vocabulary – this word follows *much*, so must be a singular noun (*it has already been mentioned*) ....

3 Read the second paragraph and fill in the answers that are immediately obvious. Don't spend time thinking about difficult items. Don't fill in anything you're not sure of at this stage, because you need to keep an open mind when you look back at the gap.

Causes of conflict between adolescents and their parents

The relationship between adolescents and their parents is sometimes stressful, and some interesting discoveries have been (1) *made* by psychologists studying the nature of this conflict. One notable feature is that they seldom argue about such major topics (2) *as* sex, drugs, religion or politics. This is surprising (3) *given* that great differences often exist between the attitudes of parents and adolescents (4) *on* such issues. Researchers speculate that these differences may not lead to much (5) *conflict* because they (6) *do* not affect many day-to-day interactions among family members. It appears that what is not directly relevant (7) *to* family life is (8) *not* discussed. Instead, (9) *parents* and their adolescent children tend to (10) *fall* out over everyday family matters like jobs in the house and disagreements over siblings.

Despite the many changes that have (11) .... place over the past fifty years, adolescents appear to have the (12) .... kinds of arguments with their parents as their parents had (13) .... they themselves were young. It seems to come (14) .... to the conflict between the adolescent's desire for independence (15) .... the parents' authority. Teenagers emphasised their right to be (16) .... of restrictions, while parents were equally (17) .... of their right to exert control, backing this up (18) .... referring to the needs of the family as (19) .... whole. Interestingly, both groups could see the other's (20) .... of view even though they disagreed with it.

4   Look through the text again and use the hints below to help you with the more difficult items.

11   part of a collocation meaning *occur*
12   part of a comparison with *as*
13   a conjunction
14   part of a phrasal verb
15   part of the structure *the conflict between (something) … (something)*
16   an adjective related to a noun that occurred earlier
17   an adjective followed by the dependent preposition *of*
18   a preposition
19   part of an expression meaning *altogether*
20   a fixed expression: *to see someone's … of view*

5   Read the text again and check that:

- the words you have added make sense in the passage as a whole, especially in terms of positive and negative words
- you haven't made any mistakes with tenses, singular and plural forms or noun/verb agreement
- you haven't made any spelling mistakes.

Exam Strategy

Remember, whenever you do a cloze you should follow these four stages.
1   Read the passage for general understanding.
2   Read it again and fill in **only** the answers that are immediately obvious.
3   Go back and work out the remaining answers.
4   Read it once more to check accuracy and ensure that the completed text makes sense.

6   Discuss the following questions.

1   Do you think the text is right about what causes arguments between parents and children nowadays?
2   Do you think your parents argued about similar things when they were young?

Speaking: passages

In Paper 5 you have to talk briefly about the content and style of a short passage. The text may be formal or informal, and it may be typical of spoken or written English. The passages in this section are all informal texts that were originally spoken.

1   Read text A and discuss the questions below with a partner.

1   Who's talking?
2   What's the situation and why is it a problem?
3   What advice would you give the speaker?

A

Whatever can I do? … everything's ready, the food's ready, the guests are on their way. I'd be letting so many people down – my family, his family, and above all him. However will he feel? It's not that I don't love him … but I just don't feel sure any more, and looking at my dress hanging there, I really can't imagine wearing it tomorrow. There's still time to say no – isn't there?

B

I've got to make up my mind about this summer … my brother's promised to pay for me to go and stay with him and his family in Miami, but my grandmother's expecting me to stay with her because I've been there every summer since I was little, and all my friends will be there. My parents want me to do a language course in England … I can't win. whatever I do I'll offend someone.

C

I've been thinking about it all night – I can't decide whether to say anything to her or not. She trusts me but if I tell her she'll be upset and she'll blame me … if I don't tell her she's going to get hurt in the long run. I wish I'd never found out about it …

2   Work with a partner. **Student A** should talk for about a minute about text B, answering the questions in Exercise 1. **Student B** should then talk about text C.

3   Compare your answers with the rest of the class. How similar or different is the advice you gave?

Grammar check: *as* and *like*

1 *as* versus *like*

Fill in the gaps in the following sentences with *as* or *like*. In which sentences do they function a) as prepositions b) as conjunctions introducing a new clause?

1 My mother practised .... a doctor until she retired.
2 She seems to me .... a very nice person.
3 Let's treat this .... our little secret.
4 I don't feel much .... going to work today.
5 He used the meeting .... an opportunity to promote his products.
6 He gave a very good speech, ... we had expected.
7 When I met him, he was nothing .... what I expected him to be.
8 I'd love to have a job .... yours.
9 I wish I could sing .... she does.
10 They live .... people did 200 years ago.

▶ Grammar reference p. 204

2 *like* and *such as*

1 Complete the following sentences with ideas of your own. Decide which pattern is more formal.

1 There have been a lot of good American programmes on TV, *like/such as* ... and ...
2 *Such* famous people *as* .... and ... have changed the course of history.

2 Rewrite the extract below to include the examples in brackets. Use *like, such as* and *such ... as*.

Household items (e.g. fridges, washing machines) were unheard of in Chiole's village in those days. Even the basic necessities of life (e.g. water, fuel) were hard to come by. But they still celebrated special occasions (e.g. births, weddings) with special food, music and dancing.

3 Verbs followed by *as*

Replace the verbs in italics in the following sentences with an appropriate verb from the box, plus *as*, and make any changes necessary. Use each verb once only. There are some verbs you won't need to use.

class	define	denounce	describe	dismiss	expose
perceive	rate	regard	recognise	think of	

1 Gunilla's teachers *thought* she was a problem child.
2 Adolescents often *say* that their parents are old-fashioned.
3 *I'd say* this film was the worst I've ever seen.

4 Many people *think* Shakespeare is the greatest playwright who ever lived.
5 We now *consider* the car to be a necessity rather than a luxury.
6 When at school, Winston Churchill was *thought* to be a failure in academic terms.
7 I suppose he could be *called* an old family friend.
8 After deceiving everyone for many years, he was finally *shown up* to be an impostor.

4 Answer the following questions individually. Then ask a partner the questions. Compare and explain your answers.

1 Would you describe the following activities as foolish or heroic?
   A climbing Mount Everest
   B bungee jumping
   C taking part in a manned space mission to Mars
   D your own idea

2 Who do you regard as the greatest novelist (playwright/poet/actor/singer) of your country? Why?

3 Who do you consider to be the most important figure of the 20th century?
   A Mother Teresa
   B Marie Curie
   C Bill Gates
   D your own idea

4 What would you rate as the most exciting discovery ever made?
   A DNA
   B the tomb of Tutankhamun
   C the mountain gorillas of Rwanda
   D your own idea

5 What do you see as the greatest threat to mankind in the 21st century?
   A UFOs
   B pollution
   C genetically modified foods
   D your own idea

Writing: descriptive composition (1)

In Paper 2 you have to write two compositions from a choice of five. One of the topics is a descriptive composition.

1 Read this writing task. How many parts does it have?

> Write a description of a person you admire, explaining why you admire them. (About 350 words.)

For this task, you could write about someone you know personally or a public figure. If you choose a public figure, be sure you know enough about them to write a composition.

To start you thinking about the topic, discuss the questions below with a partner.

1 Who do you know enough about to write a composition?
2 Do you admire this person because of what they do or the kind of person they are?
3 What qualities do you most admire in them?
4 Have they overcome any difficulties?
5 Do they help other people?
6 What examples can you think of that provide specific evidence for your answers?

2 Read the following composition, which was written in answer to the task.

1 Note down answers to these questions.

1 Who did the writer choose to describe and why?
2 What do you learn about this person's character and achievements?

*I have always liked reading about adventure and exploration, although I am not a very brave person myself. I have always felt that people who attempt to push back the frontiers of knowledge or who put their own lives in danger for others should be admired. In my opinion, a good example of **this** kind of person is the American astronaut, John Glenn.*

*<u>Throughout **his** early life</u> Glenn constantly looked for new challenges. He proved his courage and adventurous spirit <u>in 1962</u>, when he became the first American to orbit the earth. At **that** time, **this** was a major technological breakthrough and his achievement made him world-famous. <u>After</u> that spectacular trip into space, it could have been difficult for him to settle back into the routine of normal life, and indeed other astronauts who followed him into space had psychological problems later. <u>But</u> admirably, he <u>then</u> set about carving a new career for himself in politics. He became a well-respected and popular senator and made an important contribution to American politics.*

***This** in itself was an achievement that most people would have been proud of, but even then Glenn didn't rest on his laurels. <u>Instead, after</u> reaching the top in two separate professions, he decided that he wanted to go back into space to help with medical research into the process of ageing. **This** would have been a major undertaking for most people at any age, but Glenn did it at 77, an age when most people just want to sit back and relax. Not surprisingly, there was considerable opposition to his plan, as many people felt that **it** would put too much strain on him. <u>However,</u> throughout his political career he had kept himself fit and was therefore ready to undertake this final challenge.*

<u>Overall,</u> I think that I most admire Glenn's spirit and optimism. He has achieved more in his lifetime than most people ever dream of, and he has <u>also</u> set a wonderful example to others, <u>not only</u> of his own generation <u>but also</u> of mine.

2 Answer these questions about the composition.

1 How many paragraphs does the composition have?
2 What is each paragraph about? Underline the sentence that tells you. This is the 'topic sentence'.
3 What is the purpose of the first and last paragraphs? What tenses are used? Why?
4 What is the purpose of the second and third paragraphs? What tenses are used? Why?

3 Complete the following outline, which illustrates the structure of the sample composition. Use notes rather than full sentences.

Introduction
Opening comments (why the topic is important to the writer):
I have always liked ....
Statement of topic: *A good example of this kind of person is* ....

First supporting paragraph
Topic sentence: *Throughout his early life Glenn constantly looked for new challenges.*
Supporting details:
1 ....
2 *carved new career as US senator – made important contribution to American politics*

Second supporting paragraph
Topic sentence: *Even then* ....
Supporting details:
1 ....
2 ....
3 *ignored opposition – had kept himself fit*

Closing paragraph
1 *most admirable qualities = his spirit and optimism*
2 ....

4 A piece of writing needs to be organised so that it is easy for the reader to follow the development of the writer's ideas. This can be done by using:

- a clear method of development, e.g. chronological order
- reference pronouns such as *he*, *they*, *this* etc. to refer to ideas already mentioned
- linking expressions which indicate the relationship between ideas.

1 Decide what the pronouns in bold in the sample composition refer back to. They may refer to a single word, or a whole idea. They may refer to something stated in the previous sentence or an idea in the previous paragraph.

2 Group the underlined linking expressions in the composition into the appropriate category below.

Time sequence   Contrast   Summarising   Addition

3 Circle ways in which the writer introduces his/her opinion.

5 Read the following writing task. How many parts are there?

Describe a person who has influenced your life, giving reasons for your choice. (About 350 words.)

6 Here are some questions to start you thinking about the topic. You may find it helpful to jot down some notes.

1 Who will you write about? Is it someone you still have a close relationship with today?
2 In what way(s) has this person influenced you? What effect have his/her actions had on you? Think about your personality, career, etc.
3 What did he/she actually do to influence you? Think of some specific actions, events, episodes.
4 How did you feel about it at the time? How do you feel about it now?

7 Using the model in Exercise 3 to guide you, prepare your own outline to the task.

Introduction:
Introduce the person who has influenced you and explain in what way they have done so.
Supporting paragraphs:
Give specific examples of what the person did to bring this about.
Closing paragraph:
Summarise your feelings about this person and the reasons for them.

8 Now write your composition. Make sure you use linking expressions to connect your ideas within and between paragraphs.

9 Exchange your composition with a partner. Evaluate each other's work and suggest improvements. Use the checklist on page 217.

10 Write an improved version of your composition.

Exam Strategy

When you write a composition, planning in advance will save you a lot of time. For success in composition writing, get into the habit of writing an outline before you start. You can use the outline in this section as a model to guide you.

1 Match the two halves of each sentence in the following story.

1 I've been clearing up our flat
2 We'd invited a friend of my brother's to supper
3 He's easily the most inconsiderate person
4 He arrived an hour too early
5 He was lying on the sofa with his boots on
6 He took dozens of CDs off the shelves
7 He stayed

a) only minutes after he'd arrived.
b) I've ever met.
c) ever since I got up this morning.
d) because he didn't seem to know anyone.
e) until he'd finished all the food and drink we had.
f) so we hadn't finished preparing things.
g) and left them on the floor.

2 Choose the word or phrase which best completes each sentence.

1 I had several American friends as a child, but I've lost touch .... most of them.
A with B of C from D to

2 The students' efforts to find better accommodation have been in ....
A failure B despair C vain D loss

3 Her latest novel is .... in Europe, unlike her previous ones.
A placed B laid C put D set

4 There has been a decline .... the number of opportunities for graduates over recent years.
A to B of C in D on

5 It's tough having to .... with a full-time job when you are trying to study as well.
A cope B manage C run D handle

6 My leg injury means that my mobility will be .... limited for a few weeks.
A strongly B closely C tightly D severely

7 The film gives a moving .... of the great writer's early struggles for recognition.
A account B story C narrative D tale

8 It's extraordinary how rapidly words can .... a new meaning.
A bear out B turn to C take on D bring up

3 Finish each of the following sentences in such a way that it is as similar as possible in meaning to the sentence printed before it.

1 Although we have arguments occasionally, my parents and I get on well most of the time.
Despite ....

2 My friends helped me to clean the house up before my parents got home.
By the time ....

3 Emma hasn't said anything to her father about wanting to have a party for several days.
It's been ....

4 The last time you did the ironing was during the summer holidays.
You haven't ....

5 Sarah and Paul hadn't considered the matter seriously before discussing it with their families.
Until they ....

6 We were able to move to a larger house because my father was promoted.
As a result ....

7 There's been a great improvement in Hannah's relationship with her sister since she started college.
Hannah's relationship with her sister ....

8 That is the most outrageous suggestion I've ever heard!
I've ....

4 Talk about the photo.

1 Describe the photo and the situation.
2 How does it relate to the topic of the unit?
3 How important are these kinds of celebration in your culture? How important are they to you personally?

Learning for life

Speaking

1 Which of the following features do you associate with a) a traditional approach to education b) a more 'progressive' approach?

- written examinations
- individual assignments
- choice of subjects
- questioning ideas
- streaming

- continuous assessment
- collaborative activities
- fixed curriculum
- rote learning
- mixed-ability classes

Which have been features of schools you have attended?

2 The following extracts from job advertisements mention qualities which are often required in the modern working environment. Which qualities do you think are developed by schools? Which are not developed? Which of the features listed in Exercise 1 are most likely to encourage these qualities?

must be self-motivated and able to work independently

should possess well-developed leadership and communication skills

understanding of and empathy with other cultures

you will be a reliable team player with sound commercial judgement

excellent time management skills and attention to detail

good analytical ability is essential for success in this role

Reading: non-fiction

1 The following text is taken from a book by Charles Handy, an educator with many years' experience in business and public services, who has written extensively on the role of business in modern society. In this extract he evaluates how useful his own education was as a preparation for the world of work.

A PROPER EDUCATION

1 I left school and university with my head packed full of knowledge; enough of it, anyway, to pass all the examinations that were put in my path. As a well-educated man I rather expected my work to be a piece of cake, something at which my intellect would allow me to excel without undue effort. It came as something of a shock, therefore, to encounter the world outside for the first time, and to realize that I was woefully ill-equipped, not only for the necessary business of earning a living, but, more importantly, for coping with all the new decisions which came my way, in both life and work. My first employers put it rather well: 'You have a well-trained but empty mind,' they told me, 'which we will now try to fill with something useful, but don't imagine that you will be of any real value to us for the first ten years.'

2 A well-trained mind is not to be sneezed at, but I was soon to discover that my mind had been trained to deal with closed problems, whereas most of what I now had to deal with were open-ended problems. 'What is the cost of sales?' is a closed problem, one with a right or a wrong answer. 'What should we do about it?' is an open problem, one with any number of possible answers. Trained in analysis, I had no experience of taking decisions which might or might not turn out to be good. Knowing the right answer to a question, I came to realize, was not the same as making a difference to a situation, which was what I was supposed to be paid for. Worst of all, the real open-ended question — 'What is all this in aid of?' was beginning to nudge at my mind.

3 I had been educated in an individualist culture. My scores were mine. No one else came into it, except as competitors in some imagined race. I was on my own in the learning game at

Read the first and last paragraphs quickly to find out whether the writer thinks his education was a help or a hindrance to him when he started work.

school and university. Not so in my work, I soon realized. Nothing there happened unless other people cooperated. Being an individual star would not help me if it was in a failing group. A group failure brought me down along with the group. Our destinies were linked, which meant that my co-workers were now colleagues, not competitors. Teams were something I had encountered on the sports field, not in the classroom. They were in the box marked 'fun' in my mind, not the one marked 'work' or even 'life'. My new challenge, I discovered, was to merge these three boxes. I had discovered, rather later than most, the necessity of others. It was the start of my real education.

'So you're a university graduate are you?' said my new Sales Manager. 'In classics, is it? I don't think that is going to impress our Chinese salesmen! How do you propose to win their respect since you will be in charge of some of them very shortly?' Another open-ended problem! I had never before been thrust among people very different from me, with different values and assumptions about the way the world worked, or should work. I had not even met anyone more than two years older, except for relatives and teachers. Cultural exploration was a process unknown to me, and I was not accustomed to being regarded as stupid and ignorant, which I undoubtedly was, in all the things that mattered in their world.

My education, I decided then, had been positively disabling. So much of the content of what I had learned was irrelevant, while the process of learning it had cultivated a set of attitudes and behaviours which were directly opposed to what seemed to be needed in real life. Although I had studied philosophy I hadn't applied it to myself. I had assumed that the point of life was obvious: to get on, get rich, get a wife and get a family. It was beginning to be clear that life wasn't as simple as that. What I believed in, what I thought was worth working for, and with whom, these things were becoming important. So was my worry about what I personally could contribute that might not only earn me money but also make a useful contribution somewhere.

2 In the Reading paper, you have to answer multiple-choice questions on different types of text. The questions can be about:

- the main idea of the text
- details that support the main idea or give background information
- the purpose of the text and the writer's message
- the attitude of the writer.

Answer the following questions, which focus on the way Handy develops his ideas through the text and how he supports his final conclusion with evidence and examples.

Paragraph 1

1 Which is the best summary of paragraph 1?
   A Because of his background, the writer expected to succeed in business without trying very hard.
   B The writer discovered his education had not prepared him well for life after school and university.
2 Underline the sentence which helped you to decide on the answer. This is the topic sentence.

Paragraph 2

3 What kind of decisions had Handy's schooling taught him to make?
4 What kind of decisions did he have to make in his work?
5 What did he realise about what was expected of him at work?
6 Underline the topic sentence of the paragraph.

Paragraph 3

7 What attitude to other people had been encouraged by his education?
8 Why was this attitude not helpful in his working life?
9 Which sentences express the main idea?

Paragraph 4

10 What kind of people had Handy mixed with before leaving university?
11 Why was this a problem for him in his work?
12 Underline the main idea in this paragraph.

Paragraph 5

13 Does Handy decide that a traditional education is
   A a good preparation for life?
   B insufficient preparation for life?
   C a definite disadvantage in life?
   Underline the sentence that tells you.
14 What two key reasons does he give in this paragraph to support this conclusion?

3 Find the following expressions in the text and use the context to work out what they mean. Underline the words that helped you.

1 a piece of cake (para. 1)
(CLUE: *expression with similar meaning follows it*)
2 encounter (vb.) (paras.1/3)
(CLUE: *check both uses of the word*)
3 a closed problem/an open problem (para. 2)
(CLUE: *explanations supplied in the text*)
4 come into it (para. 3)
(CLUES: *parallel expression; contrast*)
5 disabling (para. 5)
(CLUE: *word formation*)

4 Now see how quickly you can answer the multiple-choice questions below. Choose the best option, **A, B, C** or **D**.

1 When the writer left university he expected to succeed
  A without needing to try very hard.
  B by excelling intellectually.
  C by knowing everything necessary.
  D by making important decisions.
  (*background information*)

2 He found that he needed to re-evaluate his approach because
  A his employers thought he was too vague.
  B he had been trained to deal with problems in the wrong way.
  C he met new kinds of problems in his working life.
  D he wanted each decision to make a difference.
  (*detail supporting main idea*)

3 Which discovery caused the biggest change in his attitude?
  A He was not good at cooperating with others.
  B He could not help a group that was failing.

C He could not work if he was not having fun.
D He needed to work as part of a group.
(*detail supporting main idea*)

4 He realised that he lacked understanding of other cultures
  A when he had to work in China.
  B when he lost the respect of his Chinese employees.
  C when he had to work with people who had different values.
  D when he found out that other people looked down on his own culture.
(*background information*)

5 What was Charles' conclusion about his education?
  A It had taught him to value money too much.
  B It had helped him to make a useful contribution to society.
  C It had done him more harm than good.
  D It had taught him that life was not simple.
(*main idea*)

5 How do you think Charles' education could have prepared him more effectively for his working life? Using information from the text, discuss whether and to what extent the following suggestions would have helped him. Give reasons for your decisions.

- more vocational or practical subjects (*give examples*)
- compulsory involvement in team sports
- school trips and exchange visits to other countries
- more cross-curricular projects
- work experience placements

Can you add any more suggestions to the list?

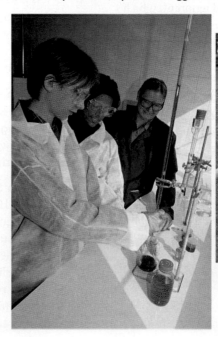

Vocabulary: style and register

Like much written English, the text on pages 20-21 contains a mixture of formal and semi-formal or even informal language. The following exercises will help you to distinguish between these types of language.

1 The following sentences are written in neutral language. Re-express them using a phrase from the text on pages 20-21 to replace the words in italics. Which of the expressions from the text are typical of formal or semi-formal language? Which are informal or idiomatic?

1 He therefore felt that starting work would be *very easy for him.*
2 He thought that he would succeed in business without *needing to work hard.*
3 The hard reality of the business world was *quite a surprise to him.*
4 He realised that he was *not adequately trained* for the demands of the business world.
5 He still felt that a well-trained mind *shouldn't be dismissed,* but that it was not enough for the world of work.
6 He had been trained specifically to deal with closed problems *but* now he needed to solve open-ended problems.
7 He felt unhappy and asked himself the question, 'What is *the purpose of all* this effort?'
8 He had previously only *met* the idea of being part of a team when he played sports.
9 He also knew nothing about *finding out about other cultures.*
10 He had assumed that the point of work was to *become wealthy,* but began to question this philosophy.

2 Phrasal verbs are a feature of a more informal style. In the text, find phrasal verbs with the same meanings as the words and phrases below. Rewrite the sentences from the text using these words or phrases, and making any other necessary changes to the structure of the sentence.

1 solve (para. 2)
2 have a particular result (para. 2)
3 make someone fail (para. 3)
4 make progress (para. 5)

Grammar check: conditionals (1), *wish/if only*

1 **Conditionals:** review of basic patterns
1 Work with a partner. Decide which of the following sentences contain mistakes in the use of tenses, and correct them. Think about these questions.

- Which sentences refer to real or possible events in the present or future?
- Which sentences refer to unlikely or hypothetical events in the present, future or past?
- If the main clause clearly refers to the future, is it necessary to use a future form in the *if*-clause?

1 If we neglect our children's education, we do society a disservice.
2 If I'm writing a long report, I always drink lots of coffee.
3 I don't advise you to study physics unless you will be very good at maths.
4 They will only let us go on the trip if we pay our own fares.
5 I'll lend you my notes providing that you won't show them to anyone else!
6 As long as you will continue to study hard, you don't have a problem passing the exam next month.
7 If I knew the solution to the problem, I will tell you. Unfortunately, I don't!
8 If you won't practise, your language will never improve.
9 If you would like to take a seat, I will fetch the Manager.
10 We would love to help if we could.
11 If there was more emphasis on working together in my school, I would have found my first job easier.
12 If he'd have travelled more, we might have found him more open-minded.

2 Check your answers by referring to the rules in the Grammar reference on page 205.

3 Complete these sentences, then compare your sentences with your partner. Have you used the right tenses?

1 If you want to get a job in my country, ...
2 ...unless I get my work finished tonight.
3 If I had the chance to go abroad to study, I ...
4 I'd never have chosen to study ... if ...
5 My parents used to let me ... as long as ...
6 We might find English easier if ...

2 wish/if only

We use *wish* to express a desire for something to be different from reality, so the tenses used after *wish* are similar to the ones used in the *if*-clause of hypothetical conditions.

1 Work with a partner. Underline the correct alternative in the following sentences.

1 I wish *I'd had/I had* the chance to do more sport when I was at school.
2 I wish our school *offered/offers* more vocational subjects. I'd like to take Information Technology.
3 I wish success *doesn't/didn't* depend so much on exam results.
4 I wish we *could/are able to* go on more school trips abroad.
5 I wish the authorities *will/would* do something to reduce class sizes.
6 I wish we *weren't getting/didn't get* the exam results tomorrow! I'm really nervous.

2 Now answer the following questions.

1 What verb form is used after *wish* when the statement refers to
   a) the past?   b) the present?   c) the future?
2 Re-express sentences 1–6 above using *if only*. Does the grammatical pattern change? Is there a difference in meaning? Which expression is more emphatic? Which is more appropriate to the context?

3 Read the following sentences. Which example in each set is wrong? Cross it out. Which rule below applies in each case?

1 a) I wish you would stop smoking so much.
   b) I wish I would stop smoking so much.
   c) I wish I could stop smoking so much.
2 a) I wish I wouldn't have to get up so early tomorrow.
   b) I wish I didn't have to get up so early tomorrow.
3 a) I wish they would give us a holiday!
   b) I wish you liked me.
   c) I wish you would like me.

* We can't use *would* when we ourselves are the subject. We have to use *could* or a past form.
* When the verb describes an action, *would* refers to the future.
* We can't use *would* with verbs that describe a state.

4 Compare these examples. What's the difference in meaning between *wish* and *hope*?

1 I wish the authorities would revise the curriculum.
2 I wished the authorities would revise the curriculum.
3 I hope the authorities will revise the curriculum.
4 I hoped the authorities would revise the curriculum.

▶ Grammar reference p. 205

3 Which of the statements in Exercise 2.1 do you agree with? Do you have any other wishes, regrets or hopes? Make similar statements using *wish/if only* and *hope* about:

* your first school or the place where you are studying at present
* your first job or your current place of work, if you have left school.

Watch Out! *meanings of* **wish** ◀

1 I wish you were here.
2 I wish you the best of luck.
3 Do you wish to make a formal complaint?

What does *wish* mean in each of the examples?

Grammar plus: unreal versus real tenses

1 as if/as though

The expressions *as if/as though* can be used interchangeably. They may be followed by a present or past tense depending on the speaker's attitude.

1 Compare the following examples. What does the choice of tense indicate about the attitude of the speaker?

1 a) He acts as if he *knows* what he *is* talking about.
  b) He acts as if he *knew* what he *was* talking about.
2 a) Why do they never go on holiday? It's not as if they *are* poor.
  b) Why do they never go on holiday? It's not as if they *were* poor.
3 a) She looks as if she *has* seen a ghost!
  b) She looks as if she *had* seen a ghost!

2 Put the main verb in each sentence above into the past tense. What happens?

▶ Grammar reference p. 205

3 Fill the gaps with the most appropriate forms of the verbs in brackets.

1 Richard behaves as though he .... that scholarship to study abroad! (already get)
2 You're looking at me as if you .... a woman in trousers before. (see)
3 They looked as if they were surprised that they .... the prize at all. (win)
4 I don't know why you're staying in bed – it's not as if you .... ill. (be)
5 I only met him recently, but I feel as though I .... him all my life. (know)

2 It's time, I'd rather/I'd prefer

1 Read the examples. What tenses and patterns can follow these expressions? What time is referred to in each sentence?

1 a) It's (high) time they *changed* the curriculum.
  b) It's time we *were going* – it's getting late.
2 a) I'd rather you *didn't* invite her to the party.
  b) We did a lot of group activities at my school, but I'd rather we *had done* more individual work.
  c) I quite like my job, although I'd rather *have worked* somewhere where I could use my language skills.
  d) I'd rather *not come* on Saturday, if you don't mind – I've got too much to do.

3 a) I'd prefer *it* if you *didn't invite* her.
  b) I'd prefer *to have done* more individual work at school.
  c) I'd prefer *to have worked* somewhere where I could use my language skills.
  d) I'd prefer *not to come* on Saturday.

2 Fill in the gaps with suitable words.

1 It's high .... messing about and got down to some serious work. You've got an exam next week!
2 'Do you mind if I smoke?' '........................ didn't, if you don't mind. I've got a horrible sore throat.'
3 I didn't really want to do this course – .... done something more practical.
4 'Are you coming to the sales conference next month?' 'Well, actually, ... not to, if you can find anyone else.'

▶ Grammar reference p. 205

3 Use of English: sentence transformations

Finish each of the following sentences in such a way that it is as similar as possible in meaning to the sentence printed before it.

1 He had problems working in a team because his education had encouraged competitiveness.
  If his education ....
2 It's a pity they don't get on with each other better.
  I wish ....
3 I hope you won't tell anyone what I've just told you.
  I'd rather ....
4 I wish he would learn to make his own breakfast.
  It's high ....
5 It's unfortunate you didn't manage to give her my message.
  I wish ....
6 I regret not having taken the chance to travel when I was younger.
  If only ....
7 I wish I had been able to study journalism rather than art.
  I'd rather ....
8 He treats his students like children.
  He treats his students as if ....
9 I would like an appointment with the managing director.
  I wish ....
10 I think you should tell him rather than me.
  I'd prefer ....

Listening: sentence completion

1 Look at the advertisement and discuss the following questions.

1 Have you ever done a puzzle like this? Was it easy or difficult?
2 What kind of mind do you think you need to be able to do this kind of puzzle?
3 Would you say you are good or bad at puzzles? Why do you think that is?

It's The World's Best-Selling Puzzle

Rubik's cube is back!
Re-launched to stretch the brain cells of a new generation, this simple-looking cube puzzle can be solved in just a few moves. That is, as long as you choose the right ones from the 43 quintillion possibilities!

2 You will hear a talk about the different ways in which we think. First, read through the incomplete sentences below. Can you predict any of the content of the talk?

> The mind's fastest processing speed could be called 'the wits' and involves ....(1)
>
> When we are consciously aware of thinking, the process is ....(2) and could be called 'the intellect'.
>
> We understand 'wisdom' the least because it is ....(3).
>
> The example of the science lesson is used to illustrate how people use ....(4).
>
> One girl was killing time ....(5) a Rubik cube.
>
> Although she appeared not to be ....(6), she was still making progress.
>
> When questioned, the girl was unaware of the ....(7) she had been using.
>
> Adults find the Rubik cube difficult because they try to ....(8).

3 Now listen to the recording and complete the sentences as far as possible. You should write only one to four words in each space.

4 Listen to the recording for the second time. Check and complete your sentences. Have you made any spelling errors?

5 Look at the list of activities and discuss the questions below, based on what you have learned from the talk you have just heard.

- doing a maths problem
- writing poetry
- choosing a holiday
- driving a car
- playing the piano

1 Decide what type of thinking is needed for each activity: wits, intellect or wisdom. Discuss why.
2 Add three more activities to the list and discuss which type of thinking they need.

6 Say it again
For some questions in the exam, you have to manipulate structures to produce a new sentence where the meaning is similar to the first one, but expressed differently. In this book you will be given regular opportunities to practise rephrasing sentences.
The following sentences are from the Listening text. Re-express them using the framework given.

1 'Wisdom' is the least understood level.
  'Wisdom' is .... the other levels. (*Use a comparative.*)
2 It'll probably come back into fashion soon.
  It's .... come back into fashion soon.
3 She seemed to be paying very little attention.
  She looked .... very little attention.
4 She explained it to the best of her ability.
  She explained it as ....

Vocabulary: idiomatic expressions

1 Read the following sentences. Can you work out the meaning of the expressions in italics?

1 You need to *keep your wits about you* in Paper 3 of the Proficiency exam.
2 I've tried everything I can think of, but I still can't get him to agree – I'm *at my wits' end*.
3 I was *scared out of my wits* all alone in that huge empty house.
4 *To the best of my knowledge,* the project's going ahead as planned.
5 Didn't you realise he was married to that actress? I thought it was *common knowledge*.
6 I've got that song *on the brain* – it's driving me mad!
7 Can I come and *pick your brains*? I'm having problems with my new computer software.
8 I've been *racking my brains* trying to remember where I'd met him before.

2 **Use of English:** key word transformations
For Question 4 of Paper 3 you have to write a new sentence as similar as possible in meaning to the original, using a given word. In the following task, you need to replace the words in italics with an expression containing the word given. You can find the expressions you need in Exercise 1 or in the dictionary extracts on page 218.

Note: You must not change the word given, but you may need to change other parts of the original sentence.

1 Have you *decided* where you want to go yet? **mind**
....

2 After *thinking about it for some time*, he decided to opt for early retirement. **turning**
....

3 *As far as I know*, they've never set eyes on one another. **best**
....

4 The possibility of doing it on my own never *entered my head*. **crossed**
....

5 I had to *think very hard* to find the answer. **brains**
....

6 I *really can't decide* whether to go now or later. **minds**
....

7 You *mustn't allow yourself to be distracted* when you're working with explosives. **wits**
....

8 *He certainly wasn't considering* looking for a job. **last**
....

3 **Phrasal verbs with *think***
Complete the following sentences with a particle or preposition from the box. Use each word once only. There are two extra words that you won't need.

across	back	of	on
over	through	up	

1 They're still trying to think .... a name for the baby.
2 When I think .... to childhood holidays, it's the long, lazy days on the beach that I remember.
3 I wonder how anyone could ever have thought .... such a complicated story.
4 Why don't you think it .... for a while, and give me your answer in a few days?
5 Your plan isn't going to work – you haven't thought it .... carefully enough.

4 Take turns to interview a partner, using the following questions.

1 Have you ever been scared out of your wits in a film? What was the film/scene about?
2 What's the most important thing you've ever changed your mind about? What would have happened if you hadn't changed your mind then?
3 Is there anything you've particularly set your mind on doing in the next few years?
4 If I ask you to name a man or woman who's in the news at present, who immediately springs to mind? Why?
5 When you think back to your first school or job, what do you remember most vividly?
6 Think over what you've done in class today. What do you think you've learned?

Exam Focus

Paper 3 Use of English (Section B, summary)

In Paper 3, Section B, you have to read a passage of about 600 words, answer detailed comprehension questions and summarise one or more aspects of the writer's argument in a given number of words.

In this section, we focus on the summary task only. The passage is shorter than exam length, but the steps to summary writing are the same. You'll practise extracting and summarising points from one part of the passage only.

1 To write a good summary, you first need to understand the passage thoroughly. Read the following passage quite quickly to find the main idea. Ignore the underlining for now. Decide which is the best title for the whole passage and highlight the words in the text that justify your answer.

A **Planning for the future of education**
B **The problems of our present education system**
C **The future of work**
D **Current trends in education**

2 Now read the passage again for more detailed understanding and answer the following questions.

1 What is meant by a 'holistic approach to education'? (line 1)
2 What does the writer mean when he refers to education as 'society's investment in its own posterity'? (line 6)
3 What is the main problem when it comes to planning future education programmes?
4 What four trends related to employment patterns are mentioned in paragraph 2?
5 What qualities does the writer indicate will be needed as a result of each of these trends?
6 What is the writer suggesting when he says 'if the nuclear family is to continue to survive'? (line 27)
7 What trend means that it will be necessary to help people prepare for retirement?
8 Why is it 'not enough to conceive of the school curriculum as a list of subjects', according to the writer? (line 35)

A holistic approach to education which involves subjects, ways of thinking and the methods by which children learn and teachers teach is a good starting point for schools in the 21st century. Children in
5 school now may live to be ninety, and some may see the 22nd century — so if education is really society's investment in its own posterity then a long-term strategy would seem to be vital. All education is a vision of the future, and failure to have such a vision
10 would be a betrayal of youth. Unfortunately it is not so simple to describe what the future might look like, and so planning for an appropriate education for the citizens of tomorrow's society is not clear-cut.

Some trends seem clear. The numbers of unskilled
15 and semi-skilled workers are in decline, therefore a much higher level of knowledge and skill will be required from those wishing to enter or to remain in employment. The ability to get on with others will become more valued as more jobs are created in
20 service, leisure and recreation rather than in factories. People may have to retrain significantly several times in their careers, so flexibility and willingness to continue learning are important. Many more people will take part-time jobs or work from
25 home; thus qualities of independence, resourcefulness and adaptability come into their own. In family life, if the nuclear family is to continue to survive, education in the art of creating stable relationships will be needed. The increasing length of
30 time spent in healthy retirement must also be prepared for, as the average life span is increasing and older people are making up a greater percentage of the population.

All of these factors must have an impact on the
35 education programming of the future. It is simply not enough to conceive of a school curriculum as a list of subjects, however important these may be. In order to develop the range of talents needed for a prosperous future, children must learn in a variety of
40 ways and for a variety of purposes.

3 The next step is to identify the relevant points required by the summary question.

1 Read the summary task. The key words that tell you what information you have to include have been underlined.

> In a paragraph of 60–80 words summarise the <u>main trends</u> which the writer feels should <u>influence 'education programming of the future'</u>.

2 Now answer these questions.

1 Look back at the passage. Which paragraph, 1, 2 or 3, contains the information you need for the task?
2 Read the task again. Do you have to write about:
   a) trends only?
   b) the implications of these trends?
   c) both a) and b)?
3 Which six points should you include in your summary? Underline or highlight them in the passage. The first two have been done for you. **Don't** underline anything which isn't relevant to the topic of the summary!
4 Which trends relate to changes in employment patterns, and which are social and demographic?

4 The next step is to make notes.

1 Look at the points you underlined in the text. Circle key words and phrases in each sentence. The first two have been done for you.

2 Now compare the following notes with the text. In what ways has the text been paraphrased to make the notes as short as possible? What sorts of words have been omitted altogether?

CHANGING EMPLOYMENT PATTERNS

1 fewer unskilled/semi-skilled workers

2 more jobs in service sector cf.* industry

3 more frequent retraining

4 more part-time jobs and working from home

SOCIAL AND DEMOGRAPHIC TRENDS

5 family life: nuclear family may not survive

6 increasing proportion of older people

* Note: *cf.* is the abbreviation of 'compared with'.
Get used to using abbreviations when making notes.

5 Next, you should use your notes to write a paragraph consisting of 4–6 sentences in your own words as far as possible. Look only at your notes, not at the text, to avoid 'lifting' phrases.

Complete the following paragraph. You may need to change the form of some words in your notes.

> The writer identifies six main trends. There will be .... Changing employment patterns will result in .... compared with industry. People will need to .... , and .... Changes in family life mean that .... At the same time, the proportion ....

6 Now check and edit your summary, using the following questions as a guide.

- Have you included all the relevant information?
- Count the words in your paragraph. Is it within the given word limit? (If not, you will lose marks.)
- Is there any irrelevant information that should be deleted?
- Have you used any phrases from the text that could have been paraphrased rather than lifted?
- Is your paragraph well constructed? Have you made use of connectors to ensure it's coherent?
- Have you made any spelling or punctuation errors?
- Are there any serious grammatical mistakes?

If you wish, exchange the edited version of your summary with a partner for a final check.

> **Exam Strategy**
>
> Follow these steps whenever you answer a summary question.
> 1 Read the passage to make sure you understand its main idea and supporting details.
> 2 Highlight the key words in the summary question.
> 3 Find and highlight in the passage the points required by the question.
> 4 Make brief notes, following the order of the passage.
> 5 Expand your notes into a well-structured paragraph, using your own words as far as possible.
> 6 Edit the summary for length and check it for accuracy.

Vocabulary: education

1 Put the words in the box into the correct column below. Some words can go in more than one column.

an exam	a course	a subject	History	lessons
homework	a module	revision	a test	notes

do	take	sit	study	pass	make	follow

2 Read the following text and fill in the gaps using verbs from Exercise 1. Try to use each verb at least once.

In secondary schools in England, students have to (1) .... 10 different subjects until they are 16, and these must include English and Maths. After that they specialise, and from age 16 to 18 they usually (2) .... a maximum of three or four subjects. Sometimes time-tabling problems in the school mean that not all the students are able to (3) .... the course of their choice. In their final year they (4) .... the final school exams, which are known as A-levels.

If students want to (5) .... a particular subject at university, they must normally have (6) .... the same subject, or a related one, at A-level. It's very difficult to go to university unless you have (7) .... your A-level exams with good grades. However, it is always possible to (8) .... the exam again to get a better grade. Although in the majority of courses, students (9) .... just one exam at the end of the course, many new courses involve modules where the student (10) .... smaller tests and builds up credits. These are popular with students because they are less stressful.

3 The following words are sometimes confused. Underline the best word for each sentence below.

1 The *format/formula* of examinations in the British educational system is changing.
2 The emphasis is moving towards a more *practical/practicable* approach to testing.
3 This involves a process of *continuous/continual* assessment done by the teacher throughout the course.
4 It has the advantage that if the student makes one *mistake/fault* they will not necessarily fail.

5 Instead, they can improve their *grade/level* in the next piece of work they do.
6 Many students like this form of testing because it is less *stressful/agitating* for them.

4 Now answer these questions.

1 How similar or different is the English education system to the one in your country?
2 Describe the way in which students qualify for university in your country. What is your opinion of the system?

Speaking: interactive communication

One of the criteria you are assessed on in the Speaking test is 'interactive communication'. This involves being able to keep a conversation going by:

- responding to what the other speaker says e.g. 'Yes, that's a good point ... '
- expressing your own opinion or making a new point e.g. 'It seems to me that ... '
- inviting a response from the other speaker e.g. 'What do you think ... ?'

1 Read the statement below. Do you agree or disagree? Think of some points for and against the statement.

'There can be no better way to test students' progress than through a formal written exam at the end of the course. It will show exactly what they have learned.'

2 Now listen to two English speakers discussing the statement. Which point of view do you agree with?

3 Listen again and note any useful expressions you hear under the following headings.

- Acknowledging an opinion before disagreeing
- Disagreeing
- Agreeing
- Asking for opinions

4 Work in pairs. Discuss points for and against this statement.

'There is no point testing what students know – it is much better to find out what they can do. And the best way to do this is by continuous assessment.'

Writing: descriptive composition (2)

For the descriptive composition in Paper 2, you may be asked to describe an experience or event in the past and assess it or reflect on it in some way.

1 Read this writing task. How many parts does it have?

> Describe your first day at primary or secondary school, and how the experience affected you.
> (About 350 words.)

To start you thinking about the topic, interview a partner about his or her first day at school. Use the following questions to get your information. Find out as much detail as you can.

1 Did you have any expectations before you went to the school? What were they?
2 Did your parents or anyone else try to prepare you for the experience in any way?
3 Was the reality better or worse than you had expected?
4 How did the experience affect you?
5 What did you learn from it?

2 The text below is an extract from an autobiographical novel, *Cider With Rosie*, by Laurie Lee (1914–98). Laurie Lee was educated at a small village school in the south-west of England. In this extract, he describes his first day at primary school. The dialogue in the extract reflects the local accent, and Laurie is referred to as 'Loll', a nickname used by his family.

Read the extract, then discuss these questions.

1 Was the writer's experience similar to yours in any way?
2 How do you think the experience he describes might have affected his life?

CIDER WITH ROSIE

A The morning came, without any warning, when my sisters surrounded me, wrapped me in scarves, tied up my bootlaces, thrust a cap on my head, and stuffed a baked potato in my pocket.

'What's this?' I said.

'You're starting school today.'

'I ain't. I'm stopping 'ome.'

'Now, come on, Loll. You're a big boy now.'

'I ain't.'

'You are.'

'Bo-hoo.'

They picked me up bodily, kicking and bawling, and carried me up to the road.

'Boys who don't go to school get put in boxes, and turn into rabbits, and get chopped up Sundays.'

B I felt this was overdoing it rather, but I said no more after that. I arrived at the school just three feet tall and fatly wrapped in my scarves. The playground roared like a rodeo, and the potato burned through my thigh. Old boots, ragged stockings, torn trousers and skirts, went skating and skidding round me. The rabble closed in; I was encircled; grit flew in my face like shrapnel. Tall girls with frizzled hair, and huge boys with sharp elbows, began to prod me with hideous interest. They plucked at my scarves, spun me round like a top, screwed my nose, and stole my potato.

I was rescued at last by a gracious lady – the sixteen-year-old junior-teacher – who boxed a few ears and dried my face and led me off to The Infants. I spent that first day picking holes in paper, then went home in a smouldering temper.

C 'What's the matter, Loll? Didn't he like it at school, then?'

'They never gave me the present!'

'Present? What present?'

'They said they'd give me a present.'

'Well, now, I'm sure they didn't.'

'They did! They said: "You're Laurie Lee, ain't you? Well, you just sit there for the present." I sat there all day but I never got it. I ain't going back there again!'

3 Answer the following questions, which focus on how the Laurie Lee extract is organised.

1 How did the boy feel when he went home at the end of the day?

a) frightened   b) angry   c) miserable

2 Find and underline evidence in the text to support the following points.

1 He did not want to go to school.
2 He was bullied in the playground.
3 He was bored in class.
4 He misunderstood what the teacher had said to him.

Which was the most important factor in making the boy feel the way he did? When do we find out?

3 Match the sections of the extract, **A**, **B** and **C** to their function.

Section .... describes the main events.
Section .... provides a commentary on the events, with a surprise element.
Section .... explains the background to the events.

4 In descriptive writing, it's important to choose interesting verbs and adjectives to make your writing more vivid and help create a 'picture' in the reader's mind. Replace the words in italics with their more dramatic equivalents from the text.

1 *put* a cap on my head
2 *put* a baked potato in my pocket
3 kicking and *shouting*
4 *made a very loud noise* (like a rodeo)
5 *torn* stockings
6 The *crowd came towards me and surrounded me.*
7 Tall girls ... and *very big* boys ... began to *press their fingers into me.*
8 They *pulled repeatedly at* my scarves.
9 a *kind* lady
10 in a *bad* temper

5 Careful use of direct speech can help create added interest.

1 What is the effect of using direct speech in sections A and C of the text? Try re-expressing each section without using it. What's the difference? Why do you think it is not used in section B?

2 Correct the punctuation mistakes in this extract.

'you have to go to school! Shouted his sister
'Why do I have to'? wailed the boy
You must' she replied, pushing him out of the room,
'It's compulsory.

6 Read the following writing task.

> Describe the best day of your school life, giving your reasons for choosing that particular day. (About 350 words.)

Here are some questions to start you thinking about the topic. Use them to help you make some notes.

1 How did you feel at the start of the day? Did you know it was going to be a good day?
2 Did something good happen to you? For example:
 • did you find out you had passed an important examination?
 • did something good happen to a friend that made you feel good as well?
 • did you do something good for someone else?
3 What was the high point of the day?
4 How did you feel at the end of the day?

7 Decide which of the two tasks in this section you can write most about and prepare an outline. (See the model outline in Unit 1, page 18.)

8 Now write your composition. Remember to include the features of good descriptive writing that you have studied in this section. Don't forget to reflect on the experience you have described.

9 Exchange your composition with a partner. Evaluate each other's work and suggest improvements. Use the checklist on page 217.

10 Write an improved version of your composition.

> ### Exam Strategy
>
> When you write a descriptive composition, remember to follow these four stages.
> 1 Plan carefully, to leave enough time for the second, reflective part of the composition.
> 2 Make your description as vivid as you can, using a variety of language.
> 3 Include references to feelings and reactions.
> 4 Use direct speech for dramatic effect, but don't over-use it.

1 Complete these sentences by putting the verbs in brackets into the correct form.

1 The class told their teacher that they'd rather they .... individual assignments this week. (give)

2 Since starting her degree, Molly wishes she .... greater attention during Maths lessons at school. (pay)

3 Judging by their expressions on leaving the exam, it looks as if the others .... it dead easy. (find)

4 I wish our teacher .... us to express our opinions sometimes. (allow)

5 If you .... me earlier that you haven't got a computer, I .... you to do those calculations. (tell) (not ask)

6 As teachers, we wish we .... continuous assessment for all subjects, but it's not practicable. (introduce)

7 It's high time students in this school .... to study subjects relevant to the world of work. (begin)

8 If only my teachers .... me running this company – they .... totally amazed. (see) (be)

2 Fill each of the gaps in the passage with one suitable word.

As a teacher, I'm well aware that education has undergone changes since I was at school myself. Thinking (1) .... , I realise now that my first school was a (2) .... one, for its time. We were in mixed (3) .... classes, where able and less able children worked together and where we were encouraged to (4) .... ideas before accepting them, while at the same time learning to be reliable (5) .... players. It seems to have been effective, because when I encountered (6) .... at a later stage, I was usually put in the top group. I'd learned at an early age how to (7) .... through the advantages and disadvantages of a course of action and this helped me to (8) .... up my mind when I was faced with a (9) .... of subjects in my teens. There was no (10) .... assessment in those days, so I spent my last years in school preparing for (11) .... examinations. Some of my teachers said I rarely paid sufficient attention (12) .... detail and was unlikely to (13) .... on very well at university, so I (14) .... my mind on proving them wrong. And I did!

3 For each of the sentences below, write a new sentence as similar as possible in meaning to the original sentence, but using the word given. This word must not be altered in any way.

1 Can you help me tackle this problem? **deal**
....

2 Few university students are adequately trained to cope with life in industry. **ill-equipped**
....

3 With his education, he shouldn't find it very hard to write a report. **undue**
....

4 My brother was making soup at the same time as doing his homework. **simultaneously**
....

5 She never took any exams, as far as I know. **knowledge** ....

6 The young engineer said that she'd invented the system herself. **thought**
....

7 I just can't forget the end of that film. **mind**
....

8 What is the point of this research? **aid**
....

9 Many children find it difficult to articulate their feelings. **words**
....

10 We had not expected the teacher to give us a test yesterday. **warning**
....

4 Read the passages below. Decide where they may have been taken from and how they link with the general theme of the unit. What do you think should be included in the ideal curriculum?

1. There is no point in teaching subjects that pupils do not enjoy. They will not learn. The curriculum should be adapted to the needs of the pupils who are actually in the schools, not those ideal students who wish to study for its own sake – these are few and far between. In my view the way forward is pragmatism – accepting the situation as it really is – and a curriculum that mirrors the real world.

2. I'm not learning just for me – OK, I know that I'm going to benefit personally but I think it's my responsibility to put something back into society as well. I'm being educated for the good of my country and my generation and I have to do whatever I can to pay that debt back. It's selfish to think that education is just for the individual.

UNIT

3

The moving image

Speaking

1 Discuss the following quotations. What common theme links them?

> 'The telephone has too many shortcomings to be seriously considered as a means of communication. The device is inherently of no value to us.'
>
> *Western Union internal memo, 1876*

> 'Who the hell wants to hear actors talk?'
>
> *H. M. Warner, Warner Brothers, 1927*

> 'The wireless music box has no imaginable commercial value.'
>
> *Business response to appeal for investment in radio during the 1920s*

> 'Television will never be a serious competitor for radio because people must sit and keep their eyes glued to a screen; the average American family hasn't time for it.'
>
> *The New York Times, 1939*

> 'I think there is a world market for maybe five computers.'
>
> *Thomas Watson, chairman of IBM, 1943*

2 Imagine you could talk to one of the people quoted. Explain how wrong their prediction was, using evidence from today's world.

3 What do you think has been the greatest advance in communications in the last ten years?

Reading: literary text

In Paper 1, the third reading text is usually an extract from a novel or literary work. You may have to answer questions on:

- the development of the narrative
- individual characters and the relationship between them
- the theme or main idea
- the writer's attitude
- the language used.

Exercises 1–3 below focus on these aspects of the text and will help you with the multiple-choice task.

1 You are going to read an extract from a novel called *The God of Small Things* by the Indian writer Arundhati Roy. The novel is set in a small town in southern India and the extract describes how the installation of satellite TV affected the lives of an old woman called Baby Kochamma and her servant, Kochu Maria.

Before you read, think of some of the older people you know and discuss these questions.

1 How important is TV in their lives? Do they watch it a lot?
2 Name some of the programmes they like to watch. How selective are they about what they watch?
3 How far are the programmes they watch relevant to their own lives?

2 Read the passage through once and write the correct paragraph number next to each topic below.

a) Kochu Maria's favourite TV programmes ......
b) Description of the main characters ......
c) The effect of TV on their way of life ......
d) The arrival of television at Ayemenem ......
e) Fears aroused by the TV programmes ......
f) Baby Kochamma's favourite TV programmes ......

TELEVISION COMES
to
AYEMENEM

▶ Baby Kochamma and Kochu Maria, the vinegar-hearted, short-tempered, midget cook were the only people left in the Ayemenem house now. Baby Kochamma was eighty-three. Her eyes spread like butter behind her thick glasses, and her tiny, manicured feet were puffy with oedema*, like little foot-shaped air cushions. Her hair, dyed jet black, was arranged across her scalp like unspooled thread. And because the house was locked and dark, and because she only believed in 40-watt bulbs, her lipstick mouth had shifted slightly off her real mouth.

▶ But Baby Kochamma had a new love. She had installed a dish antenna on the roof of the Ayemenem house. She presided over the World in her drawing room on satellite TV. The impossible excitement that this engendered in Baby Kochamma wasn't hard to understand. It wasn't something that happened gradually. It happened overnight. Blondes, wars, famines, football, sex, music, coups d'état – they all arrived on the same train. They unpacked together. They stayed at the same hotel. And in Ayemenem, where once the loudest sound had been a musical bus horn, now whole wars, famines, picturesque massacres and Bill Clinton could be summoned up like servants.

▶ And so, while her ornamental garden wilted and died, Baby Kochamma followed American NBA league games, one-day cricket and all the Grand Slam tennis tournaments. On weekdays she watched *The Bold and The Beautiful* and *Santa Barbara*, where brittle blondes with lipstick and hairstyles rigid with spray seduced androids and defended their empires. Baby Kochamma loved their shiny clothes and the smart, bitchy repartee. During the day disconnected snatches of it came back to her and made her chuckle.

▶ Kochu Maria, the cook, still wore the thick gold earrings that had disfigured her earlobes for ever. She enjoyed the WWF *Wrestling Mania* shows, where Hulk Hogan and Mr Perfect, whose necks were wider than their heads, wore spangled Lycra leggings and beat each other up brutally. Kochu Maria's laugh had that slightly cruel ring to it that young children's sometimes have.

▶ All day they sat in the drawing room, Baby Kochamma on the long-armed planter's chair or the chaise longue (depending on the condition of her feet), Kochu Maria next to her on the floor (channel surfing when she could), locked together in a noisy Television silence. One's hair snow white, the other's dyed coal black. They entered all the contests, availed themselves of all the discounts that were advertised and had, on two occasions, won a T-shirt and a Thermos flask that Baby Kochamma kept locked away in her cupboard.

▶ Baby Kochamma loved the Ayemenem house and cherished the furniture that she had inherited by outliving everybody else. Mammachi's violin and violin stand, the Ooty cupboards, the plastic basket chairs, the Delhi beds, the dressing table from Vienna with cracked ivory knobs. She was frightened by the BBC famines and Television wars that she encountered while she channel surfed. Her old fears of the revolution had been rekindled by new television worries about the growing numbers of desperate and dispossessed people. She viewed ethnic cleansing, famine and genocide as direct threats to her furniture. She kept her doors and windows locked, unless she was using them. She used her windows for specific purposes. For a Breath of Fresh Air. To Pay for the Milk. To Let Out a Trapped Wasp (which Kochu Maria was made to chase around the house with a towel).

oedema: a swelling due to the collection of water in body tissues

3 Answer these questions about the passage on page 35.

Paragraph 1

1 What does the adjective 'vinegar-hearted' indicate about Kochu Maria's character?
2 Find details that suggest Baby Kochamma was
    a) unhealthy and unattractive.
    b) vain.
    c) mean.

Paragraph 2

3 What image does the writer use to emphasise Baby Kochamma's sudden access to a wide range of TV programmes?
4 What can we infer about Ayemenem and the two women's lives before TV arrived?
5 What is the effect of juxtaposing 'picturesque' and 'massacres'?

Paragraphs 3/4

6 What detail in Paragraph 3 indicates that watching TV caused Baby Kochamma to neglect other things?
7 What aspect of each woman's character is reflected in the programmes they particularly enjoy?

Paragraph 5

8 What details suggest that Kochu Maria is treated
    a) like a servant?
    b) like a member of the family?
9 What does the expression 'locked together in a noisy Television silence' indicate about the effect of TV on their lives?

Paragraph 6

10 What negative feeling did TV bring to Baby Kochamma? What effect did this have on her life?
11 Why are capitals used for the phrases 'For a Breath of Fresh Air' etc. at the end of the paragraph?

4 Now answer the multiple-choice questions. Choose the best option, **A, B, C** or **D**.

1 What impression of Baby Kochamma is created in the first paragraph?
    A She is bitter and bad-tempered.
    B She is lonely and pitiful.
    C She is ill and irritable.
    D She is vain and unattractive.

2 What was the main effect of the arrival of television on Baby Kochamma?
    A It ended her loneliness.
    B It made her aware of other people's problems.
    C It made her aware of a different world.
    D It attracted many visitors to the house.

3 What is the attitude of the two women towards the television?
    A They feel that it helps them to understand the world.
    B They enjoy the wide range of entertainment it offers.
    C They each find very different programmes enjoyable.
    D They are critical of some of the programmes they watch.

4 What is the effect of television on the relationship between the two women?
    A They quarrel over programmes, and tension develops.
    B They become jealous of one another.
    C It makes Kochu Maria neglect her work.
    D It gives them some shared interests.

5 Why does Baby Kochamma keep her doors and windows closed?
    A She doesn't like fresh air.
    B She is afraid of thieves stealing the TV.
    C She wants to protect her inheritance.
    D She wants to keep insects out of the house.

6 Overall, what does the writer suggest about the effect of television on the two women?
    A It improved the quality of their lives.
    B It took the place of real experiences.
    C It gave them a greater understanding of the world.
    D It allowed them to enter more competitions.

5 Discuss the following questions.

1 Do you think that young children could also be affected by television? How?
2 The writer implies that reporting catastrophes such as famine and wars on television makes them less shocking and more like entertainment. If you were a TV programmer, how would you respond to this criticism?
3 If you had the power, would you ban or restrict foreign programmes on TV? Why/Why not?

Vocabulary: fixed phrases and idiomatic expressions

Fixed phrases, which may be literal or idiomatic, may be tested in Paper 1, Section A and Paper 3, Questions 3 and 4.

1   Match the sentence halves. The expressions in **bold** form fixed phrases with the pattern *noun + of + noun*.

1   I'm just going out for **a breath**
2   I didn't get **a wink**
3   Everything he told her was **a pack**
4   She showed great **presence**
5   Whether it's right or wrong is **a matter**
6   The next time he saw her, she showed no **sign**

a)   **of opinion** – there's no definite answer.
b)   **of mind** in the emergency.
c)   **of fresh air.**
d)   **of lies** – he made it all up.
e)   **of recognition**, but just walked right past him.
f)   **of sleep** all night – the baby kept crying.

2   Read the statements 1–6, and answer the questions a)–f) below.

1   'I can't go on like this – if I don't have a holiday, I'll collapse!'
2   'I didn't think about it – I just got on a plane and went!'
3   'Don't worry – if I help you revise, I'm sure you'll get through the exam.'
4   'I really wish I hadn't insulted him – it's just that I was so angry.'
5   'He looked so embarrassed I thought he was lying, but it turns out he was telling the truth.'
6   'You only just made it – another few minutes and he would have drowned.'

a)   Who acted on the spur of the moment?
b)   Who's at the end of her tether?
c)   Who arrived in the nick of time?
d)   Who has provided a ray of hope?
e)   Who said something in the heat of the moment?
f)   Who jumped to the wrong conclusion?

3   Complete the sentences below with a suitable phrase from the box. They all follow the pattern *verb + noun + preposition*. Use the preposition in the sentence to help you choose the right phrase.

| draw the line | put one's back | throw light |
| have a go | make sense | spare a thought |

1   If we really .... into it, we could be finished by tonight.
2   The instructions are so complicated I can't .... of them at all.
3   I'd like to .... at running my own business.
4   His explanation did little to .... on the mystery.
5   I believe in freedom of choice, but I .... at letting children choose whether or not to go to school.
6   Not everyone is as lucky as you – .... for those who are out of work.

4   Choose the word or phrase which best completes each sentence.

1   She's just .... to conclusions – there's no real evidence.
    A skipping   **B** hopping   **C** springing   **D** jumping

2   We searched the empty house but could find no .... of a struggle.
    A signal   **B** sign   **C** show   **D** sight

3   Politicians might do well to .... a thought for people struggling on low incomes.
    A save   **B** keep   **C** use   **D** spare

4   His behaviour just doesn't make any .... to me.
    A reason   **B** sense   **C** meaning   **D** significance

5   Fill each of the blanks with a suitable word or phrase.

1   The cashier had the .... mind to press the alarm button immediately.
2   Doctors hope this research will .... on the causes of the disease.
3   If you .... back into it, we haven't a hope of making the deadline.
4   What with all this stress, I've just about come .... tether.

6   Write a new sentence as similar as possible in meaning to the original sentence, but using the word given. This word must not be altered in any way.

1   I didn't sleep at all because of the noise from the party. **wink**
2   I don't mind doing overtime, but I won't work on Sundays. **line**
3   Let's at least make an attempt to climb to the summit. **go**
4   She hadn't been planning to go to Corsica, but she went anyway. **spur**

7   Find out if these statements are true of a partner.

1   I like to do things on the spur of the moment.
2   I tend to jump to conclusions without thinking first.
3   I draw the line at lying to help a friend.

Grammar plus: emphasis (1) (inversion)

1 Read the pairs of sentences below and tick the sentence in each pair which is more emphatic. Underline the structural differences between the sentences.

1 a) The old woman <u>had never in her life</u> experienced such excitement.
  b) <u>Never in her life had</u> the old woman experienced such excitement.

2 a) Nowhere else in the world will you find scenery like this.
  b) You won't find scenery like this anywhere else in the world.

3 a) You must not leave your baggage unattended at any time.
  b) On no account should you leave your baggage unattended at any time.

4 a) I didn't realise how cold it was until I went outside.
  b) Not until I went outside did I realise how cold it was.

5 a) Only recently did they get the chance to visit the city.
  b) They only got the chance to visit the city recently.

▶ Grammar reference p.206

2 Rewrite these sentences using standard word order to make them less emphatic.

1 Nowhere in the world are people free from the influence of television.
People ....

2 Not since the printing press has there been an invention which so radically affected society.
There ....

3 Rarely do you find a family without a television set these days.
You ....

4 Seldom can busy parents resist the temptation to use the television as a childminder.
....

5 Not only does television discourage conversation, but it also encourages anti-social behaviour, some claim.
....

6 However, not a single case of violence have researchers found that could be directly linked to a television programme.
....

3 *hardly/no sooner*

1 In these examples the underlined expressions indicate that two actions take place in rapid succession.

1 They had <u>hardly</u> finished cleaning up the mess, <u>when</u> their parents arrived home.
2 The car had <u>no sooner</u> arrived <u>than</u> it was surrounded by journalists.

Note: *when* introduces a time clause. The expression *no sooner ... than* is a comparative.

2 Inversion of the subject and verb may be used with these expressions to increase the dramatic effect.

1 <u>Hardly</u> had they finished cleaning up the mess when their parents arrived home.
2 <u>No sooner</u> had the car arrived than it was surrounded by journalists.

3 Combine the sentences below using the words in brackets. You will also need to make some changes in the tense. What tenses will you use?

1 She got on the bus. She realised she had left her money at home. (no sooner)
2 The game began. It started to pour with rain. (hardly)
3 They got to know one another. She was offered a job in America. (hardly)
4 He settled himself down in front of the television. The phone rang. (no sooner)

4 **Use of English:** sentence transformations
Finish each of the following sentences in such a way that it is as similar as possible in meaning to the sentence printed before it.

1 The minute she left, the meeting broke up.
No sooner ....

2 Immediately after solving one problem, I was faced with another.
Hardly ....

3 The colour of that jacket suits you, and it fits you perfectly.
Not only ....

4 The minute he set eyes on her, he fell in love.
No sooner ....

5 You must remember to pay that bill, whatever you do.
On no account ....

6 He did not start to feel ill until after the meal.
Only when ....

Use of English: cloze

1 Discuss these statements. Which do you agree with?

'Digital television will mean the end of decent programmes … all we'll have will be hundreds of channels all showing the same rubbish.'

'It's wonderful … I can tune into whatever I want whenever I want, and in whatever language I want. It's so liberating.'

2 What changes have you seen in television in your lifetime? What changes might you see in the future?

2 Read through the text below to get the overall meaning, then answer the following questions. Don't try to fill in any gaps yet. Remember, if you understand the text, you will be able to think of the missing words much more easily.

1 Is the text mainly about technical changes or social changes?
2 What does it suggest will be the main effects of the increased number of channels available?
3 What does the last sentence suggest about the effects of global television on national culture? Do you think that this is already happening?

3 Now fill in the gaps following the procedure you practised in Unit 1 (see page 15). Use the hints provided to help you if necessary.

4 Read through the completed text and check that:

• the passage as a whole makes sense
• tenses, plural forms and noun/verb agreement are all correct
• there are no spelling mistakes.

The future of television

The increase in the number of available TV channels world wide is bound to have far reaching effects. Up to now, television has been a uniquely unifying national phenomenon. (1) .... before have so many people had (2) .... a common core of shared cultural experiences. (3) .... creates a durable communal bond. You (4) .... not know the names of your next-door (5) .... , but you can be fairly sure that over the past few days they have seen some of the same programmes you have.

Before (6) .... , with the vast expansion of television programming, everyone will be able to watch (7) .... different – 'Me TV' perhaps – just as each Internet user (8) .... explore a different selection of websites. The television will become a personal (9) .... of equipment more like a mobile phone (10) .... a communal source of entertainment. But it is also possible (11) .... on these personalised machines, people will actually (12) .... up watching fewer programmes: that television will become more (13) .... the movie business, with a number of blockbusters attracting vast global (14) ....

Viewers in all countries will (15) .... day be able to pick their programmes in a global market. (16) .... may still choose to watch their own national programmes since programmes (17) .... at international markets, with the partial exception of those from America, (18) .... to have smaller audiences than do national products. But, armed (19) .... a credit card and a remote control, people will eventually order television programmes from (20) .... they choose. The television business will then become truly global. So, perhaps, will the cultural values it instils.

Hints

1 negative adverbial
2 adverb intensifying the adjective
3 reference pronoun
4 modal
5 noun (collocation)
6 part of an adverbial phrase
7 pronoun
8 modal
9 noun
10 part of a comparative structure
11 conjunction introducing a clause
12 phrasal verb
13 word meaning 'similar to'
14 noun
15 determiner
16 reference pronoun
17 verb (with dependent preposition)
18 verb (with dependent preposition)
19 preposition
20 word referring to place

Exam Focus

Paper 4 Listening (note-taking)

In Paper 4 you may have to listen and complete notes. For this type of task, you have to note down points of information from the text in response to given prompts. The focus is mainly on factual information and you need to listen carefully for the specific details required. Most answers require no more than a word or phrase (up to about four words), but your spelling must be correct.

Exam Strategy

Don't try to write too much. You won't get any extra marks if you include extra details and you risk losing marks if some of the details you include are wrong, or if you are too busy writing to listen properly.

Here is a procedure for all exam listening tasks.

- You will have a short time **before listening:** use this to read through the questions and get an idea of what the listening is about.
- You will hear the recording twice. During the **first listening**, answer the questions you are sure of.
- During the **second listening**, check the questions you have done and complete the remaining questions. (If you're not sure, put something – it may be right, and if it isn't, no marks will be deducted.)

 1 You will hear an extract from a radio programme in which a film critic talks about Hollywood. For questions 1–12, complete the notes with a word or short phrase.

- The first films were made in France. Types:
  .... (1)
  .... (later) (2)
- Film-makers attracted to Hollywood by: light and climate conditions
  .... (3)
- Features of film-making in Hollywood in 1920s and 30s included:
  .... (4)
  development of film genres
  .... (5)
- Two important technological developments were:
  .... and .... (6)
- In the 1950s and 1960s, Hollywood studios faced:
  competition .... (7)
  take-over .... (8)
  increasing expense
- Films like Star Wars depended on
  .... (9)
  .... (10)
- Important genres of films from 1970s to present include:
  science fiction
  .... (11)
- Other developments:
  (Present) - Imax cinemas
  (Future) - digital video,... (12)

2 Discuss these questions.

1 Can you think of a film you have enjoyed recently that was **not** made in the USA?
2 How important is the film industry in the country where you live, and what sorts of films are produced?

3 Say it again
Re-express the following sentences from the Listening text beginning with the words given.

1 What brought the film industry to Hollywood?
  Why did ....
2 It was in France that it all began.
  It all ....
3 People completely lost interest in silent movies.
  There was a ....
4 The arrival of colour was more gradual.
  Colour ....

Vocabulary: dependent prepositions

Some questions in Paper 1, Section A and Paper 3 require a good knowledge of the particular prepositions that must follow certain verbs, adjectives and nouns, for example:

(Paper 3, Question 2)
This is similar to what we've seen before.
This is not *very different from what we've seen before.*

1 Verb + preposition

1 Read these extracts from the Listening text and fill in the missing preposition.

1 At first they stuck .... short documentaries.
2 ... the focus shifted .... the other side of the Atlantic.
3 France produced experimental films made to much lower budgets than the Hollywood studios were working ....

2 Fill in the gaps with an appropriate verb from the box in the correct form, together with the preposition. There is one extra verb that you won't need.

amount	agree	conform	contribute
object	react	resort	

1 I strongly .... the decision to allow the rebuilding work to go ahead.
2 As they wouldn't listen to reason, we had to .... threats.
3 There is a lot of media pressure on young people to .... popular fashion trends.
4 The problem was small and only .... a storm in a tea cup.
5 Many people .... charities by making regular donations.
6 The director .... the decision to cut the budget by walking off the set.

3 Add a preposition where necessary in the sentences below. What's the difference in meaning between the verbs with and without the preposition?

1 a) The secretary answered .... the letter.
   b) The suspect answered .... the description in the newspaper.
2 a) He confessed .... the crime.
   b) He confessed .... his sins.
3 a) She succeeded .... the throne of England.
   b) Queen Elizabeth II succeeded .... King George VI as monarch.

2 Adjective + preposition

1 Adjectives with related meanings or functions are often followed by the same preposition. Match the prepositions in the box to the sets of adjectives **A–F**.

about	at	from	in	on	to

A bad   efficient   hopeless   adept
B similar   contrary   preferable   applicable
C happy   worried   anxious   curious
D dependent   keen   reliant   intent
E different   free   distinct   exempt
F deficient   lacking   involved   successful

2 Most of the expressions above can be followed by both noun and gerund. How many exceptions can you find?

3 Complete the following sentences with an appropriate adjective and preposition combination from Exercise 2.1.

1 He is .... predicting the right moment to sell shares.
2 No-one should be .... prosecution if they have committed a crime.
3 Some diets are .... iron, which causes medical problems.
4 The film industry seems .... maximising profits by producing ever more ambitious blockbusters.
5 Her parents aren't very .... her plan to go back-packing in the Himalayas.
6 Organically grown food is .... chemical additives.

3 Noun + preposition

Nouns derived from verbs and adjectives are often, though not always, followed by the same preposition as their related forms. Fill in the gaps below with an appropriate preposition.

1 His involvement .... the robbery is beyond doubt.
2 We place a great deal of reliance .... the co-operation of our customers.
3 The director made an enormous contribution .... the success of the film.
4 She showed great efficiency .... organising the conference and ensuring it went off successfully.
5 It is the right of every person to live in freedom .... fear.
6 I grant you complete freedom .... action in this matter.

Grammar plus: participle clauses (1)

1 Read the short film reviews below and discuss these questions.

1 Which of the films have you seen? How far do you agree with the reviewer?

2 Which film would you most/least like to see? Why?

Jurassic Park. By extracting the blood from a prehistoric mosquito preserved in amber, scientists are able to develop living dinosaurs. Billionaire John Hammond masterminds an epic theme park for the dinosaurs, but before revealing his secrets to the public, he invites a small group of people to visit. Big mistake …

Spielberg drew on a budget of $60 million for the film, creating an astonishing range of prehistoric creatures that move, breathe and attack like the real thing. Although the human characters are less convincing, it has to be said that the film is an exhilarating and often intensely frightening experience.

Robin Hood Prince of Thieves. Opening with a man having his hand cut off in Jerusalem, this film hurtles back to England and never stops. Witchcraft, comic villains and large-scale battles fill the screen until your head aches. Kevin Costner comes over as an unsympathetic Robin, not thinking twice about putting an arrow through a colleague's hand, and the rest of the cast are equally unconvincing. Another overblown, overscored, overbudgeted Hollywood excess story.

Heavenly Creatures. Exploring the emotional experience that makes a murderer, New Zealand director Peter Jackson charts the true story of two schoolgirls, Pauline (played by Melanie Lynskey) and Juliet (played by Kate Winslet, outstanding in her debut film performance). Both were bright, imaginative girls who were trapped in a provincial world that was stifling them. Seeking to escape from it through the power of their imaginations, they resorted to a murder to preserve their unique universe. The intensity of the young actresses' performances and the superbly realised fantasy sequences make this a memorable film.

2

1 Rewrite the following sentences using participle clauses, as in the examples below. (Participle clauses are clauses in which a finite verb – i.e. a verb with a tense – is replaced by an *-ing* or *-ed* participle.)

EXAMPLES:
Before he reveals his secrets to the public, John Hammond invites a small group of people to visit.

Before revealing his secrets to the public, John Hammond invites …

Spielberg drew on a budget of $60 million for the film, and as a result he created an astonishing range of prehistoric creatures.

Spielberg drew on a budget of $60 million for the film, creating an astonishing range …

1 The film opens with a man who is having his hand cut off in Jerusalem. It then hurtles back to England and never stops.

....

2 Kevin Costner comes over as an unsympathetic Robin, since he doesn't think twice about putting an arrow through a colleague's hand.

....

3 New Zealand director Peter Jackson explores the emotional experience that makes a murderer and charts the true story of two schoolgirls.

....

4 They were seeking to escape from it through the power of their imaginations, so they resorted to a murder.

....

2 Now compare your sentences with the texts.
Note: Sometimes more than one option may be perfectly acceptable.

3 Match your sentences to the rules in the Grammar box.
Note: There are more rules than sentences!

1   **Participles** can replace *and* in sentences with two main clauses,
e.g.: *He sat there waiting.* (= *and waited*)

2   **Participle clauses** can indicate the sequence of events.

   a) We use the **present participle** when the action in the participle clause and the main clause happen at about the same time, e.g.:
   Looking up, I realised I was not alone.
   (= *When I looked up, I realised ...*)
   He stormed out, slamming the door behind him.
   (= *He stormed out and slammed ...*)

   b) We use the **perfect participle** when we want to make it clear that there is a time difference between two actions, e.g.:
   Having finished school, he entered his father's firm.

3   **Participle clauses** can replace *adverbial clauses* of reason, result and condition, e.g.:
   Not being a film buff, I can't remember who made that one. (reason)
   Having starred in a string of box-office hits, this actress can now command $1M per movie. (result)
   Given enough stimulation, a baby will start talking very early. (condition: *If it is given enough stimulation, ...*)

4   **Participle clauses** can be introduced by the following prepositions and conjunctions: *despite, on, before, after, when, while, since*, e.g.:
   On hearing of his success, I immediately wrote to congratulate him.
   While travelling in the USA, I met many interesting people. (time)
   While understanding your arguments, I cannot agree with them. (concession)

   ▶ Grammar reference p. 206

4   Why do you think participle clauses are common in written English, particularly in short pieces of writing such as summaries, film reviews etc.?

3   Combine the following sentences using a participle clause.

1   I used to be shy and lacking in confidence. Then I read your book.
Before ....

2   I met her for the first time. I was struck by her resemblance to the actress Audrey Hepburn.
On first ....

3   He started his preparations early. However, he did not manage to finish on time.
Despite ....

4   He was kept waiting for three hours. Then he finally saw the Minister. (*Remember this is a passive.*)
After ....

5   I appreciate the fact that you have a limited budget. However, I feel that more money needs to be spent in this area. (*Do you need the link word 'However'?*)
While ....

6   We hadn't expected to win an Oscar for the film. We were completely bowled over by the news! (*Think about the tense.*)
Not ....

7   This car will give you many years of service. However, it must be looked after properly.
....

8   The number of hotels in the city has increased substantially. As a result, it is now much easier to find a room.
....

4   Shorten the film review below and add variety of sentence structure by using some participle clauses. Make any changes necessary, e.g. to the word order.

Marion sees money as the solution to all her problems, so she steals $40,000 from her employer and drives off to start a new life with her lover. She stops for the night at the Bates Motel because she feels tired after her long journey. When she checks in, she meets the owner, a shy young man called Norman. After she has unpacked, she decides to take a shower. She does not hear the approach of the murderer, as she is deafened by the sound of the water . . . We see the terrifying shadow of a hand with a knife behind the shower curtain and we know what is going to happen. After forty years, Hitchcock's *Psycho* remains as terrifying as the day it was made.

5

1   You have been asked to write a review of your favourite film for the Movie Choice page of a student magazine. You have to include both a brief synopsis of the plot and your opinion of the film in no more than 100 words. Write your review.

2   Submit your review to the Editorial Panel of the magazine. They should choose the best four reviews for the Movie Choice page.

Writing: narrative composition (1)

One of the tasks in Paper 2 is to write a story. You may be given the first line, the last line, or the title. In this section you will work on a story where you are given the last line.

1 Read the following writing task.

> Write a story ending with the line:
> *Leaving the building, he walked away without looking back.*
> (About 350 words.)

Before you start to write, you need to think of ideas for a plot. Work in pairs or groups and note down answers to the questions below.

1 Who is 'he'? Is he young or old?
2 What sort of building is it?
3 Why did he go there? What happened to make him leave?
4 Are any other characters involved in the story? Who are they?
5 How does he feel as he leaves? Think about the words 'without looking back'. What do they suggest?

2 Read the following story, which was written in answer to the task. Do you think the writer has answered all the questions in Exercise 1 successfully?

VERSION 1

Alex knew that Peter had always wanted to go into films. Peter had seen an advert in the local paper which called for new young actors for a part in a new TV drama, and had suggested that he and Alex should go to the audition. Alex, as always, had wanted to take the boat out instead. But now he was standing in a long queue waiting to get in to the auditorium. Peter had told him that it would be fun, but it wasn't. Then, when he saw his friend's face, he knew it had been the right thing to do.

When they were finally called into the auditorium, they were given long lines of dialogue to look at. Alex felt very unhappy. In the background he could hear the producer

3 Look at the list of features that make a good story. Tick the features illustrated in the story you have just read. How effective is the story?

Feature	Version 1	Version 2
• a single key event or incident as the focus of the story		
• a dramatic opening paragraph to capture the reader's interest and make him/her want to read on		
• sufficient background details to provide an explanation for the events		
• a strong ending that rounds the story off in a satisfactory way		
• believable and interesting characters		
• description of feelings and reactions		
• interesting and varied vocabulary		
• careful use of direct speech for dramatic effect		

saying something, but he was so nervous he couldn't move. Peter hadn't noticed and had gone on stage ahead of Alex. Alex stepped back and handed his script to the boy behind him. He wished Peter good luck silently. He watched from the auditorium, and saw Peter give a very good performance. Then he heard the producer make his choice and call Peter over to discuss terms for the contract.

Alex realised that he wasn't needed any more. He had supported Peter when he needed him, and now he could go. Leaving the building, he walked away without looking back.

4 Now read a second version of the same story and do the exercises that follow.

VERSION 2

Alex had never wanted to go to the audition. The thought of it terrified him. It had been Peter's idea, and Alex also bitterly resented the time it was taking up. He could have been out in his boat, sailing round the bay, making the most of the gusting winds and good weather. Instead, he was stuck in the queue waiting to get into the auditorium, standing with hundreds of other hopefuls, feeling foolish and distinctly nervous.

'It'll be fun!' Peter had said, brandishing the newspaper in front of Alex and jabbing his finger at the advert that said YOUNG ACTOR WANTED FOR TELEVISION DRAMA. AUDITIONS ON SATURDAY AT THE TOWN HALL. 'I've always wanted to be on TV – it's my big chance! But I don't want to go alone and you do owe me a favour.'

So Alex had allowed himself to be persuaded. But it wasn't fun at all, and he wished he hadn't come. Then, seeing his friend's eager face gazing round excitedly, he knew he had had no choice. Sighing, he pushed the thought of the boat to the back of his mind. No sooner had he done so than they were called onto the stage and given their scripts. Alex's heart sank. He hated it. He felt stupid and vulnerable, and a sickening feeling hit him in the pit of his stomach. His hands started sweating, his heart pounded, the world spun round, and he felt as if he was going to faint. He was dimly aware of the producer shouting, but he was rooted to the spot. He could not have moved forward to save his life. Stepping back, Alex handed his script to the boy behind him. In his mind, he whispered to Peter, 'Good luck – go for it!' Watching in the wings, he saw his friend give the performance of his life, and heard the producer say 'That's the one!'

With relief, Alex realised that his obligation was over – he had done his best for his friend. Now he was free. Leaving the building, he walked away without looking back.

5 **Adding detail and interest**

1 Answer the following questions about version 2 of the story.

1 How did Alex feel about the situation? Why was this? Why did he agree to go?
2 What do you know about the character of each boy?
3 What was the situation outside the auditorium? How did Alex feel then?
4 How did Alex feel at the crucial moment? What did he do? Why did he do this?
5 What do you know about Alex's feelings after Peter's audition?
6 How did the incident affect Alex afterwards?

2 Compare the two versions of the story. What extra information is included in version 2? Use your answers above to help you.

3 Look back at the list of features that make a good story. How many can you find in version 2?

6 **Variety of tenses and structures**

1 What tenses are used in paragraph 1 of version 2? Why do you think this is?

2 Rewrite the sentences below from version 1 using participle clauses.

1 Then, when he looked at his friend's face he knew it had been the right thing to do.
2 Alex stepped back and handed his script to the boy behind him.
3 He watched from the auditorium, and saw Peter give a very good performance.

3 Look back at version 2 and compare your answers. Underline any other examples of participle clauses in version 2.

4 Underline an example of inversion in paragraph 3 of version 2. What does the inversion emphasise here?

7 Interesting vocabulary

1 Compare the two sentences below. Which one is more interesting, and why?

1 He could not have moved forward at all.
2 He could not have moved forward to save his life.

2 Rewrite the following sentences.

1 Alex wanted to take every chance of enjoying the good weather.
Alex wanted to make .... the good weather.
2 He was unable to move because he was standing in a long queue.
He couldn't move because he was .... queue.
3 He knew that he couldn't do anything else.
He knew that he .... choice.
4 He tried to stop thinking about the boat.
He pushed the thought .... mind.
5 He couldn't move.
He was .... spot.
6 He watched his friend give a very good performance.
He watched his friend give .... life.

3 Now check your answers with version 2 of the story.

8 Vivid verbs

Version 2 of the story describes the physical effects that fear had on Alex at the most important moment in the story. This adds interest and helps to bring the character of Alex to life.

1 Find and underline the verbs and expressions used in paragraph 3 which contribute to this effect.

2 Match expressions from the box below to the correct parts of the body. There are two phrases for each part of the body.

churned	fell open	filled with tears
shook	sweated	pounded
turned over	went dry	sank
opened wide		

1 My hands ....
2 My heart ....
3 My stomach ....
4 My mouth ....
5 My eyes ....

3 Is the verb being used literally or metaphorically? Can these phrases suggest any other feeling than fear?

9 Read this writing task.

> Write a story ending with the following line:
> *Walking up the hill towards home, I knew I had made the right choice.*
> (About 350 words.)

Choose one of the following synopses and develop it into a story ending with the line given.

Synopsis 1
- woman/man has been unsuccessful in life
- discovers an unexpected talent
- has great success
- returns to home and family

Synopsis 2
- boy/girl is forced to move away from city with family
- hates new home near sea
- has problems in school life
- makes a friend in an unexpected way

10

1 Exchange your story with another student. Evaluate each other's stories using the list of features in Exercise 3 to help you. Check that the last line has been prepared for. Suggest any improvements.

2 Write an improved version of your story.

Exam Strategy

What will your strategy be in the exam, if you choose the narrative composition?

- What will you do before you start to write your story?
- How will you organise your story?
- How will you make it interesting, so as to impress the examiner?

1 Find and correct the errors in the following sentences.

1 Contrary from what you might expect, I have in fact completed my assignment.
2 Not once has he asked me whether I agree with his ridiculous scheme.
3 I'm prepared to keep quiet about what I know, but I draw a line at lying.
4 She's adept in finding plausible excuses for not doing as much work as she should.
5 Not only have you my evening ruined, but you've offended my friends as well.
6 With maturity, we are less inclined to conform in the expectations of our peers.
7 Only now I am free to do what I want with my life.
8 Whether you're ready or not, filming will start tomorrow as scheduling.
9 This supposedly comic story is singularly lacking of humour.
10 There are means and ways of evading taxes, but I wouldn't advise you to try any of them.

2 Choose the word or phrase which best completes each sentence.

1 Your criticism is simply not applicable .... the type of films children enjoy.
   A on   B of   C about   D to

2 The posters were delayed at the airport and only arrived in the .... of time.
   A spur   B nick   C slice   D wink

3 The heroine spends her time .... to conclusions and causing chaos.
   A jumping   B running   C falling   D climbing

4 The actor said that he objected very .... to the changes made to his role.
   A severely   B strongly   C staunchly   D stoutly

5 The director's assistant attends .... all the detailed arrangements about re-shooting scenes.
   A to   B about   C for   D on

6 .... a more generous budget, we could have had really impressive special effects.
   A Provided   B Accepted   C Given   D Agreed

7 I was .... aware of a noise behind me, but was too involved in my work to pay any attention.
   A mildly   B nearly   C slightly   D dimly

8 Our eyes were .... to the screen as the mystery unfolded.
   A fixed   B glued   C stuck   D fastened

9 At one point, the main character is .... by a gang of thugs.
   A beaten up   B knocked on   C whipped up   D smashed in

10 The film industry in this country is unduly reliant .... foreign capital.
   A of   B from   C on   D to

3 FIll each of the blanks with a suitable word or phrase.

1 Under no circumstances will .... a member of the public to enter the film studio today.
2 The telephone was originally scorned by many companies as .... of communication.
3 So .... he by the film that he saw it four times.
4 The film crew stood about .... to the actors until the visitors had left..
5 No sooner had they started filming .... to rain.
6 You really .... twice before giving up your job to become an actor.

4 Talk about the photos.

1 Describe the different media pictured.
2 How do the photos relate to the topic of the unit?
3 Which of the media do you think has already had the greatest effect on modern life? Why?
   Which one do you think will have the most long-lasting effect? Why?

The hard sell

Speaking

1 Look at the company logos. Can you identify the companies? What products do they sell?

2

1 Think of some consumer products you have bought recently, such as an item of clothing, a CD, electrical equipment, etc. Which of the factors in the list below influenced your choice? Can you add any other factors to the list?

- brand name
- brand loyalty (you had bought the same brand before)
- a friend's recommendation
- pressure from your peer group
- advertising
- price
- accompanying special offers or gifts

2 Compare and discuss your answers with other students.

3 What are the advantages and disadvantages of advertising for:

a) the consumer?
b) the manufacturer or producer?

Use of English: comprehension and summary

Paper 3, Section B involves answering comprehension questions on a passage and then writing a summary in response to a question about the passage.
In Unit 2 you practised writing a summary of a short passage. In this section you will practise answering comprehension questions, as well as writing a summary.

1 You are going to read a newspaper article which discusses an important issue facing consumers today.

1 Read the headline and look at the photograph. Can you predict what the issue is? Who are the 'tiny targets'?

2 Read the first paragraph (introduction) and last paragraph (summary/conclusion) only, to see if you were right, and answer these questions.

1 What is the main concern expressed by the writer?
2 What does he think should happen?

3 Underline the parts of each paragraph that give you the answer.

2 Before you read the rest of the article, predict which of the following examples could be used to support the main idea introduced in the first paragraph. Circle the appropriate letters.

Big companies ...
a) use sports stars and celebrities to endorse their products. ......
b) give away free gifts with their products. ......
c) advertise their products on children's TV. ......
d) use well-known cartoon characters on packaging. ......
e) use shocking images in advertisements. ......
f) give away educational material incorporating the company logo to schools. ......
g) offer discounts for regular customers. ......
h) encourage children to buy things to be like their friends. ......
i) display sweets at children's eye-level in supermarkets. ......

Study Tip

Before reading a text in detail, try to predict what it is about by looking at the title or headline, as well as any sub-headings or pictures. You may already know something about the topic. If so, you can use this to anticipate what you are going to read.

3

1 Now read the rest of the article and check if your predictions were right. Underline the phrase or sentence in each paragraph that gives you the information.

2 Write the number of the paragraph next to those examples in Exercise 2 mentioned by the writer.

Big sell, tiny targets

Big companies are using increasingly intensive marketing techniques to promote their products – so what is new about that? They have been doing it for years. But what is disturbing is the fact that they are now targeting the very young, aiming to establish brand loyalty at an age when children have no ability to be discerning or to recognise the exploitative nature of the advertising wars being waged against them.

Anyone who doubts this should watch the commercial breaks on children's television in the early afternoon or on a Saturday morning. Some of the advertisements for toys may be more or less acceptable to parents although the pressure on parents to scour the shops for the latest craze in toys can be irritating and is always expensive. But many ads are for foods and soft drinks, most of which have high fat and sugar contents and are not particularly good for children. Sweden has banned ads during children's television programmes, and other countries have introduced restrictions at these times.

Even if television advertising is controlled, what happens when the family hits the supermarket? Marketing people say that the big sell to the tinies began for them with the invention of the child-carrying supermarket trolley. Their most powerful weapon in the fight to sell is sitting right under the nose of the parent, bored, seeking attention and absolutely bound to spot anything whose packaging features a logo or a cartoon character seen regularly on the television.

Children are easy targets. They begin pestering their parents to buy brand-name items almost as soon as they can talk, and the pressure doesn't let up. It takes until the age of about six for the young consumer to understand the difference between an advert and a programme on the television, and even longer to appreciate what the ad is trying to do. Even then, the child does not necessarily care. Marketing managers are well aware of children's desperate need to keep in with the peer group. If they can start a craze with, for example, collectable toys given away in packets of cereal or

crisps, sales of that product will probably go through the roof.

It does not stop with leisure and pleasure pursuits. It is a small step from the playground into the classroom, and the marketing men have already taken it. Most schools are acutely short of cash. Who can blame them for welcoming offers of wonderful 'freebie' educational resource packs? Does it matter that these include subtle or not so subtle references to the products of the generous donor? Even exercise books are now donated by companies who make sure that their logos are prominently displayed on the covers.

Such marketing is aimed at a very impressionable age group, and although companies claim that it is the responsibility of parents to monitor what their children eat, drink or play with, it may be that the time has come for a little more social responsibility to be shown by these people who are exploiting children for their own financial gain.

4 Now answer the questions below. These focus on:

- the relationship between the main ideas of the passage and supporting detail
- the meanings of specific words or expressions in context
- what is implied or suggested by specific parts of the passage (e.g. by choice of words, use of stylistic devices, etc.)
- what reference pronouns such as *it* or *this* refer to in the passage.

Remember to use your own words when the question asks you to. You don't need to write complete sentences.

1 According to the writer, who are the companies' campaigns aimed at in 'advertising wars' (line 9)?
2 What could not be doubted by anyone watching the advertisements on children's TV?
3 What can we infer about the writer's attitude to ads for toys and ads for foods and soft drinks?
4 During which particular times do some countries place controls on TV advertising?
5 What is the 'most powerful weapon' referred to by the writer? (line 28)
6 What is the significance to the marketing people of the fact that the child is 'bored'? (line 30)
7 Explain in your own words how young children try to make their parents buy advertised products.
8 When children reach the age where they can understand what an advertisement is trying to do, what is their main priority?
9 Explain in your own words why starting 'a craze' might cause sales to 'go through the roof' (line 46).
10 Why do you think the word 'freebie' is in inverted commas? (line 53) Suggest two reasons.
11 Who is the writer referring to in the phrase 'the generous donor' (line 55) and what is he actually implying here?
12 What type of marketing is 'aimed at a very impressionable age group' (line 59)?

Study Tip

In addition to being used to show direct speech, inverted commas may be used:
- to show that a word or phrase is unusual in some way – e.g. made-up or slang – or is assumed to be new to the reader, e.g.:
  ... offers of wonderful 'freebie' educational resource packs
- to indicate that the writer does not really believe that the word is appropriate in this case, e.g.:
  Her 'friends' all disappeared when she was in trouble.

---

5 Read the following summary task carefully, and answer the questions which follow.

> In a paragraph of 70–90 words, summarise what marketing managers know about young children's leisure activities and the way they use this information to promote their products.

1 How many parts are there in the summary? Underline the key words.
2 Should you include the writer's opinions?
3 Look back at the passage. Identify the three paragraphs which contain the information relevant to this question.
4 Underline or highlight the points you should include. Then compare with the notes in Exercise 6.

6 Complete the notes below.

WHAT IS KNOWN	MARKETING TECHNIQUES USED
children watch TV at particular times	show ads for .... during commercial breaks
parents take young children to supermarkets – they get bored	use packaging with .... or .... from TV to attract their attention
older children want to be like	start a craze by ....

7 Expand your notes into a paragraph. Remember to look only at your notes, not at the passage itself, to avoid copying phrases from the text as far as possible.

1 You will need to start your summary with an introductory sentence. However, this should not just repeat the words in the question. Decide which sentence below is appropriate and why.

A Manufacturers know about children's leisure activities and use this information to sell their products.
B Manufacturers use information about children's leisure activities to target them in three main ways.

2 Complete your paragraph, using appropriate expressions from the box below a) to introduce the facts and link them to the techniques b) to link the main points.

> They know that ... , so ...
> They realise that ... ; therefore ...
> They are aware that ... , and consequently ...
> Firstly, ... Secondly, ... Thirdly, ... Finally ... *and/or*
> In addition, ... Also ...

8 Check the number of words in your paragraph and edit it if necessary. See the advice given in Unit 2, page 29.

9 Finally, read through your completed summary and check the grammar, spelling and punctuation. If you wish, exchange your summary with a partner for a final check.

Vocabulary: metaphor

A **simile** makes a comparison between two different things using the words *like* or *as*, e.g.:

*Her tiny, manicured feet were **like** little foot-shaped air cushions.* (text p. 35)
*Her hair was white **as** snow.*

A **metaphor** implies a resemblance between two distinctly different things without using *like* or *as*, e.g.:

Life is a bowl of cherries.

You may need to recognise and interpret the metaphorical use of language in the Reading paper and in the comprehension passage in Paper 3.

1 Metaphorical use of language ranges from single words or phrases to whole sentences. Read the following examples from the texts on pages 35 and 49. Explain the literal and metaphorical meaning of the words in bold. What image does the use of the metaphor create in each case?

- Single words
  *The TV programmes **rekindled** her fears of revolution.*
  *... what happens when the family **hits** the supermarket?*

- Compound words
  *The **vinegar-hearted** cook*

- Phrases
  *Sales will ... **go through the roof**.*

- Extended metaphors: sentences and beyond
  *Blondes, wars, famines – they all **arrived on the same train**.*
  They unpacked together. They stayed at the same hotel.

  *It is **a small step** from the playground into the classroom, and the marketing men **have already taken it**.*

2 Read these further extracts from the text on page 49 and answer the questions below.

*Children have no ability to recognise the exploitative nature of the advertising **wars being waged against** them.*
*The most powerful **weapon** in the **fight** to sell ...*
*Children are easy **targets**.*

1 What is the common theme of the metaphors?
2 What does this choice of metaphor indicate about the writer's attitude towards advertising?

3

1 For each the following sets of sentences, identify a) the topic area and b) the common theme of the metaphors.

2 Are there any similar patterns in your language? Think of some examples.

1 a) The audience was *enchanted* by the play.
   b) The storyteller held his audience *spellbound*.
   c) A *magical* production that will delight all age-groups.
   d) Within moments, Sinatra's voice had *cast its spell* on the audience.

Topic area: entertainment
Common theme of metaphors: ....

2 a) Her eyes sparkled with excitement.
   b) Suddenly a smile lit up her face.
   c) A grin flashed across his face.

Topic area: ....
Common theme of metaphors: bright light

3 a) He fell ill.
   b) I'm feeling a bit low.
   b) He came down with flu.
   c) I'm a bit under the weather today.

Topic area: ....
Common theme of metaphors: falling, downwards movement

4 a) Details of the plan were leaked to the press.
   b) People started trickling into the conference room around 8.30.
   c) We've been flooded with complaints.

Topic area: movement of people and information
Common theme of metaphors: ....

Exam Focus

Paper 3 Use of English (key word transformations)

In Question 4, Section A, you have to rewrite eight sentences using a given word, to produce sentences similar in meaning to the original. This question tests your knowledge of phrases, idioms and sentence patterns.

You mustn't change the word given and you must include all the information from the original sentence. There isn't always one right answer. There may be more than one way to use the given word in a phrase, or there may be various ways in which it can affect the structure of the whole sentence. However, try not to change the structure of the sentence unless you are sure it is necessary. You won't get extra marks for unnecessary changes.

EXAMPLE: The new coffee commercial is nothing like the old one. **bears**

ANSWER: *The new coffee commercial bears no resemblance to the old one.*

(This tests a fixed phrase and no other changes are necessary.)

EXAMPLE: The government has changed its policy completely since the election.
undergone

ANSWER: *The policy of the government has undergone a complete change since the election.*

(This tests a noun-verb collocation, and the change also affects the structure of other parts of the sentence.)

EXAMPLE: We all knew that he didn't like the new manager.
dislike

ANSWER: *We all knew about his dislike of the new manager.*
(This tests your knowledge that the same word may be more than one part of speech. The temptation is to use 'dislike' as a verb, but this would mean changing the given word.)

1 Look at the answers suggested by students for the item below and tick the ones that you think are possible. Check that:

- all the information has been included
- all necessary changes have been made
- the new sentence is grammatically correct.

The business has been more profitable since we installed the new computer system. **increased**

a) *The business has increased since we installed the new computer system.*

b) *The profits of the business increased since we installed the new computer system.*

c) *The profits of the business have increased since we installed the new computer system.*

d) *Our installation of the new computer system has increased the profits of the business.*

e) *Installing the new computer system has increased the profits of the business.*

2 For each of the sentences below, write a new sentence **as similar as possible in meaning to the original sentence**, but using the word given. This word must not be altered in any way.

(a) The information revolution began when the first printing press was made. **invention**

....

(b) A new exhibition opens this week and shows the work of modern artists. **featuring**

....

(c) If inflation continues at this rate, prices will increase dramatically. **roof**

....

(d) Lots of people have complained about last night's programme. **floods**

....

(e) The ship sank and no sign of it was ever found. **without**

....

(f) The authorities should do something to reduce traffic congestion. **steps**

....

(g) You should try to stay friendly with Benson – he has a lot of influence. **keep**

....

(h) The brochure didn't say anything about any extra charges. **reference**

....

► Exam Maximiser

Listening: multiple-choice questions

1   You will hear a woman talking about her job. Before you listen, read through all the questions. Can you predict:

a) what she does?
b) what her job involves?

Remember, for any listening task, always read the questions **before** you listen, so you can try to anticipate what you are going to hear.

1   The speaker says her job involves
   A   launching electrical goods.
   B   advising on how to manufacture good products.
   C   persuading people to buy new products.
   D   taking products to markets.

2   What is the main attraction of the ice-cream product described, according to the speaker?
   A   Its convenience.
   B   Its taste and texture.
   C   The fact that it is healthy.
   D   The number of different varieties available.

3   Both the name and the packaging of the ice-cream
   A   must be suitable for the target consumer.
   B   must be original and striking.
   C   must be aimed at children.
   D   must reflect the nature of the product.

4   What aspect of the product should the price reflect?
   A   It is a special occasion treat.
   B   It is bought by housewives.
   C   It is not something people plan to buy.
   D   It is very high quality.

5   The speaker suggests that the ice-cream will probably be sold
   A   in supermarkets.
   B   in expensive restaurants.
   C   in large cafés in tourist centres.
   D   from small outlets.

6   What does the speaker recommend about promotional campaigns ?
   A   They should use a wide variety of media.
   B   They should be carefully planned.
   C   They should include special offers.
   D   They should not target the very young.

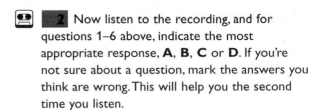

2   Now listen to the recording, and for questions 1–6 above, indicate the most appropriate response, **A, B, C** or **D**. If you're not sure about a question, mark the answers you think are wrong. This will help you the second time you listen.

3   Listen again to complete and check your answers. Make sure that at the end you have only **one** answer to each question.

4

1   According to the speaker, a product will be successful if the business gets the 'marketing mix' right. The marketing mix is often referred to as the '4 Ps'. Complete the explanation below.

To meet customers' needs a business must develop the right p............ to satisfy them, charge the right p............ , get the goods to the right p............ and make the existence of the goods known through effective p............ .

2   Work in groups. Think of a product you all buy regularly, such as an item of confectionery, a magazine, etc. Decide how effective the marketing mix for your selected product is by asking yourselves these questions.

- Does the product meet the requirements of the customers for whom it is intended?
- Is the price right?
- Can consumers get it when and where they want it?
- Is the marketing successful?

5   **Vocabulary:** connectors
In Paper 1 and Paper 3, Section A, you may be tested on your knowledge of connectors, or linking expressions. Replace the connectors in the following sentences with an alternative expression which includes the word in brackets.

1   We've been considering who it's for, *that is to say*, the target market. (in)
2   *Most importantly*, it's got to be right for the consumer. (Above)
3   *Of course*, the price has to be right. (saying)
4   *Incidentally*, you can sell something too cheap. (way)

 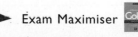

Speaking: simulation

In Part 3 of Paper 5 you may be asked to take part in a simulation. The examiner will describe a situation and ask you to complete a task related to it.

1 Read the situation described below.

'You work for a marketing company that plans promotional campaigns for different products. You have been asked to plan an advertising campaign to launch a new product, either:

- a combined shower gel/shampoo
- a new type of pen
- a new hi-fi system *or*
- a new camera'

Work in pairs or groups. Each group should choose one product. Using the notes below, discuss and decide together what kind of advertising campaign will achieve the best sales for your product.

- target market – *old/young? male/female/both? people with high/low disposable income?*
- special features – *convenience? quality? innovation?*
- price – *present as luxury item or value for money?*
- name/packaging – *ideas for name? luxury or economy? image?*
- advertising techniques – *celebrity endorsement (who?) use 'before and after' images? music? humour?*
- media to be used in campaign – *cinema? posters? TV? magazines?*

2 When you have planned your campaign, you should be prepared to present it to the rest of the class for approval.

In an oral presentation, it's important to organise your ideas as clearly as possible. Connectors, or linking expressions, are important 'signposts' which make it easier for the listener to follow the development of your ideas.

1 Read the following presentation, ignoring the gaps for the moment. What is the product and how is it going to be marketed and promoted?

'Good morning everyone. In my presentation this morning, I'm going to tell you about our plans for marketing a brand new soft drink. *First of all*, I'll explain the type of consumer we think we should be aiming at, then I'll discuss some of the features of this product that we think make it special. *After that*, I'll move on to talk about our ideas on how to present and price the product, and *finally* I'll discuss how we think it should be advertised.

To begin with, then, research has indicated that there is a need for a new non-alcoholic drink which appeals to (1) .... and *so* we have aimed our campaign particularly at (2) ....

Moving on to the product itself, the main feature we'll be focusing on is (3) .... *. In addition to this* we'll be mentioning that (4) .... and *accordingly* we'll be stressing the fact that (5) ....

The packaging will reflect this healthy, sophisticated image – for *example*, (6) ....

It will be marketed as a luxury product and *consequently* (7) .... We're considering using a foreign word for the name, maybe Italian or, *better still*, (8) ....

As far as advertising media are concerned, we've found that (9) .... and *for this reason* we're planning to advertise mainly through (10) ....

So, *to sum up*, the emphasis will be on the fact that (11) ....

2 Now fill in the gaps with phrases from the list below. Use the connectors in italics to help you.

A a name that sounds vaguely Scandinavian
B it will be sold in a bottle, not a can
C it won't be cheap
D its delicate, subtle taste
E it's healthy
F people in their 20s and 30s with a reasonable amount of disposable income
G television advertisements
H the more sophisticated consumer
I there are no artificial additives
J this age group doesn't go to the cinema so much
K this is a high-quality, luxury product

3 Listen to the recording and check your answers.

4 Read the text again and suggest a different expression to replace each of the connectors in italics.

3 Now take turns to present your own campaigns to the class. When all the proposals have been presented, the class should decide which campaign sounds the most interesting.

Grammar plus: emphasis (2) (preparatory *it*)

1 Read the information about the uses of *it* and do the exercises.

> The pronoun *it* may be used in four main ways.
> 1 To refer back to something that has already been mentioned.

What does *it* refer to in this extract from the Listening text on page 53?

> New products are being launched all the time … but a lot of them sink without trace after just a short time. And this isn't just to do with how good the product is; a lot of *it* is to do with how it's marketed to the public.

> 2 As an 'empty' or 'dummy' subject.

Can *it* be replaced by any other subject in the following sentences? If so, what is the effect?

> *It* was the middle of summer. *It* hadn't rained for several weeks and *it* was extremely hot. *It* was almost midnight before the air cooled.

> 3 As a 'preparatory subject' in order to postpone the subject of a sentence to a later position. This may be done if the subject is long, for example a clause, or if the speaker/writer wants to focus our attention on the subject by placing it towards the end of the sentence.

Underline the subject in the following examples. Then rewrite each sentence starting with *It*. Decide which sentence sounds better and why.

1 <u>From the playground to the classroom</u> is a small step.
   It is a small step

2 To monitor what young children watch on TV is the responsibility of the parents.
   ....

3 For the young consumer to understand the difference between an advert and a programme on the television takes until the age of about six.
   ....

4 That the price has to be right goes without saying.
   ....

5 That the company can't just send the product off to the shops and hope for the best is obvious.
   ....

6 Does the fact that these educational resource packs include references to the products of the generous donor matter?
   Does it
   ....

7 That you can sell something too cheap is worth remembering.
   ....

> 4 As a 'preparatory object' in order to postpone a clause in object position.

Underline the object clause in each sentence. In which **one** sentence can you replace the pronoun *it* with the object clause without changing the form?

1 I find *it* enjoyable working here.
2 Parents may consider *it* easier to give in to their children's demands.
3 We owe *it* to him that the campaign has been a success.

► Grammar reference pp. 206-207

2 Introductory *it* can be replaced by other structures which may change the focus of the sentence without changing the meaning.
Look at the way the following sentences have been rewritten. Underline the words that have been changed or added.

1 It is the responsibility of parents to monitor what young children watch on TV.
   <u>Monitoring</u> what young children watch on TV is the responsibility of parents.

   Parents are responsible for monitoring what young children watch on TV.

2 It would be a good idea to have a code of advertising practice.
   To have a code of advertising practice would be a good idea.

   The introduction of a code of advertising practice would be a good idea.

3 We owe it to him that the campaign has been a success.
   We owe the success of the campaign to him.

► Grammar reference pp. 206-207

3 Use of English: sentence transformations

Finish each sentence so that it is as similar in meaning as possible to the one printed before it.

1 From Algiers to Niamey by road is a long and difficult journey.
It ....

2 Making a speech to a large audience can be very frightening.
It ....

3 Inviting them to take part might be a good idea.
It ....

4 I am honoured to be here tonight on this very special occasion.
It ....

5 No one can predict the future accurately.
It ....

6 The loss of his job turned out to be a good thing.
It ....

7 A management course wouldn't be particularly useful to you.
It ....

8 It's no excuse that a danger warning was printed on the packaging.
The fact ....

9 I'll leave it to you which brand we choose.
I'll leave the ....

10 I owe it to him that I was promoted so rapidly.
I owe my ....

Register: spoken and written English

The ability to use the appropriate register when speaking and writing is an important skill in English, and is tested in the exam in Papers 2, 3 and 5. The following exercises give you practice in recognising and using different registers.

1 Read the introduction to a magazine article about the fashion designer Stella McCartney, then answer the question below.

Stella McCartney is the daughter of Paul McCartney of the famous pop group, the Beatles. She studied fashion design and after her graduation in 1995 she was almost immediately made head of a Paris fashion house at the young age of 25. Some felt that this rapid success was due in part to the influence of her father. But in fashion, talent is more important than influence.

Do you think the article will be mainly about
a) Stella's relationship with her father?
b) her career as a fashion designer?
c) something else?

2 Read the two passages A and B below, and discuss the following questions.

1 What information do the passages give you about Stella McCartney?
2 Which passage is more like spoken English? Which is more like written English? What features tell you?
3 Which passage is more likely to be an extract from a later part of the magazine article about Stella?

A

Despite the fame, it's the most normal family I know and it's close – we all love each other so much, and get on so well. My parents have always told me I was great.

At the weekend I was down in the country at their place baking cookies and I was a bit stressed out about work and Dad came up to me and said 'Stella, just stop for a minute and look at me and remember you are a lovely girl.' My Dad's so funny – he'll say, 'So, Stella, I think it's kilts with tassels this season, what do you reckon?' Oh dear, I wish I hadn't told you about that – I want to hold back my private life.

What's funny is that in his interviews people have started asking him about me. The first time I realised that my Dad was incredibly famous was when he performed a concert in Rio in front of 20,000 people. Suddenly it dawned on me. Actually, my Dad is the coolest dude alive.

B

Her 1995 graduation show featured top models Kate Moss and Naomi Campbell, while other students were relying on friends to model. Although this made her unpopular, she is unrepentant. Somewhere in this irresistibly photogenic young woman is the talent of a modest, diligent worker who asks that we swallow our vague sense of injustice and look at how eagerly she has beavered, how hard she has tried.

She was the only student at college to use a thimble because, dissatisfied with the tuition in tailoring, she enrolled for evening lessons with an old Savile Row* friend of her father's. The dedicated work ethic is partly explained by a fear of being dismissed as a rich girl dilettante. Partly, too, it is the influence of parents who made it clear from the start that their children would be expected to make their own way. And finally it is the knowledge, boldly stated, that genius alone would never be enough.

* Savile Row: London Street famous for its expensive tailors' shops

3   The majority of written English, especially newspaper and magazine articles, is neither very formal nor very informal in style, but somewhere in between. Some informal writing may share features of spoken English. The degree of formality depends on the target reader, the reason for writing, and the type of publication.

Look at the table of features that distinguish formal and informal written English. Underline examples in passages **A** and **B**. Do any features of formal and informal written English occur in both texts?

4

1   Read passage A again. Think of an alternative for each colloquial word or expression you underlined, for example: _stressed out – worried_

2   Rewrite the passage in a more formal written style. Use the following framework to guide you.

Despite being so ... , my family is as normal as any other. We are ... and ... . My parents have always made me feel ... .

One weekend, ... them in the country. I was feeling ... . Then, while I ... , my father tried to ... , telling me ... .

It is interesting that my father is now being asked ... . It was not until I ... that I realised ... .

Feature	Informal	Formal
1 Choice of vocabulary	colloquial and slang expressions phrasal verbs	formal expressions; one-word verbs of Latin origin; abstract nouns
2 Tone	personal tone with use of first person	impersonal tone, avoidance of first person
3 Personal/impersonal structures	use of active structures	use of passive and impersonal constructions e.g. _It is said that..._
4 Contractions/full forms	contractions used _It's, doesn't_	full forms used e.g. _It is, does not_
5 Sentence patterns	short sentences or long sentences with several main clauses joined by _and_	complex sentences with subordinating conjunctions e.g. _although_; use of participle clauses
6 Emphatic structures	some limited use of inversion e.g. _Not only did we lose our way, we got drenched too!_	use of inversion for emphasis e.g. _Should you need further information ..._
7 Punctuation	use of dashes and exclamation marks for emphasis; use of commas to link clauses where conjunctions are needed	correct use of commas, use of semi-colons; use of parentheses or dashes for explanatory insertions
8 Coherence and cohesion	may not be clearly or logically organised	clear organisation sign-posted by linking words; repetition of or rephrasing of vocabulary items throughout a text (lexical cohesion)
9 Stylistic devices		deliberate repetition of a structure; rhetorical questions

5

1 Make a list of different genres or types of written English, for example: novels, newspaper articles, textbooks, instruction manuals, notes and messages, etc.

2 Decide which genres are concerned:

a) with expressing feelings and emotions, creating images and associations in the reader's mind (i.e. creative writing)?

b) with presenting facts, issues, ideas and opinions, and persuading the reader to agree (i.e. expository writing)?

3 How would you expect them to differ in the way they are written? Which ones would you expect to be most like spoken English?

6 Read and compare passages C and D below and discuss these questions.

1 Which passage is an example of creative writing? of expository writing?
2 What type of publication do you think each passage is taken from?
3 What are the main features that distinguish the two types of writing?

Creative writing
- *focus on feelings*
- *personal tone*
- *detailed description of physical sensations, emotions*
....

Expository writing
- *focus on facts and opinions*
....
....
....
....

C

The successful art auction house presents itself as a temple of civilised style and judgement, but its essential function is to uncivilise the judgement of at least two normally balanced people and entice them to bid and counter bid for any given object as far as possible above the price it would command in a shop. The appeal is to cupidity and recklessness. The trick is to persuade people who already possess more than their fair share of worldly goods that their happiness depends on acquiring even more.

D

It seemed as if I had been sitting at the back of the hall for hours. Finally the auctioneer announced Lot 64 and held up the small, dark painting in its ornate frame. He looked round the room impassively as he invited bids. My heart began to pound. Five hundred, six hundred, seven hundred … . The bids came from every corner of the room, but still I couldn't move.

'Nine hundred pounds to the gentleman in the corner. Am I bid more? Going at nine hundred pounds. Going once, …' – the tension was mounting – 'going twice …'

Suddenly I was on my feet. I heard myself shout, 'A thousand pounds!' A sea of faces turned to look at me. The auctioneer paused, looked round the room and seeing no further signals, brought his hammer down with a crash to confirm the sale. Drained of all emotion, I sat down again slowly.

7 In Paper 5 you are asked to read a short text and say where it may have been taken from. To do this, you need to be able to recognise features of formal and informal language. Read the short extracts below (these are shorter than in the exam).

1 Decide which extracts are:
   a) spoken English.
   b) written English.
   c) written-down spoken English.
2 For extracts in Group a) decide who is the speaker and what is the context.
3 For Groups b) and c) decide what genre of written English the extract belongs to (see Exercise 5).

1
Pin the sections of the bodice together, matching the darts. Tack the seams loosely using the coloured thread.

2 I should like to state publicly, here tonight, that I shall be proud to be a candidate in the forthcoming election.

3 It's great – he'll put us up for free in his flat and it's really close to the beach. It couldn't be better! So let me know what you think – I need to let him know if we're taking him up on his offer.

4 Have you heard about Jonathon? Well, I've heard that he's getting married next week – yes, I know, I couldn't believe it myself but apparently it's true. Sorry? Oh, to Susan!

5
And it's Wright running down the wing ... he passes to Thompson ... Jones ... oh, and it's a wonderful move ... back to Wright ... he's clear in the box and it's in the back of the net! What a goal!

6 News is coming in of an avalanche in the Austrian Alps. Unconfirmed reports say that there are three people unaccounted for.

7
Although she published both poetry and novels, it is perhaps for her critical and philosophical works that Kathleen Nott will be principally remembered.

8 The father and son boarded the train and waited for it to move in the company of buzzing flies and passengers struggling on and off.

8 Select three extracts from Exercise 7 and rewrite them in a different style.

Writing: formal letter (1) (complaint)

In Paper 2 there is always a task-directed question in which you have to produce a piece of writing (about 300 words) appropriate to a specified context, such as a formal letter, a report, or an article.

For this type of task it is very important to:

- think about the purpose of writing and the target reader
- use a style, tone and register suitable for the task
- use a consistent register – you will lose marks if you mix registers in your answer.

1 You are going to write a letter of complaint about an advertisement you have seen. First, read the information below about the UK Advertising Standards Authority and discuss these questions.

1 What is the function of this organisation?
2 Is there a similar organisation in your country?
3 Who would you write to if you wanted to complain about an advertisement?

ASA

The Advertising Standards Authority was set up in 1962 and acts independently of both the advertising business and the government to make sure that the millions of advertisements that appear in the UK each year are:

✓ legal   ✓ decent   ✓ honest and truthful

The Authority safeguards the public by applying the rules contained in the British Codes of Advertising and Sales Promotion to all advertisers. The Codes stipulate what is and is not acceptable in newspapers, magazines, poster and direct marketing sales promotion, cinema, video and electronic media. Advertisers who break the Codes' rules risk receiving damaging adverse publicity and they will be refused space to advertise.

In addition to the Codes' general rules, advertisements are subject to the following requirements:

- They should contain nothing that is likely to cause offence on the grounds of race, religion, sex or disability.
- They should contain nothing that condones or is likely to provoke violence or anti-social behaviour.

The ASA handles around 10,000 complaints each year.

WR TE
One letter is all it takes

2 Read the following case study and discuss these questions.

1 Which code do you think the advert may have broken?
2 Do you think complaints 1 and 2 were upheld or not upheld? (You can check your answers on page 223.)

Complaint: Objections were raised to a double-page trade press advertisement. One page showed a picture of a nuclear power plant, the other page showed sheep grazing on green fields and a man fishing in a pond. The complaints challenged:

1. the implication, in the claim that "BNFL* can transform old nuclear installations into land that can be used again" and the picture, that land used for nuclear installations could be re-used for any purpose; and

2. the claim ".. we've perfected ways to deal with all types of nuclear waste."

Adjudication:

*BNFL: British Nuclear Fuels plc

3 Work in pairs. **Student A**, look at the advert opposite. **Student B**, look at the advert on page 222. Take turns to describe your advert to your partner. The adverts are intended to be shocking. How do you react to them?

4 Think of some advertisements that you have seen recently in your national press, in magazines, on posters or in the cinema. Describe them to a partner. Your partner should decide if any of them could be accused of breaking the rules laid out in the Codes described on page 59.

5 Any formal letter should follow a similar pattern, no matter what the purpose of the letter is. Each section should have a separate paragraph. Put the sections below into the order you think they should appear in the letter.

- ☐ any requests for more information or action
- ☐ clarification of situation
- ☐ further action to be taken, details of any enclosures
- ☐ further details
- ☐ reason for writing

Note: In the exam you don't need to worry about letter layout, unless the task specifically asks you to include addresses or follow the conventions of letter-writing.

6 Read the following writing task. How many parts does it have? Look back at Exercise 5. Which section of the letter will each of these parts come in?

> A company has put up a large advertising hoarding in your local town centre. The advertisement seems to you likely to provoke unacceptable behaviour. Write a letter of complaint to your local council, explaining why you object to it and what you would like them to do about it. (About 300 words.)

7 Read the following letter, which was written in answer to the task, and answer these questions.

1 What kind of advert is the writer complaining about?
2 What is the reason for his complaint?
3 What does he want done?
4 How does he round off the letter?
5 Are the tone and register appropriate to the task? Are they consistently maintained?

Dear Sir,

I am writing to complain about the car advertisement currently being displayed on the hoarding outside the main post office in the centre of town.

The advertisement shows a car speeding away from a set of traffic lights, with the caption, '0—100 in under 10 seconds'. I feel that this claim is misleading and irresponsible. For a start, there is so much traffic on the roads these days that it is extremely unlikely that anyone could reach a speed of 100 kilometres per hour in a town. The advertisers also seem to have forgotten that there are speed limits on most roads. In my view, this type of advertising only encourages drivers to break the law.

Furthermore, the advert suggests that the best cars are the fastest cars and places undue emphasis on the power of this car in particular, implying that its best feature is its speed. I would argue that this can only encourage those people who buy the car to drive fast in order to maintain that image. However, we all know that speed kills, and more often than not it is the innocent pedestrian who is the victim of the speeding driver. Don't you think car companies should be focusing on safety, and behaving responsibly in trying to reduce fatalities on our roads by giving safety a better image?

May I request that you have this advertisement taken down as soon as possible? While I have no objection to cars being advertised, I feel strongly that this type of advertising should not be allowed. I have already written to the company concerned, requesting that they remove this advertisement from their campaign and giving them my reasons in detail. I enclose a copy of this letter for your information.

Thank you in advance for your help. I look forward to hearing from you.

Yours faithfully,

Sam Broadbent

Sam Broadbent

Encs.*

Encs: short for 'enclosures'

8

1   A letter of complaint is usually written in a formal style, and it clearly states the writer's point of view. Underline the formal phrases or set expressions that the writer uses to indicate his own views.

2   Now underline the expressions that mean the following.

1   on show at the moment (para. 1)
2   giving the wrong impression (para. 2)
3   make something seem overly important (para. 3)
4   cut down the number of deaths (para. 3)
5   I don't mind about ... (para. 4)

9   Read the following writing task. What do you need to include?

> You have seen a commercial on your local television station which appeared during a children's programme. You feel that an advertisement of this type is not suitable for showing on children's TV. Write a letter of complaint to the television company, explaining why you object to it and what you would like them to do about it. (About 300 words.)

10   Plan your letter before you write. How many paragraphs will it have? What will each contain?

11   Write the letter. Make sure you state your point of view clearly and use a consistent tone and register. After you have written your letter, exchange it with a partner. Evaluate each other's work and suggest improvements.

1 Choose a suitable word or phrase from the box to fill each of the gaps in the following letter.

accordingly   as a result   because of this
better still   first of all   for example   furthermore
last but not least   likewise   what's more

Dear Mr Perkins,

I wish to bring to your attention some problems which I encountered at your hotel when you yourself were absent.

(1) ...... , when I booked, I clearly stated that we required one double and two single rooms on the same floor. When we arrived, we were informed that this was impossible and (2) ...... that it should not have been promised, as all single rooms are on the top floor. (3) ...... , I had explained when booking that we are vegetarians and I was reassured that there is always a vegetarian option on the menu. (4) ...... , I did not request special dietary arrangements. To our horror, we discovered that the vegetarian option is always the same and (5) ...... we had baked aubergine three times in two days. (6) ...... , the dining-room staff were extremely slow and forgetful. (7) ...... , it took three requests to get a simple jug of iced water! (8) ...... , I must inform you that the manner of your deputy was far from polite when these matters were raised with her.

Our stay was by no means the pleasant experience we had anticipated and (9) ...... , I feel that at least an apology or (10) ...... a refund is due to us.

Yours sincerely,

Jack Lawrence

Jack Lawrence

2 Decide whether each of the following sentences is formal (F) or informal (I) and underline the features which indicate this.

1   Given the speed with which the popularity of film stars can diminish, there may be risks in using one to promote our new line of products.

2   We're all getting really fed up with film stars who only give interviews when they want to plug their latest release.

3   Last summer, my parents had their silver wedding and asked all of us and our kids down to their place for a whole weekend, and so there was this really great bunch of us all celebrating together.

4   The weather has proved to be unexpectedly mild, attracting considerable numbers of visitors to the town and hence increasing the likelihood of traffic congestion in the evening.

3 Finish each of the following sentences in such a way that it is as similar as possible in meaning to the sentence printed before it.

1   Will it matter that he is unable to speak Greek when he starts the new job?
Will his ....

2   It had been snowing for several hours by the time we left.
Snow ....

3   Getting from this part of the country to the coast doesn't take long.
It ....

4   Might it be helpful for us to have professional advice regarding this issue?
Might professional ....

5   Our being late for the concert didn't matter, as the singers were too.
The fact ....

6   It was nearly midnight before we got home.
We didn't ....

7   Under the circumstances, learning French quickly was essential.
It ....

8   It really wasn't necessary for you to apologise.
Your ....

9   Recognition as market leader is currently the aim of this company.
It ....

10 The fact no one checked with the MD before speaking to the press is very much to be regretted.
It's highly ....

4 Read the passage below. Decide where it may have been taken from and how it links with the general theme of the unit. What aspects of shopping nowadays do you enjoy and what do you not enjoy? Why?

Shopping is the greatest feel-good factor in modern life. You feel bad – it's OK, a quick trip to the shops, a few impulse buys and you feel better. Trouble with the boss? A new outfit soon puts it into perspective. Fed up with the family? A new CD and you can put them out of your mind. The problem is, of course, that it's a quick fix but not a solution – and with mounting credit card bills you're really in trouble.

5

Tough justice

Vocabulary: crime

1 Read the newspaper extract below, and discuss the question that follows.

US murder rates collapse

THE VIOLENT crime rate in the United States has fallen to the lowest level since standardised records were first collected in the early 1970s.

New York City is heading for a remarkable achievement: the lowest number of murders since 1964. Its rapidly declining murder rate is part of a nationwide trend towards lower crime figures and in particular a rapid decline in murders in the big cities.

Which of the following do you think could be the main reasons for the decline in crime rates? Choose three.

- zero-tolerance policing (no crime is ignored)
- improved surveillance techniques (e.g. closed-circuit TV)
- improved detection rates
- re-introduction of the death penalty in some states
- better economic conditions in the cities
- more effective rehabilitation of offenders
- more visible police presence
- a growth in the prison population

2 Discuss these questions.

1 What types of crime are most/least common in your country?
2 Are crime rates falling or rising in your country?
3 What explanations can you suggest for this?

3

1 Match each of the following verbs with a word or phrase on the right to form a collocation connected with a British court of law.

1	commit	a)	guilty/not guilty
2	plead	b)	to an offence
3	pass	c)	the defendant (*to* + time period)
4	convict/acquit	d)	evidence in court
5	admit	e)	someone in custody
6	serve	f)	a crime
7	give	g)	on a jury
8	cross-examine	h)	sentence on someone
9	appeal	i)	a witness
10	sentence	j)	against a sentence/verdict
11	remand	k)	someone with an offence
12	charge	l)	someone of a crime

2 Which of the actions or procedures above are carried out by each of the following people?

- a judge
- a member of the public
- a criminal
- a police officer
- a lawyer/(barrister *UK*)
- a juror/the jury
- a witness
- the defendant

3 What differences between the British legal system and your own are indicated by the collocations?

4 Interview a partner using the questions below. Compare your experiences.

Have you or has someone you know ...
1 ever been the victim of a crime?
2 witnessed a crime?
3 reported a crime to the police?
4 been called to give evidence in a court of law?
5 been called to do jury service?

Reading: newspaper article

1 Read the newspaper headlines and answer the following questions.

1 What problem are the headlines highlighting?
2 How big a problem is this in your country?
3 What measures are available to the police and the courts to deal with it?

Youth gangs prey on city centre shops
Petty theft reaches record high

Young offenders not deterred by court sentences
Study finds 90% of young criminals re-offend.

2 You are going to read an article about a new method of dealing with young offenders recently pioneered in the USA.

Skim the text to find the answers to the questions below. Which parts of the text will you read?

1 What is the new method being tried out?
2 How successful is it? What is the main reason for its success?

Peer pres

1 An armed police bailiff guards the proceedings and the black-robed judge is "your honour". He addresses the jury as "ladies and gentlemen" but there any resemblance to an orthodox American court ends. These jurors are not even voting citizens. They are fellow juvenile miscreants who judge their contemporaries in a unique youth court in San Francisco aimed at halting delinquency at its first manifestation. It is attracting widespread notice for its astonishing success; a re-offending rate of only five per cent compared with over a third for the mainstream juvenile system.

2 To a foreign visitor, the youth court's replacement of a punishing judge with a true jury of peers is most intriguing in an authoritarian US legal system that jails more of its citizens than any other industrialised nation. The court handles only minor offences: drinking alcohol, vandalism, graffiti, and battery. The most common is petty theft, often shop-lifting. As all offences have been admitted beforehand, there is no trial. Names are withheld and schools concealed to avoid factionalism and possible gang identification.

3 On this Wednesday evening, 42 youngsters file in for jury service in a court normally used for civil litigation. As the hearing begins, the jurors cas[t] knowing looks at the first defendant whom we will call John. Like him, the[y] are admitted offenders. Indeed, sitting o[n] these juries is part of their rehabilitation. After John admitted his offence, he an[d] his parents agreed to co-operate with th[e] court to avoid the harsher route throug[h] the juvenile court system. John, nearly 17 has shoplifted two Walkmans and thre[e] cartons of cigarettes from a discoun[t] store. The police report says he was wit[h] his mother when he concealed the item[s] in specially tapered baggy trousers. Joh[n] says that it was the first time he had stolen and that the goods were intende[d] as Christmas presents to save mone[y]. Then he awaits jurors' questions.

4 They are hard and shrewd. The judg[e] tells me afterwards that the jurors are tougher on defendants than adults woul[d] be. One boy does not believe that it wa[s] John's first time because he went about i[t] too professionally. A girl asks sarcasticall[y,] "How would your friend feel about you[r] Christmas present if he was busted fo[r] receiving stolen goods?" Another juro[r] puts a question encouraged by th[e] counsellors, "How did your offence affec[t] the community?"

5 The jury retires to privat[e] deliberations, while another panel take[s] its place to deliberate on another case[.]

sure

Later, John's jury returns with a sentence. John receives 85 hours of compulsory community work (which will probably include jury duty) plus 400-word apologies to the store and his mother. He must also write 850 words on "thinking before acting" and another 850 on the consequences of stealing. The programme requires that parents also attend counselling, and the director of the scheme has received grateful letters from parents marvelling at how family life had improved as a result of being forced to examine what was wrong in their relationship with their children.

The success rate of the programme is attributed to the children being involved in the process; the offenders understand why they need to be rehabilitated. The problem with the regular juvenile system is that by the time they get to court they may have broken the law several times.

The session ends with a harangue from the formidable police supervisor; a juror has disrespected the court with inappropriate clothes. Her peers add ten extra community hours on her then and there. Tough justice, juvenile style.

3 The following questions will help you to interpret both the factual and implied information in the text. Decide if each statement is true or false and underline evidence in the text to support your answers.

1 A judge in an American court would normally be addressed as 'ladies and gentlemen'.
2 Offenders sentenced in San Francisco's Youth Court are unlikely to commit crimes in the future.
3 The writer implies that the legal system of the USA is in general excessively harsh.
4 The court has to decide whether the offenders are guilty of minor offences or not.
5 In order to protect the victims of the crime, some information is not revealed.
6 It is hoped that sitting on the jury will encourage young people not to re-offend.
7 In the Youth Court, John was found guilty of stealing items from a shop.
8 The writer implies that the punishments suggested by the jury are often rather too severe.
9 The jury questioned John to make him think about the implications of what he did.
10 Punishment may involve sitting on a jury for another case.
11 The Youth Court is part of a wider programme aimed at helping young offenders and their families.
12 One member of the jury is given an additional punishment by the police supervisor.

4 Discuss your reaction to the Youth Court.

1 What are the advantages and disadvantages?
2 Would this system be appropriate in your country? Why/Why not?

5 Find the following words in the article and use the context to work out their meaning. Note down a synonym, definition or example to explain the meaning.

Paragraph 1
1 orthodox
2 miscreant (formal)
Paragraph 2
3 petty theft
4 factionalism
Paragraph 3
5 file in

6 litigation
7 knowing
8 tapered
Paragraph 4
9 shrewd
10 bust someone/get busted

6 Find the following words in the article.

1 What part of speech are they – noun or verb? What do they mean?

Paragraph 1
1 guard
2 notice
Paragraph 2
3 handle
Paragraph 3
4 cast
5 discount

Paragraph 5
6 deliberate
7 programme
Paragraph 7
8 harangue

2 Think of a sentence using each of the words above in a different part of speech without changing the form of the word. How does the meaning change? Does the word stress change?

7 As part of his punishment, John has to write 850 words on 'the consequences of stealing'. Imagine you are his friend, and he has asked you to help him write the composition. Brainstorm the topic with a partner. Use these headings as a guide.

The consequences of stealing
• for the thief
• for the victim/shop
• for the community

Grammar check: modal verbs (1)

Modal verbs may be tested in Paper 3, especially in Question 1 (cloze) and Question 3 (gapped sentences).
Other expressions for describing the same functions may also be tested, for example in Question 4 (key word transformations).

1 Use of English: gapped sentences

1 Fill in the blanks with a suitable phrase including a modal verb.

1 I'll .... pay the fine or I'll be sent to prison.
2 You're looking rather pale – perhaps you .... a doctor.
3 I .... gone to the party if I'd wanted, but I didn't really feel like it.
4 You .... a taxi – if you'd let me know you were coming, I'd have picked you up.
5 You .... that curried fish unless you like very spicy food.
6 You .... play near the railway tracks, children – it's very dangerous.
7 'I wonder if I .... possibly .... your phone?' 'Of course you ....'
8 Being brought up in a bilingual family, she .... English fluently by the time she was five!
9 He .... more sense than to lend money to Susie. He'll never get it back.
10 We absolutely .... a move on – we're going to be terribly late.
11 'Do you know where School Lane is, please?' 'I'm afraid I .... you – I'm new around here!.'
12 The nurses were wonderful – they were so busy, but they .... more helpful.

2 Which of the sentences 1–12 refer to the past and which to the present/future?

3 Match sentences 1–12 above with the meanings below.

a) obligation
b) prohibition
c) advice (positive)
d) advice (negative)
e) opportunity/free choice
f) lack of necessity
g) permission
h) ability
i) necessity

► Grammar reference p. 207

Watch Out! *may/might*

The modal verbs *may* and *might* used in requests are very polite and formal. With a certain intonation, they can sound sarcastic and unpleasant. Which of these sentences is polite and which sarcastic?

1 I wonder if I might ask you a big favour?
2 Perhaps I might suggest that you do this in your own time?
3 And what have **you** been doing, may I ask?

---

2 Find the mistakes in the following sentences and correct them. Complete the rules below.

1 You needn't to come with me if you don't feel like it.
2 We needn't have gone to work last Monday, so we went to the beach.
3 You mustn't help me, but you can if you want to.
4 The child was struggling in the deep water but fortunately his mother could rescue him just in time.
5 I found I must pay extra for a single room.
6 You didn't need to do that – I could manage on my own.
7 You hadn't to give him that tip – the service was awful!
8 In my view zoos should have to be educational if they are to be allowed at all.
9 I can have had a great career as a singer if I hadn't got married!

• When *need* is used as a modal verb, it is followed by ...
• When an action was unnecessary in the past and **didn't** happen, we use ... , but when it **did** happen we use ...
• The negative of *must* is ... for prohibition, but ... for lack of necessity.
• We use ... for general ability in the past, but ... when referring to a single occasion.
• We use ... *have done* to talk about unfulfilled opportunity or ability in the past.
• To express an opinion about right or wrong in the past, we use ... *have done*.

► Grammar reference p. 207

---

3 Instead of using modal verbs, we can express obligation, advice, etc. in other ways. Read the following examples and match them to the meanings in Exercise 1.3. Try re-expressing them using an appropriate modal verb.

1 All students are required to attend the fire drill at 5.00 p.m.
2 I don't recommend the lamb dish here – last time I had it, it was disgusting.
3 It's entirely up to you whether you stay or go.
4 She's quite capable of managing on her own.

5 Students are not to use dictionaries in the exam.

6 Please feel free to browse – you are under no obligation to buy.

7 You'd be better off getting a taxi – the buses are always full.

8 You aren't supposed to smoke in here.

9 There's no need to get impatient – I'm doing my best!

10 Hadn't you better go home? Your family will be looking for you.

11 I didn't quite manage to finish the job on time.

Watch Out! *be supposed to/suppose*

These verbs are often confused. Match each example to the correct meaning below.

1 Why are you watching TV? Aren't you supposed to be doing your homework?
2 I don't suppose you know where Peter is, do you?
3 I hear he's supposed to be a talented artist.
4 The danger is not as great as many suppose.

   a) be meant to   b) think, consider

---

4 **Use of English:** key word transformations

For each of the sentences below, write a new sentence as similar as possible in meaning to the original sentence, but using the word given. This word must not be altered in any way.

1 You'd be better off doing what he says. **recommend**
2 You can do whatever you want. **free**
3 It is not necessary for you to wear formal clothing. **need**
4 You don't have to do military service in this country. **compulsory**
5 She is not to play in any further matches this season. **banned**
6 He's already proved he can do it himself. **capable**
7 I think exams should be voluntary for all students. **compelled**
8 They say he's writing a new novel. **supposed**

Use of English: cloze

1 Read the first sentence in the cloze text below. Without using a dictionary, discuss the difference in meaning between the three terms in italics. Give an example of each.

2 Read the rest of the passage quickly without filling in any of the gaps to get a general understanding of what it is about. Underline the first occurrence of each of the three terms which were introduced in the first sentence. Were your ideas in Exercise 1 correct?

RULES, LAWS AND NORMS

Any discussion of criminal behaviour requires understanding of the difference in meaning of *rules*, *laws* and *norms*. Rules (1)............ be unwritten, or formal and written. The rules of dress or of how we eat are unwritten guides. (2)............ contrast, the rules of a factory, for example safety regulations, are usually (3)............ down and serve (4)............ strict regulators of behaviour.

Laws are perhaps the (5)............ example of written, formal rules and (6)............ decided upon by powerful and influential groups in society. In order to ensure that everyone adheres (7)............ the laws, there are specific penalties, including fines or imprisonment, for those (8)............ guilty of (9)............ them. Unlike other rules, (10)............ as rules of dress or of grammar, laws can always be enforced by agencies (11) .... the police and the courts.

A norm is very much (12)............ general term; it is an expected (13)............ of behaviour shared by (14)............ of a social group. Norms can be thought of as unwritten rules. (15)............ of these are that parents should play with their children, or that (16)............ should respond in the appropriate (17)............ to a 'good morning' greeting. Norms are (18)............ of the culture of a society and are (19)............ on from (20)............ generation to the next over time.

3 Now fill in the gaps, following the procedure suggested in Unit 1, page 15.

4 Discuss and justify your answers with a partner. For example:
'Number 1 has to be a modal verb – there isn't another verb in the sentence, and the gap is followed by "be".'
'I think Number 2 is " ... " – it's part of a linking expression.'

5 Discuss this question.

Laws are not universal. They change over time, and from one place to another. Can you think of:
• a law that used to be enforced in your country, but which no longer exists?
• a law which is enforced, but which you think should not be?
• a law which does not exist, but which should exist!

Listening: three-way choice

Paper 4 may include a question where you have to decide whether a list of statements reflects the views of the speakers. The choice is often between two speakers, and each statement may reflect the view of one or both of them.

To do this type of question you need to listen for:

- the stated facts
- the attitudes and opinions of the speakers
- whether they agree with one another or not.

You may also need to understand colloquial language.

1 Read the following information about Angus and Rick, who are both convicted offenders.

Angus comes from Glasgow but ran away to London when he was 15. He is now 19. He has convictions for breaking and entering, and petty theft.

Rick is 18 and has always lived in London. He has been in trouble with the police on and off since he was 11. He was recently convicted of petty theft and minor assault.

2 You will hear Angus and Rick discussing their respective punishments. Before you listen, read through the list of statements below. What can you predict about the content of the Listening? What do you think 'Community Service' involves?

1	The influence of friends led him astray.	1
2	Community Service is preferable to prison.	2
3	Community Service was not an easy experience.	3
4	People don't like dealing with violent criminals.	4
5	Community Service led to further conflicts with those in authority.	5
6	Community Service can be rewarding.	6
7	Time passes slowly when doing Community Service.	7
8	The experience has changed him.	8

3 Now listen to the recording. Indicate which of the opinions listed are given by each speaker. In each box, write either:

A (Angus)

or **R** (Rick)

or **B** (both Angus and Rick)

4 Listen again and check your answers.

5 Discuss these questions.

1 Who do you think has benefited most from his experience of community service? Justify your answer.
2 Who do you think is more likely to re-offend? Why?

6 **Say it again**

Re-express the sentences from the Listening text using the key word given.

1 There's only so much you can get away with.
   limit
2 Violence is about the worst thing you can do.
   nothing
3 He was really in favour of community service.
   idea
4 Maybe people will treat me seriously.
   taken

Speaking: discussion

1 Read these statements. What point is each one making about punishment?

'The success rate of the [rehabilitation programme for young offenders in San Francisco] is attributed to the children being involved in the process; the offenders understand why they need to be rehabilitated.' (text, p.65)

'[Working at the youth club] I'm starting to prove myself – show there's more to me than a police record [...] maybe people will see the real me and treat me seriously [...] I think I've got the chance to make something of myself.' (Listening, p.68)

2

1 You are going to hear an English teenager, Neil, discussing the question below. Before you listen, read the following task and think about what you would say.

> On the basis of what you have read and heard so far in this unit, which of the views of punishment below would you agree with? Give reasons.
>
> 1 An eye for an eye, a tooth for a tooth.
> 2 We need punishment as a deterrent to stop people offending.
> 3 The legal justice system should aim to rehabilitate offenders, not take revenge on them.

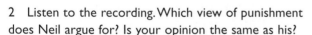 2 Listen to the recording. Which view of punishment does Neil argue for? Is your opinion the same as his?

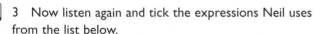 3 Now listen again and tick the expressions Neil uses from the list below.

a) I think (that) ...
b) It seems to me that ...
c) The main argument for ...
d) However, the argument against this ...
e) As well as that ...
f) So let's look at the alternatives ...
g) Another related point is that ...
h) Finally, the idea that ... seems to ...
i) Some people think that ...
j) All in all, I suppose ...

4 Notice how Neil deals with each point.

1 He gives his opinion.
2 He gives arguments for and against.
3 He discusses the alternatives and gives reasons for rejecting them.
4 He summarises - by restating his original opinion.

Which of the expressions above could be used at each of these stages?

3 Work in groups or pairs. Each of you should choose one of the crimes described below. Using the model you have heard to help you, give your views on which punishment you think is most appropriate, together with your reasons for rejecting the alternatives. Your partner should listen carefully and then say if he/she agrees or not.

Crimes

1 A teenager hacks into an airline company's computer system and deliberately introduces a virus.
2 A man is attacked by muggers on the subway, defends himself with a gun and shoots his assailants dead.
3 A small business is caught selling pirated CDs.

Punishments

* long prison sentence/short prison sentence
* community service
* fine
* caution (a formal warning)

4 Write a paragraph summarising your views, using some of the expressions from Exercise 2.

Grammar check: modal verbs (2) (degrees of likelihood)

We use the modal verbs *may, might, could, must* and *can't* to express possibility, likelihood and logical deduction. To speculate about past events we use these verbs followed by the perfect infinitive. We use *should* and *ought to* to say if we think something is possible or true.

1 Agatha Christie (1890–1976) is one of the best-known crime writers of the 20th century. Have you read any of her books or seen a film based on any of them? What was it about?

2 Look at the poster below. What happened to Agatha Christie in December 1926?

BERKSHIRE CONSTABULARY, WOKINGHAM DIVISION.
9th. December 1926

MISSING

From her home "Styles" Sunningdale in this Division.
Mrs. Agatha Mary Clarissa CHRISTIE
(WIFE OF COLONEL A. CHRISTIE)

AGE 35 YEARS, HEIGHT 5 ft. 7 ins., HAIR RED (Shingled), NATURAL TEETH, EYES GREY, COMPLEXION FAIR, WELL BUILT.

DRESSED—Grey Stockingette Skirt, Green Jumper, Grey and dark Grey Cardigan, small Green Velour Hat, may have hand bag containing £5 to £10.   Left home in 4 seater Morris Cowley car at 9.45 p.m. on 3rd. December leaving note saying she was going for a drive.   The next morning the car was found abandoned at Newlands Corner, Albury, Surrey.

Should this lady be seen or any information regarding her be obtained please communicate to any Police Station, or to
CHARLES GODDARD, Superintendent,
WOKINGHAM.
Telephone No. 11 Wokingham.
PRINTED AT THE "BERKSHIRE GAZETTE" OFFICES, PEACH STREET, WOKINGHAM.

3

1 Now read and listen to the following conversation between two policemen involved in the case. What explanations do they come up with for her disappearance?

A: Well, it's a strange case. We found the car in a ditch last Saturday. She must have been driving too fast and lost control. But where is she now – or where's the body?

B: Well, she might have hit her head in the accident and lost her memory – she could just be wandering around somewhere.

A: But that was six days ago – she couldn't possibly have been wandering around for six days like that, everyone's been looking for her.

B: I suppose not. Well, what about her husband, the Colonel? Do you think he may know more than he's saying?

A: Well it's not impossible – it's common knowledge that things haven't been right between them. There could be another woman. I suppose he might conceivably have had more to do with it than he's letting on.

B: Yes, he seems very keen on this idea that she's lost her memory – too keen, maybe. I think he could well be implicated …

A: Mind you, it's quite a coincidence, isn't it? A famous writer of mystery stories – and then her own disappearance is the biggest mystery of all. Have you thought it might not have been an accident at all?

B: You mean, the Colonel …

A: No, I mean Miss Christie. Has it occurred to you that she may have engineered the whole thing?

B: If so, she's probably sitting in some nice comfortable hotel laughing at us.

A: Yes – and I suspect we could end up being accused of wasting the tax-payers' money. This search must have cost a fortune already.

2   Read the dialogue again and underline all the phrases including modal verbs. Number them 1–12. Match each phrase to the appropriate explanations below.

The speaker
a) is sure this happened.
b) thinks it is possible this happened.
c) thinks it is possible this didn't happen.
d) is sure this didn't happen.
e) thinks it is possible this is the case or will happen.

▶ Grammar reference p. 208

3   What do **you** think was the most likely explanation for the mystery? You can check your ideas by referring to page 219.

Watch Out!

1 He could at least have offered to drive you home!
2 He could have forgotten the date of the meeting.
3 He might have hurt someone, driving so fast!
4 He might have told us he wasn't coming, after all!

Which sentence expresses
   a) possibility?
   b) annoyance?
   c) criticism?

4   Instead of using modal verbs, we can express degrees of likelihood in other ways. Re-express the following sentences in as many different ways as possible, using appropriate expressions from the box below.

1 Our team should win the Cup easily.
   There's every chance of our team winning the Cup.
   It's odds on that our team will win the Cup.
2 He could very well have been the murderer.
   It's highly likely that ...
3 I'm afraid we may not arrive in time for the start of the film.
   I doubt if ...
4 It must have been Peter you saw last night – no-one else fits that description.
5 They certainly won't have managed to solve the mystery yet.

6 No-one can have survived the crash.
7 I suppose they might conceivably decide to double our salaries.
8 They can't have got married secretly – Anna always wanted a big wedding!

It's highly (un)likely that ...
(He/She) is highly unlikely to have + p.p.
There's a strong/faint possibility that ...
There's every chance/likelihood that .... / of + object + -ing
(He/It) is bound/certain/sure to ...
The chances are that ...
I bet (that) ... / It's odds on that ...
I doubt if ... / It's doubtful that ...
There's not much chance that ... / of + object + -ing
I can't see + object + -ing / I can't see why ...
The odds are against + object + -ing
The prospects of ... are good/small.

5   **Use of English:** gapped sentences
Fill each of the blanks with a suitable word or phrase.

1 Her bag is still on the desk, so she .... home yet.
2 I might .... something would go wrong – it always does!
3 John is .... to get the job – he's the best qualified candidate.
4 Our .... winning the Cup have never been better.
5 She .... a very important person for the police to mount such a massive murder hunt.
6 There's only .... of the government lowering taxes before the next election.
7 I waited for two hours! You .... phoned to let me know you were held up!
8 He only got 10% in the test – he .... attention in class.

Use of English: cloze

1 Methods of crime detection have improved enormously since Agatha Christie wrote her detective novels. Nowadays the police can use a number of methods to help them, including:

- forensic evidence (blood, hair, fingerprints)
- DNA fingerprinting
- psychological profiling
- geographic profiling.

What do you know about these methods?

2 Now read though the cloze passage opposite without trying to fill in any of the gaps yet. How was the robber 'caught' by his jeans?

3 Fill each of the numbered blanks in the passage with one suitable word.

4 Do you foresee any danger in the development of sophisticated techniques such as the ones mentioned in this section? Which of the statements below would you agree with?

'With improved techniques at their disposal for the detection of crime, the police can ensure that law-abiding citizens no longer need go in fear of their lives and property.'

'The development of ever more sophisticated techniques for surveillance and detection increases the likelihood that innocent people will be harassed and possibly wrongly convicted and imprisoned.'

Robber caught by his jeans

WHEN GANG MEMBER Charles Barbee woke up and considered how to prepare for the first of two bank robberies, he made a crucial (1) .... He slipped (2) .... his jeans. This decision helped to (3) .... him in jail for two life (4) .... plus 64 years. That day he was (5) .... on camera during a bombing and robbery that he helped to commit. (6) .... he wore a mask to disguise his face, his jeans were clearly visible.

And (7) .... was all the forensic scientist Vorder Bruegge and his team needed to (8) .... him positively. Police gave them a pair of jeans from Mr Barbee's bedroom and they noticed (9) .... were distinctive lines worn into the fabric. They then enlarged the surveillance photograph (10) .... by the bank's camera. They found almost two dozen features (11) .... the jeans from Barbee's bedroom to the jeans (12) .... by the suspect in the photograph.

"Jeans (13) .... usually be identified more easily than any other type of clothing, (14) .... their owners tend to keep them until they are absolutely worn (15) .... ," says Mr Vorder Bruegge.

The analysis technique was disputed by the defence at the trial, who brought along 34 apparently (16) .... pairs of used jeans in an attempt to (17) .... the theory. However, Vorder Bruegge was (18) .... to check them against his list of distinguishing (19) .... from the photo and show the court that each (20) .... failed to match them.

The jeans analysis has since been used in hundreds of trials in the US.

Exam Focus

Paper 1 Reading (Section A, multiple-choice vocabulary)

In Paper I, Section A, there are 25 multiple-choice questions. You have to choose a word or phrase from a choice of four to fill in a gap in a sentence. The questions test your knowledge of:

- collocations and fixed expressions
- words with similar meanings or forms
- the grammatical patterns that words are used with
- connectors and adverbial phrases
- phrasal verbs.

Here is a procedure for this task.

- Read the sentence carefully.
- Decide what type of word the sentence needs. Think about the possibilities listed above.
- Read the choices carefully. You may be able to eliminate one or two immediately.
- If several of the words look similar, think carefully about their meanings. They may in fact be very different.
- If several words have similar meanings, think carefully about their grammatical use. The words before and after the gaps may suggest a particular grammatical pattern.
- If you aren't sure, take a chance and go for the one that 'feels' right.

1 Choose the word or phrase which best completes each sentence below.
In this exercise there are some hints to help you.

1 Since he has a watertight alibi, he can't be accused of having .... the crime.
   A done **B** made **C** committed **D** performed
(HINT: *Only one of these verbs collocates with crime.*)

2 He was .... guilty of fraud and sentenced to five years' imprisonment.
   A admitted **B** found **C** called **D** shown
(HINT: *This is a collocation.*)

3 The criminal must have had an .... – he can't have done this alone.
   A assistant **B** accomplice **C** aide **D** accessory
(HINT: *These are all words with similar meanings. You need to think of the exact meaning of the word in this context.*)

4 He's a bit .... – he's been caught stealing several times.
   A light-fingered **B** light-footed **C** heavy-handed **D** heavy-set
(HINT: *The distractors have the same form but different meanings.*)

5 The physical evidence .... with the eye-witness accounts was enough to convict the mugger.
   A related **B** joined **C** added **D** coupled
(HINT: *Think about grammatical constraints – only one word can be followed by **with**.*)

6 .... having been found with the stolen goods in his pocket, the young boy was allowed to go free.
   A Although **B** In spite **C** Despite **D** Even though
(HINT: *Think about the grammatical structures these connectors are used with.*)

7 The jury disagreed among themselves at first but eventually they all came .... to the same point of view.
   A along **B** across **C** round **D** back
(HINT: *This is a phrasal verb.*)

2 Choose the word or phrase which best completes each sentence below. Decide which type of vocabulary is being tested in each case by matching the question to the checklist in the introduction to this section.

1 It is believed that there is a .... between pollution and global warming.
   A comparison **B** combination **C** connection **D** communication

2 The shop assistant .... on the customer's complaint to the manager.
   A passed **B** gave **C** moved **D** conveyed

3 She failed the driving test but .... she knew she had done her best.
   A at least **B** at once **C** at first **D** at most

4 The success of the marketing campaign was .... to the eye-catching artwork on the posters.
   A applied **B** awarded **C** assigned **D** attributed

5 .... the reasons, there are fewer teachers entering the profession than there were ten years ago.
   A Whatever **B** Whichever **C** However **D** Wherever

6 The critics were completely .... by the commercial success of the low-budget film.
   A bypassed **B** baffled **C** distracted **D** diverted

7 The editor of the newspaper .... in for heavy criticism when he allowed the publication of the pop star's private letters.
   A let   **B** went   **C** came   **D** fell

8 Tourists are .... across to the island in a small boat.
   A lifted   **B** ferried   **C** shipped   **D** fetched

9 When I went to the museum I found that several important artefacts were not on ....
   A scene   **B** exhibition   **C** sight   **D** show

10 The tourists hadn't enjoyed being stranded on the island but admitted that .... the experience had been interesting.
   A moreover   **B** alternatively   **C** nonetheless   **D** similarly

11 David is always starting new projects but he rarely gets .... to finishing them.
   A through   **B** around   **C** on   **D** up

12 Shuttle buses from the hotel went regularly to and .... taking holiday makers to the beach.
   A from   **B** fro   **C** back   **D** between

13 The athlete's gold medal was .... as her greatest victory to date.
   A claimed   **B** observed   **C** noticed   **D** hailed

14 .... the poor reviews it received, it is amazing that the book has become a best-seller.
   A Considering   **B** Seeing   **C** Remarking   **D** Evaluating

15 The craze for collecting phone cards has really .... on in some countries.
   A taken   **B** caught   **C** come   **D** held

16 There was an increased police presence at the peace talks .... security.
   A in the interests of   **B** at the behest of
   C in the event of   **D** with regard to

Writing: formal letter (2) (recommendation)

In Unit 4 you wrote a letter of complaint. Another type of letter which you may be asked to write in Paper 2 is one in which you describe a situation and make recommendations for taking action.

1 Read this writing task.

1 Underline the three parts of the task and add them as headings to the table below.

> Your local radio station has invited listeners to contribute ideas to a documentary programme on ways of reducing crime in your area. They are planning to include some of the ideas below, and would like feedback on them before making the programme.
> • improving leisure facilities
> • expanding the police force
> • providing help with security
> • improving video surveillance
> • giving talks in schools
> Write a letter to the programme makers, identifying the main problems leading to crime in your area and saying which of the ideas above for reducing crime should be included in the programme and your reasons. (About 300 words.)

2 Discuss what ideas you might include under the three headings in the table above. Remember to think about the topic areas that were suggested in the question. Write your ideas in the table.

2   Read the following letter, which was written in answer to the task. Notice how each problem mentioned is followed by a suggested solution to the problem and a reason for including it In the programme.
Answer these questions.

1   How many problems does the writer mention? Add any new points the writer makes in the letter to the table in Exercise 1.
2   How does he justify his recommendations? Add the points he makes to the table on page 74.

Dear Sir,

I was very pleased to learn about your plans to do a documentary on crime, as this is an important issue for those of us who live in this area, and I am writing to you with my suggestions for what to include.

It seems to me that one of the biggest problems in our area is overcrowding. When people live too close together, they can get angry and frustrated, so it's no wonder that they sometimes take out this aggression through vandalism. I thought that the idea of improving video surveillance was a good one; in fact, I'd take it one stage further and suggest setting up cameras in shops and poorly-lit places. Of course this would be expensive, but it would mean that the real criminals could be identified. Then not all young people would be under suspicion! I would be very interested in hearing a discussion on this.

Another problem is that schoolchildren are being lured into crime by older boys. I think it would be really useful if the police were to visit schools on a regular basis, just so that they could talk to the children about ways of avoiding crime. This would also make the police a more visible presence in the city generally. I would like to hear other people's views on this idea.

Finally, it has occurred to me that a lot of crime is actually caused by boredom. Where I live there is nothing for anyone to do in the evenings and I'm sure that is part of the problem. There's a real need for more leisure activities and I think a discussion on possible types of entertainment could throw up some interesting ideas.

I'm looking forward to hearing the programme.
Yours faithfully,

Steve Chalmers

STEVE CHALMERS

---

3   Read the sample letter again.

1   Highlight any words and expressions and other features which suggest the letter is semi-formal rather than formal. (Compare this letter with the one in Unit 4, p.61 and refer to the list in Unit 4, page 57 to help you if necessary.)

2   What amendments would you make to vocabulary and sentence structure to make the letter more formal?

4   Read the following writing task.

1   How many parts does the task have? Underline them.

You have been involved in a project to provide unemployed young people with things to do in their free time, in an attempt to prevent them from turning to crime. Your committee has been considering the following ideas.

• youth club
• working with old people
• voluntary training programme
• sports activities
• music lessons

Choose two of these to recommend to your local council. Write the letter, making your recommendations and giving the reasons for your choice. (About 300 words.)

---

2   Think about the advantages and disadvantages of each suggestion, and make notes of your ideas.

3   Decide which projects you will recommend in your letter and why.

5   Plan the sections and paragraphs of your letter, including the opening and closing sections. Each project suggested should be described in a separate paragraph, with the reasons for your choice.

6   Write your letter. Remember to use the appropriate phrases for each section of the letter and make sure you maintain a consistent register.

7   When you have written your letter, exchange it with a partner. Evaluate each other's work. Use your partner's comments to help you write an improved version.

1 Choose the word or phrase which best completes each sentence.

1 They had to cancel the show as the lead singer had .... with chickenpox.
A made off   B come down   C fallen out
D caught up

2 I think you should write a letter of complaint, or .... still, phone them up.
A rather   B just   C even   D better

3 Our seaside holiday .... my father's boyhood enthusiasm for sailing.
A reminded   B rekindled   C relived   D resurrected

4 I can't understand how he expected to .... away with such an obvious lie.
A get   B make   C run   D do

5 It was felt that a(n) .... police presence would minimise the risk of violence.
A apparent   B remarkable   C clarified   D visible

6 .... his attitude to homework, it's not surprising he does so badly at school.
A Given   B Accepted   C Provided   D Considered

7 This sort of complex research needs to be carried out by someone with a trained ....
A brain   B sense   C mind   D wit

8 He comes .... as rather pompous, but I think he's just shy.
A over   B in   C to   D about

9 The company rejected celebrity .... as an inappropriate marketing strategy for their products.
A endorsement   B appreciation   C exploitation
D reinforcement

10 Adolescents tend to care more for the opinion of their peer .... than their parents.
A gang   B group   C set   D crowd

11 Attending nursery school is considered useful for the development of social .... as well as for learning.
A manners   B ability   C skills   D behaviour

12 Mike's car broke down and .... he found himself making his way along the main road on foot.
A necessarily   B naturally   C consequently
D successively

13 Whether she's a good artist is a .... of opinion, but she's clearly serious about her work.
A matter   B subject   C difference   D debate

14 This jacket was a(n) .... buy which I'm already regretting.
A style   B impulse   C fashion   D fantasy

15 The film's not much good, but some of the special .... are worth seeing.
A results   B shots   C effects   D designs

16 On the spur of the .... , she decided to visit her friend.
A instant   B second   C hour   D moment

17 He was commended for his .... to detail in the preparation of his report.
A attention   B concentration   C carefulness
D consideration

18 We're unsure whether our documents .... the requirements of the officials.
A reach   B meet   C achieve   D complete

19 His objections to the plan were .... as irrelevant by other people at the meeting.
A refused   B disdained   C dismissed   D reported

20 I don't know what started the .... for these toys, but every child in the school seems to have one now.
A madness   B whim   C fantasy   D craze

21 We find that if we .... the pupils as responsible individuals, they generally behave sensibly.
A treat   B behave   C conduct   D lead

22 At the end of the evening, we found to our horror that a large sum of money was unaccounted ....
A to   B for   C on   D in

23 I've been getting so .... out about the exams I've decided to take a day off and relax.
A stretched   B tensed   C stressed   D drawn

24 The children made an extremely useful .... to the discussion on improving the general appearance of the school.
A suggestion   B addition   C opinion
D contribution

25 After a whole day alone with three children, the *au pair* was at the end of her ....
A tether   B halter   C bridle   D reins

2 Finish each of the following sentences in such a way that it is as similar as possible in meaning to the sentence printed before it.

1 After seeing the film for himself, my father has stopped criticising it.
Since ....

2 It is a shame he had to leave before the end of the show.
I wish ....

3 No sooner had the witness begun to speak than the judge interrupted her.
The minute ....

4 It is impossible to accept your explanation without a thorough investigation.
Your explanation ....

5 Martin needn't have paid for all our tickets.
It ....

6 John hasn't done any revision since the spring term.
The last time ....

7 My parents think I should go to university rather than start a job immediately.
My parents would prefer ....

8 There haven't been such long queues at the cinema since the release of the last blockbuster.
Not ....

9 It is extremely unfair that no witnesses were questioned.
The fact ....

10 You may not be able to find a parking space in the city centre.
I doubt ....

3 Fill each of the blanks with a suitable word or phrase.

1 If only I .... the same opportunities as you, I wouldn't be doing this boring job now.

2 I wish my brother .... on coming to parties with me.

3 The boys were so .... on winning the final that they overcame their nerves.

4 It .... a very smart restaurant, if you managed to get in wearing jeans!

5 Aren't we .... ask permission before we come in here?

6 Don't wear anything that might attract .... of the security guard.

7 Does .... you have a university degree make any difference to your salary?

8 By the time the stadium opened, a large crowd .... in the road outside.

9 Scarcely .... left the room, than they started arguing again.

10 There's not much .... getting to the cinema in time with all this traffic.

4 For each of the sentences below, write a new sentence as similar as possible in meaning to the original sentence, but using the word given. This word must not be altered in any way.

1 Will such lenient punishment put others off committing crimes?
deterrent
....

2 His father is bound be angry with him, I'm afraid.
chances
....

3 I wouldn't ask his advice, if I were you.
recommend
....

4 Shouldn't we check with someone before we go in?
better
....

5 He's supposed to be a brilliant artist, but I can't see it myself.
say
....

6 The trial will almost certainly last another week.
likelihood
....

7 I doubt whether the teacher will agree to let us off school early.
see
....

8 The court does not publish the names of young offenders.
withheld
....

9 Fewer people buy this product now than in the past.
declined
....

10 The manager knew perfectly well that his staff were underpaid.
aware
....

6 Bright lights, big city

Speaking

1 The photos on this page were selected to promote the following cities. Can you identify the cities?

- Berlin
- Bilbao
- Kuala Lumpur
- Jeddah
- New York
- Hong Kong

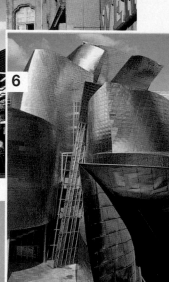

2 Discuss these questions.

1 What image of the city does each photo convey? For example
   - cosmopolitan and sophisticated
   - a place where history lives
   - bustling and dynamic
   - a city of the future
   - green and clean
   - a city of culture
2 Why do you think these particular pictures were chosen? Who are they aimed at?
3 In what types of publications might you see pictures like this?
4 Which picture do you find most striking? Which city would you most want to visit or live in? Why?

3 If you were asked to submit a photograph to promote your own town, city or region, what image would you choose? What image do you think your parents or grandparents would have chosen 25 years ago – the same as you, or something different?

Exam Focus

Paper 4 Listening (multiple-choice questions)

In Paper 4, you may have to answer multiple-choice questions about a passage. As well as factual details, these questions can test your understanding of abstract ideas and the attitudes and opinions of speakers, either stated or implied. The questions generally follow the order of the text, but the final question may test global understanding of the passage as a whole.

Here is a procedure for this task.

- You will have a short time **before** listening to read through the questions.
- During the **first** listening, eliminate the answers you're sure are wrong.
- During the **second** listening, choose the correct answer. (If you're not sure, put something.)

1 You will hear a conversation between two friends, one of whom lived for many years in Jeddah, a city in Saudi Arabia. For questions 1-7 circle the most appropriate response **A, B, C** or **D**.
Follow the recommended procedure and use the hints to help you choose the correct answer.

1 When the speaker first arrived in Jeddah, there were no
   A tall buildings.
   B cars in the city centre.
   C modern buildings.
   D large commercial buildings.
(HINT: *Statements and questions containing negatives can be confusing. Try underlining any negatives in the stem so you don't overlook them when answering the question.*)

2 The city
   A had an industrial area near the sea.
   B didn't have easy access to the sea.
   C was built to the north of the port.
   D had roads which were very unsafe.
(HINT: *You may hear expressions in the recording that seem similar to words in the question, but in fact mean something quite different. Listen carefully for the context.*)

3 According to the speaker, a positive side to the changes was that
   A old houses were pulled down.
   B old houses were restored.
   C buildings had traditional features.
   D there were no tourists.
(HINT: *You need to think about the speaker's attitude. The statements are all true, but the speaker only indicates she is pleased about one aspect.*)

4 It wasn't easy to find places in the city because
   A the city was so large.
   B there were no street names.
   C there were no maps.
   D there were few natural landmarks.
(HINT: *Here you are looking for a definite reason, not an implication.*)

5 The bicycle was
   A a statue.
   B an abstract painting.
   C part of a fountain.
   D 12 metres high.
(HINT: *You will hear the information needed for the answer before the key word in the stem – 'bicycle' – is actually mentioned. Don't worry. You can check this type of question the second time you listen.*)

6 The speaker suggests that an important aspect of life in Jeddah was
   A the fact that entertainment was not commercialised.
   B the closeness of family relationships.
   C the fact that much of life was lived outdoors.
   D the way that life was influenced by the climate.
(HINT: *You need to infer the main emphasis of the last section.*)

7 Overall, what was the speaker most conscious of during her time in Jeddah?
   A its sense of history
   B its beauty
   C its rapid development
   D its convenience
(HINT: *The word 'overall' tells you that you need to think about the meaning of the whole passage, not just the last section.*)

2 In multiple-choice listening activities you need to be able to match phrases in the recording with the items on your question paper and then decide if the meanings are the same or different. To analyse your answers, look at the extracts from the tapescript and the notes on page 219.

3 Say it again
Re-express these sentences from the Listening using the framework given.

1 What was really incredible was the speed with which the city expanded.
   The speed .... incredible.
2 It was really difficult to find your way around.
   .... was really difficult.
3 There weren't many natural features like rivers or hills.
   Natural features like .... existed.
4 They'd planted trees and bushes along the central reservation.
   The central reservation ....

4 Think of ways in which the place where you live has changed in recent years. Do you consider these changes to be for the better? Why/Why not?

Vocabulary: phrasal verbs, verbs + *way*

1 Complete the sentences below using an appropriate verb from the box in the correct form. Then match the meanings of the particle *up* to the definitions below.

clean	end	put	start	speed	do

1 I was offered a job for ten weeks and .... up staying ten years.
2 An ambitious programme of restoration was .... up.
3 The old houses were .... up instead of being demolished.
4 The streets were .... up and piles of rubbish were cleared away.
5 The city authorities .... up statues at all the main roundabouts.
6 It was a very interesting time to live through, like seeing history .... up.

The particle *up* can:
a) suggest increase, or progress to a higher position e.g.: *turn up* (the volume), *bring up* (children).
b) intensify the meaning of the verb, adding the idea that the action has been completed, e.g.: *cut up, smash up, sell up.* In this case the particle can often be omitted.

2 Complete the sentences below using an appropriate verb from the box in the correct form. What two general meanings or functions can you suggest for the particle *down*?

get	fall	go	stand	pull	let	put	break

1 The lifts in this building are always .... down.
2 The street has several neglected old buildings that look as if they're about to .... down.
3 All this waiting and delay are really .... her down.
4 This neighbourhood has really .... down in the last few years.
5 The villagers felt that they had been .... down when the council cut the bus services.
6 They were forced to .... down the old theatre as it was unsafe.
7 He had to .... down as candidate for Mayor when it was discovered he'd been involved in fraud.
8 Our neighbour's dog had to be .... down after it attacked the postman.

Study Tip

Knowing that particular particles and prepositions often have a meaning or function can help you understand and remember the meaning of a phrasal verb. When recording phrasal verbs, it may help to record them by particle/preposition. See if you can identify patterns of meaning for yourself.

3 A number of verbs are typically used in the following pattern.

- *Motorists have to **edge their way** carefully through the narrow, busy streets of the old town.* (Listening text)

Complete the following sentences with an appropriate verb from the box in the correct form. Use each verb once only.

find	inch	talk	worm	force	make

1 After the picnic we slowly .... our way home across the fields.
2 She remembered bitterly how he .... his way into her confidence and then betrayed her.
3 He .... his way forward through the undergrowth to get a better view of his quarry.
4 The President has finally gone too far – he'll never manage to .... his way out of it this time.
5 The thieves seem to have .... their way in through the window.
6 We'll never .... our way back in the dark without a map.

Vocabulary: collocation

1 This exercise practises six different types of collocation.

1 Choose the word or phrase which best completes each sentence.

1 The population of the city is .... rapidly.
   A expanding B stretching C going out
   D spreading out
2 The authorities should .... funds to restore public buildings and monuments.
   A make B develop C exploit D raise
3 The road .... are in desperate need of repair.
   A layers B coatings C crusts D surfaces
4 A number of .... beautiful buildings have sadly been pulled down.
   A acutely B considerably C exceptionally
   D drastically

5 A major disaster was .... averted when a monument was found to be in danger of collapsing.
   A closely   **B** narrowly   **C** purely
   D positively

6 The area is very flat and has few natural .... of interest.
   A features   **B** factors   **C** facilities
   D functions

2 Identify the collocation patterns in sentences 1–6 above.

3 Do any of the statements apply to your own home town? Give examples.

2 Adjective + noun collocations

1 How many combinations can you make with the sentence halves below? Which combinations are **not** possible?

1 There has been a tremendous growth ...
2 There has been a dramatic improvement ...
3 There has been a noticeable increase ...

a) in the use of public transport.
b) in shopping.
c) in the quality of life.

2 Work with a partner. Choose adjectives and nouns from the boxes below and write six true sentences about the place where you live using the same pattern as above.

EXAMPLE: *There has been a **marked deterioration** in air quality over the last few years.*

A alarming   enormous   gradual   marked   phenomenal   rapid   slight   steady   substantial   sudden

B change   decrease   decline   fall   increase   rise   growth   improvement   deterioration   explosion

3 Compare your sentences with other students. Have you written about similar things? Are your opinions similar or different?

> **Watch Out!** *in* or *of*?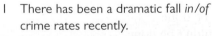
>
> 1 There has been a dramatic fall *in/of* crime rates recently.
> 2 There has been some improvement *in/of* transport services.
>
> Which preposition is correct?

Grammar check: the passive

1 Read the following extract. Can you guess which city is being described? What time period do you think it refers to? Underline and discuss any clues.

Most of the City streets were cobbled. (1) Only a line of posts reserved the rare sidewalks for pedestrians. Sometimes the road surface sloped down to a central drain; (2) rubbish usually blocked this.

Main streets were prone to traffic bottlenecks; at least no modern City driver has had to face a drove of turkeys (3) which someone is driving to their last home in City storehouses. (4) Narrow alleys barely wide enough for two pedestrians to pass punctuated side streets.

Sign boards hung from almost every house; in theory they were supposed to be nine feet off the ground, to give room for a man on a horse to pass underneath. (5) Sometimes an elaborate code conveyed their meaning. An elephant showed where (6) people could buy combs of ivory and other materials. Adam and Eve offered apples and other fruit.

Householders had a duty to hang out a candle or a lantern from dusk until nine o'clock during the winter. (7) However, from the frequency with which City regulations had repeated this duty since the fourteenth century, one can only suppose that (8) people did not generally observe it. Mostly the City streets were ill-lit or dark.

City authorities had tried for centuries, with only partial success, to discourage 'noxious' trades from operating in the City, their main market. Even when these trades obeyed the rules and stayed away from the City, (9) the wind blew airborne pollution in from across the river.

2 In the original text, the numbered sentences and clauses were written using the passive. Rewrite them as you think they were, using an appropriate passive form. Decide whether it's necessary to include the agent or not. Then read the information on the next page.

3 Uses of the passive

Read this information about the uses of the passive and look at the passive sentences you wrote for Exercise 2. What further examples can you give for each use described?

In English, the new or most important information in a sentence is usually placed towards the end: this is where we normally expect to find it. Complex phrases or clauses should also be placed towards the end, otherwise the sentence can sound awkward.

Using the passive allows us:

1 to focus attention on the **action** by putting it in end position. We may do this because the agent (the person or thing that actually did the action) is unknown ('someone'), unimportant, or obvious, or because we deliberately want to avoid saying who did the action. Compare:
An elephant showed where people **could buy** *combs of ivory and other materials.*
An elephant showed where combs of ivory and other materials **could be bought***.*

2 to focus attention on the *agent* by moving it from the beginning to the end of the sentence or clause. Compare:
Only a **line of posts** *reserved the rare sidewalks for pedestrians.*
The rare sidewalks were reserved for pedestrians only by a **line of posts***.*

3 to put long complex phrases at the end, and avoid awkwardness. Compare:
Narrow alleys barely wide enough for two pedestrians to pass *punctuated side streets.*
Side streets were punctuated by **narrow alleys barely wide enough for two pedestrians to pass***.*

4 to make previously given information the subject or topic of the sentence or clause. Compare:
… from the frequency with which City regulations had repeated **this duty** *…*
… from the frequency with which **this duty** *had been repeated in City regulations …*

Because it is less personal, the general effect of the passive is to give a statement or text a more formal, objective style. It is therefore frequently used in factual accounts, reports etc.
► Grammar reference p. 208

4

Imagine you live in the city described in the text in Exercise 1. The city authorities have asked for recommendations on ways of improving life for the citizens.

1 Read the following suggestions. What word can be removed from the *that* clauses without changing the meaning?

I recommend that the streets should be widened in order to reduce congestion.

I propose that more pavements should be built so that people aren't forced to walk on the road.

I suggest that large fines should be introduced to discourage manufacturers from polluting the atmosphere.

The verbs *suggest, recommend, propose, insist, demand* and *urge* are often followed by a *that* clause + modal *should*. In more formal English, *should* may be omitted. For example: *I suggest (that) large fines be introduced.* Here, the verb *be* is in the subjunctive form.
► Grammar reference p. 208

2 Use the prompts below to make more suggestions with the passive. Add a reason.

1 I suggest that ....
(rubbish/collect/more frequently)
2 I recommend that ....
(underground drains/build)
3 I propose that ....
(city centre/pedestrianise)
4 I demand that ....
(fines/introduce/for littering)
5 I urge that ....
(street lighting/install)
6 I insist that ....
(industry/ban/from the city)

5

Work with a partner. Think about the place where you live. Recommend changes that could improve life for a) the people who live there b) tourists visiting the area. First, discuss what you think:

1 could/can't be done.
2 should/shouldn't be done.
3 is likely/unlikely to be done.

Then decide on three major recommendations.

6 Use of English: sentence transformations

Passives may be tested in Paper 3, Question 2. The transformations may involve some other change to the structure of the sentence, including a change of word form.

Finish each of the following sentences so that it is as similar as possible in meaning to the one printed before it. You can refer to the Grammar reference on page 208 if you need help.

1   The government is considering introducing new measures to help the homeless.
    The introduction ....

2   A technically unsophisticated society could never have built the Pyramids.
    The Pyramids ....

3   Widening the streets would go some way to relieving traffic congestion.
    Traffic congestion ....

4   If they catch anyone littering in Singapore, they make them pay a fine.
    Anyone caught littering ....

5   They used to let farmers drive their animals to market through the city streets.
    Farmers used to ....

6   There are throngs of tourists in the streets in summer.
    The streets ....

7   There is soon to be a decision on the location of the new shopping centre.
    The location ....

8   They should pull that building down urgently – it's dangerous.
    That building needs ....

9   Attending this course will help young people gain additional qualifications.
    Young people ....

10 I noticed that thick mud covered both the man's shoes.
    I noticed that both ....

11 A passer-by saw her drive away from the scene of the crime.
    She ....

12 They should not have approved the plan until they had consulted the residents.
    Consultations ....

Speaking: simulation

1   Read this information.

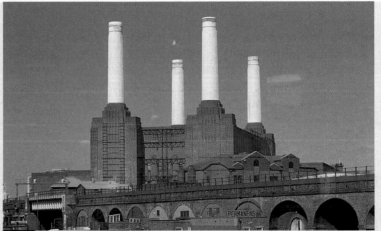

attersea Power Station, which served London with electricity for over fifty years, is one of the city's best-loved landmarks. One of the largest brick buildings in the world, it was built in the 1930s and continued to function until it was finally closed in the 1980s. The building lay empty and neglected for years, despite protests from those who regarded It as part of England's architectural heritage.

Finally the Central Electricity Generating Board announced a competition inviting the public, including schools and local residents, to suggest a use for the building. Suggestions included a theme park, a sports centre, an entertainment complex, a film production centre and an art gallery. Latest plans for the site are

Which suggestion do you think won the competition?

2   You have been invited to take part in a similar competition to consider the renovation and redevelopment of a building in your own town or city. Your proposal should cover the following areas.

- the ways in which you think the building could best be used
- any objections which might be made about the project, e.g. from people living or working in the surrounding areas, and how these might be overcome
- the overall benefit your proposal would bring to the community

Work in groups to prepare your proposal and be ready to present it to the rest of the class. First, decide which building would be suitable for development and what features make it suitable.

3   Listen to each other's presentations. Then vote to decide the winning proposal.

1 The picture shows a vision of a city of the future by an artist living in the 1930s. Imagine you could go back in time and talk to the artist about his predictions.

- Which parts of his vision have come true?
- Does anything in his vision look old-fashioned to you?
- What other developments in modern city life could you tell him about?

2

1 Read the first paragraph of the passage below. How many of the features mentioned there are illustrated in the picture?

2 Skim the entire passage. Find out what the writer considers to have been the main factor in shaping the 'city of the present'.

cities
of the future

Imagining cities of the future was a favourite 20th century sport. Film directors, novelists and architects all practised it, dreaming up with remarkable consistency gleaming towers joined
5 by skyways, aeroplanes and helicopters flitting between them like aerial buses, and buildings and people looking ever more uniform.

Now, as the next century begins, the city of the future has become the city of the present, and it turns
10 out that a few things were overlooked. If the metropolis of the 21st century does indeed have some large shiny blank buildings, it also includes such things as a theme park in the 15-year-old city of Shenzen, China, where Sydney Opera House, the
15 Grand Canyon, the Eiffel Tower and other great monuments of the world are reproduced at reduced scale.

For, as the future-gazers failed to spot, the industry that is shaping the city in the new millennium is
20 entertainment. Once the urban role models were the skyscrapers of Manhattan. Now it is Las Vegas, with its recreations of Egypt, medieval England, New York, Venice, Paris, and ancient Rome. Las Vegas is the fastest growing city in the United States and is
25 spawning imitations from Malaysia to Italy. It is the American city most people in China would like to visit.

The Disney Corporation is now one of the world's leading patrons of architecture and has built an entire
30 town in Florida inhabited by real, living, breathing people. One of the biggest powers behind the current rebuilding of Berlin is Sony. Across the developed world entertainment is becoming ever more intimate with its good friend shopping, to create malls that
35 look like theme parks and theme parks where you can do a lot of shopping.

In central London, the most rapidly changing area is what its backers call Millennium Mile, on the South Bank of the River Thames. Here is a parade of high and low-brow entertainment that includes a giant Ferris wheel, concert halls and theatres, a giant screen cinema, a major museum of modern art and a recreated sixteenth century theatre. Battersea Power Station is due to be a giant entertainment complex. In the heart of the city there is Segaworld,* Europe's largest indoor theme park. And elsewhere in London, the Museum of Natural History and the Museum of Science are replacing their display cabinets with computer animations so they can compete with Sega and Disney.

What all this means for cities is that buildings acquire more of the values of entertainment. They get more spectacular, as the Guggenheim Museum in Bilbao bears witness. They are more likely to be themed inside and, sometimes, out. There are more buildings which try to stage-manage the visitors' entire experience as if they were watching a film. In such places the rest of a city is screened off as an unwelcome distraction.

Meanwhile, other forces are at play. There are the office blocks of international finance, which obey a different set of rules. There is the fabric inherited from the past; all the mucky bits such as abandoned factories which no one knows what to do with. There are monuments to religious faith, and there are stubborn assertions of local identity and civic pride.

When these many forces come together you have oddities like County Hall, a political building now colonised by fish,** or the close proximity of a handcarved Hindu temple and a modern Swedish furniture superstore on London's busy North Circular Road. You get skyscrapers rising from ramshackle streets in Asian cities. You find things like Sunway lagoon, a theme park in Malaysia that imitates Las Vegas imitating Egypt. We have now seen the future, and it is weird.

---

* *Segaworld is a six-floor indoor entertainment park with virtual reality games, simulators, and video games.*
** *County Hall in London was the headquarters of the London County Council. It now contains London's biggest aquarium.*

3   Answer the following questions. You don't need to write complete sentences.

1   What 'sport' was 'practised' by people such as film directors in the 20th century? (line 2) Why does the writer refer to this as a sport?
2   What is the writer suggesting by the phrase 'with remarkable consistency'? (line 3)
3   In your own words, describe two general features of the city of the future as given in paragraph 1.
4   What is the main thing that was 'overlooked', according to the writer? (line 10)
5   What phrase in the first paragraph does 'some large shiny blank buildings' (line 12) relate back to?
6   Explain in your own words why people might want to visit the theme park in Shenzen, China.
7   What is the writer suggesting when he uses the phrase 'spawning imitations'? (line 25)
8   What is the significance of the phrase 'real, living, breathing people' in line 30?
9   What general point is the writer making about entertainment and commerce in paragraph 4?
10   Give two examples from paragraph 5 of types of 'low-brow entertainment' offered on Millennium Mile.
11   How have some of London's museums changed, and what reason is suggested for this in paragraph 5?
12   Where and in what way might the rest of the city be 'an unwelcome distraction'? (line 59)
13   What sort of buildings is the writer suggesting by referring to 'stubborn assertions of local identity and civic pride'? (line 67)
14   What point is the writer making about the two buildings he describes on London's North Circular Road? (lines 71-74)

4   Read the following summary task carefully.

> In a paragraph of 60–80 words, summarise the factors which the writer suggests will affect the city of the future and what their overall result will be.

Remember the procedure recommended in Unit 2, page 29 (Exam Strategy). Decide:

1   What are the key words in the question?
2   Which paragraphs contain the information you need? (For this question, you don't need to summarise points from the whole text.)
3   How many points do you need to include?

Next:

4   Make brief notes in your own words, following the order of the passage.
5   Expand your notes into a paragraph.
6   Check and edit your paragraph.

Vocabulary: metaphor

1 Read the following examples. The words in italics are being used metaphorically. Answer the questions about their meaning and effect in the sentence.

1 Pedestrians had to be careful as they could easily get *mown down* by the traffic. (Listening, p. 79)
a) Which of the following things can be mown? grass/beard/lawn
b) What does the metaphor suggest about the traffic and the pedestrians?

2 Because it was so easy to lose one's way in the suburbs, tempers used to get *frayed*. (Listening, p. 79)
a) What normally frays? What does it look like when it has frayed?
b) What does the metaphor suggest about the way the person is feeling?
c) What's the difference in meaning between 'they lost their tempers' and 'tempers became frayed'?

3 ... gleaming towers joined by skyways, aeroplanes and helicopters *flitting* between them ... (text, p. 84)
a) What usually 'flits'? What type of movement does the verb suggest?
b) What does the choice of verb suggest about the tone of the article? Is the writer being entirely serious?

4 Las Vegas ... is *spawning* imitations from Malaysia to Italy. (text, p. 84)
a) What is the literal meaning of 'spawn'?
b) Does the use of this verb have a neutral, positive or negative connotation in the context?

2 Read the postcard below.
1 What city do you think the writer could be describing? What are her three main impressions of the city? How does she feel about it?

Dear Monica,

I'm here at last and I can't tell you how great everything is. It's a huge city — you can't imagine the size of some of the skyscrapers! Everything round them is dwarfed and when you're on the 50th floor looking down the people are just like ants. Everyone and everything is in a hurry — the streets are swarming with people all day long, and it can be really difficult to push your way through the crowds. And the noise — it's never quiet, and police sirens are wailing all night. It's all so exciting, I'm so glad I'm here!

See you soon,

Love, Christine

2 Find three examples in the postcard of verbs used metaphorically. What are the usual meanings of these words? What do they suggest when used in this context?

3
1 Choose a verb from the box which can complete both gaps in the sentence pairs below. There are three extra verbs which you don't need to use.

screech	crawl	fly	freeze	melt
squeal	stampede	surge	fight	

1 a) The soldiers .... their way over the bridge.
   b) People .... their way onto the buses.
2 a) The children .... into the playground, shouting and yelling.
   b) Terrified by the noise, the cattle .... across the plain.
3 a) The bird .... angrily as the cat approached the nest.
   b) The car brakes .... as the car stopped just in time.
4 a) The baby .... across the room on all fours.
   b) The road was jammed with cars .... along at a snail's pace.
5 a) The car tyres .... as he raced round the corner.
   b) The children .... in delight when they heard they had a holiday.
6 a) As night fell, the crowd .... away.
   b) The sun came out and gradually the ice ....

2 In which sentence, a) or b), is the verb used literally, and in which is it used metaphorically? What is the effect of the metaphor in each case?

3 Now write similar pairs of sentences for the three remaining verbs from the box.

4 Work with a partner. Write sentences using some of the metaphors from this section, and others that you know, that could be included in a description of:

1 a famous landmark in your town/country.
2 rush hour in your town.
3 the crowd at a big public event.
4 your home town in 2050.
5 a car chase in a big city.

EXAMPLE: *The older buildings are dwarfed by the gleaming new skyscrapers which tower above them.*

Grammar check: relative clauses (1)

1 Read the information about Curitiba. How has it solved its public transport problem? How does the solution in Curitiba compare with your home town?

The Curitiba experience – solving the public transport problem

Curitiba in south-eastern Brazil has earned an international reputation for good city management with its innovative programmes for public transport, industrial pollution control and waste recycling. One of Brazil's fastest growing cities, it has avoided many of the problems that usually go with rapid expansion. Early in its development, Curitiba adopted a plan for linear growth along radial axes, using the areas in between for green space and leisure facilities as well as for industrial and housing development.

Curitiba has few traffic jams, despite having more cars per capita than any other Brazilian city except Brasilia. Roads running along the structural axes include special 'busways', which provide rapid transport of people to and from the city centre. A sophisticated bus system has been developed, featuring red express buses, green inter-district buses and yellow 'feeder' buses. There are regular services, which are closely linked, so that it is easy and quick to switch from one route to another. A single fare operates for all journeys within the city limits, with tickets interchangeable on all routes.

The transport network is managed by a city authority which lays down operating rules, sets timetables and routes, and monitors performance. The buses themselves are run by private companies, licensed by the city authority. The bus system Curitiba opted for is far cheaper in terms of capital cost than underground metro or light rail. It is a simple transparent system and it works – some 75% of commuters travel by bus. (In Sydney, by contrast, over 60% go to work by car; in Los Angeles, 90%.)

Another innovation has been the preservation of green space. During the last 20 years, green space per capita has increased one-hundredfold, which is all the more amazing given that this increase took place during a period of rapid population growth.

A key factor in Curitiba's civic development has been its mayors, whose enthusiasm and persistence have been maintained for over 20 years. But as they have always stressed, it is ultimately the people themselves to whom the city belongs.

2 How much do you know?

1   Read the article again and underline eight examples of relative clauses. Be careful! One is not introduced by a relative pronoun. Number the examples 1–8. Decide which ones are
a) non-defining or b) defining.

2 Read the rules below. Which of these rules are true of a) non-defining relative clauses, b) defining relative clauses, c) both? Write ND, D or ND/D next to each rule. For each rule, find one example from the text.

1   The clause gives essential information and cannot be omitted. ....
2   It may refer back to the whole of the previous clause. ....
3   We use commas to separate the clause. ....
4   The relative pronoun immediately follows the noun it refers to. ....
5   The relative pronouns *who* and *which* can both be replaced by *that*. ....
6   The clause can be introduced by *whose*, *where* and *when*. ....
7   The original subject does not stay in the clause – it is replaced by the relative pronoun. ....
8   The relative pronoun can be omitted when it is the object of the clause. ....
9   When a preposition is necessary, it can go at the beginning or end of the clause, depending on formality. ....

► Grammar reference pp. 208-209

3 Identify the mistakes in the following sentences and correct them.

1   The museum who we visited was extremely interesting.
2   New York is one of the cities that I would most love to visit it.
3   He took a pamphlet from one of the folders that they were on the table.
4   My parents would like to retire to the countryside, that they think will be quiet.
5   We met a really interesting man, the name of who I've unfortunately forgotten.
6   The man was very interesting that gave the talk on local history.
7   The people are using public transport are not very satisfied.
8   What was the name of the hotel we stayed last year?
9   The programme they adopted it was highly successful.
10   This is a village in that I would really like to live.
11   He is one of the few people to who the prize has been awarded.
12   The speed which the city expanded was incredible.

Grammar plus: relative and participle clauses (2)

1 Sentence relatives

1 Read the following examples and underline the prepositional phrases used with a relative. What type of relative clauses are they used in?

1 Stricter controls on energy use may be introduced, in which case taxes will inevitably rise.
2 The Clean Air Act was introduced in Britain in the late 1950s, since when air quality has improved massively.

2 Combine these sentences in the same way.

1 Curitiba invested heavily in public transport. As a result, pollution was greatly reduced.
2 We are expecting a full report in April. At that time we will make our decision.
3 A five-point action plan was agreed. Since then many improvements have been made.
4 People started arguing. At that point, I left.

2 With quantifiers

1 The relative pronouns *who, whom, whose* and *which* are often used after quantifiers such as *all of, the majority of, some of, both/neither of*, etc. For example:

1 I have two brothers, both of whom live abroad.
2 The city bought a fleet of garbage trucks, only three of which were still in service five years later.

2 Combine these sentences in the same way.

1 A conference is being planned. Its aim is to canvass opinion from a range of people.
2 A lot of people came to the meeting. I didn't know most of them.
3 The Lottery makes a lot of money. Only a small proportion of it goes to charity.
4 The City has had two mayors in the last ten years. Both of them were excellent.

3 Participle clauses

1 Compare these pairs of sentences.

1 a) People *who live in small villages* have close ties with their neighbours.
   b) People *living in small villages* have close ties with their neighbours.

2 a) Children *who are brought up in cities* cope well with the stresses of urban life.
   b) Children *brought up in cities* cope well with the stresses of urban life.

The clauses in italics are participle clauses in which a relative pronoun and verb are replaced by a participle. Which type of participle clause has an active meaning? Which type has a passive meaning?

2 Re-express the following sentences using full relative clauses instead of participle clauses.

1 Roads running along the structural axes include special 'busways'.
2 A sophisticated bus system has been developed, featuring red express buses.
3 The buses are run by private companies, licensed by the city authority.
4 The Disney Corporation has built an entire town in Florida inhabited by real, living people.

3 Which words can you remove from the relative clauses in the following examples without omitting any information? How are these examples different from those above?

1 The first walk begins in Placa de Catalunya, which is the nerve centre of the city.
2 The square is flanked on all sides by splendid old buildings, which are now banks and stores.

► Grammar reference pp. 208-209

4 Rewrite the following extract from a guidebook, replacing the relative clauses with participle clauses where possible.

Originally, Las Ramblas was nothing more than a river-bed which marked the outer limits of the 13th century city walls. A promenade was formed which ran parallel to the walls, through which various entrances allowed access to the town. In the course of time, these walls ceased to serve their defensive function and were destroyed. All along the Rambla, houses, hospitals and colleges were built, which formed the splendid promenade we see today. In the centre are stalls which sell flowers, birds and animals or newspapers and magazines, whilst further down are pavement cafés and stands that sell craftwork. There are also street performers, Tarot card readers and portrait artists, who are usually surrounded by curious onlookers.

5 Choose **one** of the following tasks.

1 Write a paragraph for a guidebook describing a part of your village, town or city in such a way as to make it attractive to a visitor.

2 Write a paragraph for a report on city development projects describing a problem in your town or city.

 ► Exam Maximiser

Writing: report (1)

For the task-directed exercise in Paper 2, you may be asked to write a report. You will be told what the report should be about, and who it is for.

A report:

- is normally written for a particular purpose in a business or work situation
- deals with facts
- may contain recommendations for action
- normally uses headings for each section
- is written in an impersonal, neutral to formal style.

To answer this question well, it is very important that you:

- organise your report carefully, using headings as a guide
- ensure your ideas are supported with evidence.

1   Read the newspaper headlines below. What main problems are they highlighting?

Gridlock Imminent As Traffic Piles Into City Centre

Pollution Levels Rise To Record Heights

Demands For Better Public Transport From Residents

2   Read this writing task. What type of report does it ask for?

> As part of your Urban Studies course, you have attended a presentation of proposed changes to ease traffic congestion in your town centre. Write a report on the plan, giving your opinion of the proposals and making recommendations to improve them. (About 300 words.)

To start you thinking, discuss any problems that traffic congestion causes where you live, and any measures that have been taken to ease them.

3   Read the following report, which was written in answer to the task. Are any of the problems mentioned similar to those you discussed? What are the advantages and disadvantages of the proposed solutions?

Background information

I attended a presentation by the Town Planning Officer, who began by summarising the causes of traffic congestion in the city centre and the resulting problems. He then moved on to recommend a number of changes.

Problems

The city is old, with narrow winding streets, many of which are one-way only. Offices, shops and entertainment facilities attract large numbers of people into the centre at all hours. As a result, there is a steady stream of traffic, causing jams at peak times and raising pollution levels, a situation which is both frustrating and unhealthy.

Proposed changes

It was proposed that the city centre be pedestrianised, and all private vehicles be banned. Large underground car parks should be built at three entry points into the traffic-free zone. From these entry points, special shuttle buses would run at regular intervals to convey people around the centre. Shop deliveries would only be made at night, on a rota basis. In addition, improved public transport services from the suburbs would encourage people to leave their cars at home.

Comments and recommendations

In my view, the proposals have much to recommend them. The main stumbling block, however, is the total cost. It was not stated how this money was to be raised. Presumably there would be high car park prices, in which case people may be less inclined to use them. The result could be congestion in the streets outside the traffic-free zone.

While I support the proposal in general terms, I recommend that it be implemented in stages, to spread the costs. Initially public transport to and from the suburbs should be improved, and charges for parking in the city centre should be increased. This would immediately ease the pressure of private cars. Car parks and shuttle buses could then be introduced in phase two.

4 The writer planned his report carefully by preparing an outline. Read the report again and fill in the missing information in the notes.

Background information
Presented by T. P. O
stated problems + ...

Problems
1 old town
   – narrow streets, some one-way only
2 ....
   – constant traffic, rush-hour jams
   – pollution

Proposed solutions
1 .... town centre
2 ....
3 three .... + shuttle buses
4 night deliveries
5 ....

Comments / own recommendations
Comment: main problem = ...
Recommendations: phased implementation:
Phase 1 – .... public transport
         – increase ....
Phase 2 – ....

5 Look through the report again and find examples of the following features of more formal language.

- passive and impersonal structures
- the subjunctive
- formal linking expressions
- complex sentences (i.e. with more than one clause)

How would you express the same ideas in less formal language?

6

1 Read the following task and underline the key words that tell you what information you have to include.

> Your local authority is planning to develop the area you live in to provide better sports, leisure and other facilities. Young people have been asked to contribute their ideas. As secretary of the local Youth Community Organisation, you have called several meetings to establish the main problems and opportunities facing your area. Write a report summarising your findings, identifying the most urgently needed changes and making recommendations for achieving these. (About 300 words.)

2 Read the extracts from conversations you had at your meetings. What problem does each refer to?

'Kids have nowhere to play football, so they play in the street.'

'The neighbourhood would be much more attractive if they'd just deal with the litter.'

'There are some wonderful old buildings around and they're just decaying – why don't they renovate them and use them?'

'The library only opens three times a week, and it has no money to buy new books – it's a real shame!'

3 Using some of the ideas above and adding any more of your own, write an outline for your report using the headings below.

> Background information
>
> Main problems and opportunities
>
> Most urgent changes needed
>
> Recommendations

7 Exchange your outline with a partner and evaluate each other's work.

- Are the points clear and supported by evidence?
- Is each point in the most appropriate part of the report?

8 Now expand your outline into the final report.

► Exam Maximiser

1 Rewrite the following sentences, using passive forms to avoid using the words in italics.

1 *They*'re constructing a bypass to relieve city centre congestion.

2 I think *they* ought to have done that years ago.

3 Unfortunately, *it*'ll only prevent a small proportion of the traffic jams.

4 *They* shouldn't have given permission for the developers to build all those blocks of flats.

5 *They*'ve built over all the open spaces.

6 *No-one* gave any consideration to the need for access roads.

7 *Someone* is going to have to find a radical solution before the traffic brings the city to a halt.

8 Residents are demanding that *the authorities* take action immediately.

9 *We* need to organise a meeting and draw up a plan of action.

10 *The authorities* have been neglecting public opinion for far too long.

2 Join each of the following pairs of sentences by using a relative or participle clause.

1 I recently attended a meeting. The purpose of the meeting was to discuss the modernisation of the swimming pool.

2 The pool was constructed in 1968. In those days little thought was given to the matter of access for wheelchair users.

3 Some disabled people use the pool now. Only a small number of them could attend the meeting.

4 They made a number of practical suggestions. This resulted in changes being made to the specifications.

5 We all agreed there should be a ramp as well as steps. The steps lead up to the entrance doors.

6 It should be possible to get a government grant to pay for the ramp. If that proves to be the case, we'll have enough money to re-paint the changing rooms.

7 The small pool is going to be re-opened. It was designed for use by young children and their parents.

8 We all agreed that the meeting had in fact been very useful. We hadn't been particularly keen to attend it.

3 For each of the sentences below, write a new sentence as similar as possible in meaning to the original sentence, but using the word given. This word must not be altered in any way.

1 That man's opinion means more to me than any other person's. **whose**

....

2 Since the start of the rain the protesters were no longer to be seen. **melted**

....

3 My little tent looked very small against the mountains. **dwarfed**

....

4 I'm afraid there may be something missing from your report. **overlooked**

....

5 Surely someone saw the man take the picture? **seen**

....

6 The students demanded the abolition of the regulations. **be**

....

7 You should wash your shirt right now before that stain dries. **needs**

....

8 The new one-way system has not been entirely successful. **partial**

....

9 The number of accidents has gone down steadily since the speed limit was imposed. **decline**

....

10 The spy gained access to the building by a secret passage. **made**

....

11 We're raising money for the restoration of the Town Hall. **do**

....

12 The committee recommended raising entrance charges to cover costs. **increased**

....

4 Read the passages below. Decide where they may have been taken from and how they link with the general theme of the unit. What do you think are the advantages of living in a city/living in the country?

1. I'm very much a country person; I was brought up in a village and even though I've worked in the city for many years, it's a relief to get out of the hustle and bustle every evening. Commuting is not pleasant but it's preferable to staying in the city – getting out of the train into fresh air, quiet, stillness – there's no doubt that it's worth it. It distances work and stress and means I can recharge my batteries ready for the onslaught of the next day.

2. To live in a city is a lifestyle choice, not merely an investment decision. It was Benjamin Disraeli who wrote 'London is a nation, not a city'. He was more right than he could ever have realised. Today large cities are like empires full of all races, religions and refugees. Resentment of new arrivals has turned into a celebration of cosmopolitanism and complexity, the city acting as a mirror of the values of the 21st century.

Vocabulary: the environment

1 You are going to read a text about environmental change.

1 Look at the photos and describe what is happening. What environmental issue does each represent?

2 Read the introductory paragraph below and fill in the gaps with words from the box.

resources	destruction	ecology
environment	habitats	

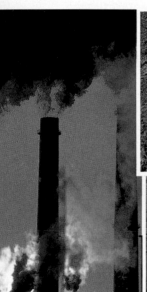

We have come to the end of a millennium of relentless and accelerating (1) .... of the world around us. While human creativity and technology have blossomed, we have steadily been destroying the (2) .... of the planet on which we depend for our survival. The sad fact is that every day the diversity of life on Earth gets poorer because of our overuse of (3) .... and our disregard for the riches of nature. Ecologically, our natural (4) .... provide services without which life on the planet would become impossible. When we tamper with the (5) .... , it is not just nature which suffers. Our own way of life is under threat.

2 Read the next part of the text and identify the key environmental issues being described. Then use words and phrases from the box below to fill in the gaps.

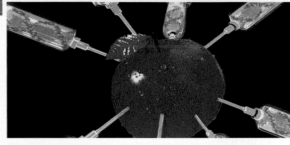

Since the industrial revolution, man has burned ever larger quantities of (6) .... , first coal and then oil, with the result that the composition of the atmosphere has started to change. Burning these fuels produces (7) .... such as carbon dioxide, which act in the atmosphere like glass in a greenhouse and trap the heat of the sun – this is known as the (8) .... The overall global temperature has already begun to rise. Global warming is expected to lead to extreme (9) .... , with more frequent floods, droughts and heat waves. No person, animal, bug or bird will be unaffected.

In addition to greenhouse gases, industrial processes produce poisonous substances which can be virtually impossible to dispose of safely. If these (10) .... are buried in underground storage sites, there is the danger that they may (11) .... into lakes and rivers, with serious long-term effects on living organisms. Emissions from industrial plants, such as sulphur, can also enter the atmosphere, where they can cause damage to the (12) .... around the planet. They may also fall back to earth as (13) .... and destroy plants and trees. All these are examples of types of (14) .... that could be prevented.

acid rain	changes in climate	fossil fuels
gases	greenhouse effect	pollution
ozone layer	toxic wastes	leach

3 Now read the continuation of the text. Fill in the gaps with words from the box below.

We drain (15) .... near rivers and coastal areas to create land for building. Through (16) ...., the large-scale cutting down of trees, the (17) .... that allow species to survive are changed and the amount of land available for (18) .... decreases. Some species are so reduced in number that they are in danger of (19) .... At this stage they are known as an (20) .... and are only one step away from total (21) ....

We are now beginning to manipulate nature in new ways, without thought for the possible consequences. Using the latest technology, we can now create (22) .... of plants which are resistant to diseases and which can survive extremes of temperature or salinity (salt content). The danger of this process of (23) .... is that producing new plants or other (24) .... like bacteria may bring disaster as well as apparent advantages, as experience has already shown.

So, with the new millennium, we need a new beginning, a fresh start. We need to reverse the major threats to our environment. Above all, we need to understand that we cannot go on consuming and polluting with no thought for tomorrow.

deforestation	wildlife
ecosystems	endangered species
extinction	genetic engineering
living organisms	dying out
wetlands	strains

4 In technical texts, the writer often helps the reader to understand difficult words or concepts by giving examples or definitions, describing causes and effects, using synonyms, and so on. In this sentence from the text, two examples of 'fossil fuels' are given, which explain the meaning of this term.

'Since the industrial revolution, man has burned ever larger quantities of fossil fuels, first coal and then oil,...'

With a partner, discuss what methods the writer has used to help the reader understand the following concepts.

1 emissions
2 deforestation
3 salinity
4 genetic engineering

5 Work in pairs. Without looking back at the text, take turns to explain the following concepts to your partner.

1 the greenhouse effect and global warming
2 industrial pollution
3 species loss
4 genetic engineering

6 **Sentence structure:** cause and result
1 Join these sentences using the words in brackets. Make any changes necessary. Then check by referring back to the text you have read.

1 Every day the diversity of life on Earth gets poorer. We are overusing resources and disregarding the riches of nature. (because of)
2 Man has burned ever larger quantities of fossil fuels, first coal and then oil. The composition of the atmosphere has started to change. (result)
3 Some species are very reduced in number. They are in danger of dying out. (so ... that)

2 Now rewrite the following sentences beginning with the words given, making any changes necessary.

1 The number of private cars has increased enormously, and this is a key factor in global warming.
A major cause of global warming is the ....
2 The Earth's temperature is rising and, as a result, the polar ice caps are melting.
The polar ice caps are melting as a result of ....
3 As sea levels rise, there is an increased incidence of flooding.
One effect of the ....
4 Sea levels may rise even more and cause whole countries to disappear.
Sea levels may rise to such an extent ....
5 Toxic waste is being dumped in the sea with the result that many fish and sea mammals have died.
Many fish .... due to ....
6 The spread of deserts is linked to deforestation and farming methods such as irrigation and excessive grazing.
.... have led to ....

7 Choose an environmental issue that you think is particularly relevant to your country. Answer the following questions using the expressions in the box to help you.

1 What are the specific effects of the problem on your country? Give examples.
2 What is being done to improve matters? Is it enough, or should more be done? What?
3 What is likely to happen if nothing is done?

A major/An urgent environmental concern/ issue/problem is ...
One of the main/major causes of ... is ...
One/Another (very worrying) effect of ... is ...
Various solutions have been tried out, such as ...
What really/urgently needs to be done is ...

Exam Focus

Paper 1 Reading (Section B, multiple-choice questions)

In Paper 1, Section B, you have to read three different texts, usually one fiction and two non-fiction, and answer 4–6 questions on each text, choosing the correct answer from four options. To avoid being confused by the options, try the following procedure.

- Read through the text to get an overall impression of what kind of text it is (e.g. fiction or non-fiction) and what it is about.
- Look at each question or stem – **not** the four options – and find the answer or completion in the text.
- Read the options and find the one that is closest to the information in the text.
- Read the text again and check all your answers.

1 Using the procedure above, read the text and answer the questions which follow.

Note: In this exercise, the last two questions each focus on global understanding of the text to show you the different ways in which this may be tested. Usually there will only be one question of this type.

> ### Exam Strategy
>
> - The questions are in the same order as the information in the text.
> - Don't be distracted by your own opinions or knowledge of the subject: the questions can all be answered from information given in the text.
> - Don't be put off by new words. Ignore them if they aren't important, or use the context to work out the meaning.

In 1951 research ships found the Barndoor skate in 10 per cent of all catches in the Atlantic Ocean off Newfoundland. Over the last 20 years, none at all have been caught there. The fish grows to a metre across, not something you would miss if you were looking out for it. But nobody was. If something the size of a Barndoor could slip away without being missed, the fate of little-known species is likely to be worse.

The enormous task of identifying and classifying the species that exist on our planet was begun in 1758 by Carl Linneaus, a Swedish taxonomist. Over the next 240 years other natural historians followed suit, establishing a local habitation and name for each of about 1.7 or 1.8 million species. With no central catalogue or inventory, the same species was sometimes recorded under one identity in one country and under an entirely separate name in another, but even when these double entries were taken out, the number was still about 1.4 million.

Then the researchers began to look a little harder. They spread nets under trees in the Amazon rainforest, dusted them with insecticide and counted just the arthropods* that fell out. The numbers astonished them. When they reached 50,000, they started to get alarmed: by that reckoning there might be 20 million species to be described, rather than two million. What was true there turned out to be equally true for coral reefs, mangrove swamps and the great plains of Africa.

This diversity is life's strongest card, as has been demonstrated repeatedly by laboratory experiments based on small, artificial worlds. We now know that many of the things that make life possible are barely visible. The recycling of air and water and plant nutrients is the business of little creatures most of us never notice. Last year Cornell scientists calculated that if humans had to pay for the services they received free from nature — pollination, water purification, crop pest control, that sort of thing — the bill would be $2.9 billion annually. The food we eat, the medicines we take and the tools we use have been fashioned for us by 500 million years of evolution.

But what is going on now is described, quite calmly, as "the sixth great extinction". According to some theorists, half of all the creatures with which humans share the planet could be on the verge of extinction, about to steal away into the eternal night simply because their homes are being destroyed by man. The world's dwindling tropical forests could be losing creatures at a conservative estimate of 27,000 a year — three creatures an hour. While the precision of these figures is disputed, the truth behind them is not. Crude counts confirm that many of the big mammal groups and a tenth of all flowering plants could be about to disappear and a tenth of all birds on the planet are seriously endangered. But 99 per cent of creation is less than 3mm long. Most of the smaller species will be gone before scientists ever find out they were here.

Creatures disappear because their surroundings change, and those surroundings are maintained for them by other sets of creatures. Biodiversity cannot be managed unless it can be understood, and it cannot be understood unless its components are identified. Unfortunately, there are just not enough resources to identify and catalogue all the species in the world. Yet human economy rests on plants. To understand and conserve crops and their wild relatives, the insects that prey on them must also be understood. Biodiversity is therefore clearly a matter of naked human self-interest. There could also be billions of dollars of useful, valuable, exploitable knowledge to be gained from almost unknown creatures in their habitats. Why do barnacles not grow on starfish? Because the starfish secrete a natural anti-fouling paint. Why do arctic fish not freeze? Because they have an antifreeze fluid to keep blood circulating. Despite these potential benefits, the twentieth century may be remembered for the most severe and rapid loss of biodiversity in history. The massacre of the species at the present rate could have baleful consequences for Planet Earth.

*arthropods: animals with segmented bodies and jointed limbs such as insects, spiders and crabs

1 The case of the Barndoor skate is particularly significant because
   A it was found off the coast of Newfoundland.
   B its virtual disappearance was not noticed.
   C it is no longer found in its previous habitat.
   D it is probably extinct.

(HINT: *All the answers give information that is mentioned in the text, but only one answer fits the question stem correctly. Here you are reading for the main idea in a paragraph.*)

2 What was the main drawback of the first inventories of species?
   A They took over 200 years to complete.
   B Only local habitations could be established.
   C They recorded the same species in every country.
   D Lack of an international system led to some duplication.

(HINT: *Be careful with answers which are very close in wording to the text. They may not have exactly the same meaning, and/or may not answer the question. Here you have to identify the details which support the main idea of the paragraph.*)

3 Researchers in the Amazon rainforests were alarmed by
   A the difficulty of locating new species.
   B the use of harmful research procedures.
   C the large numbers of species found.
   D the need to save endangered species.

(HINT: *One answer may seem to be more likely than the others from your general knowledge of the topic. This type of background knowledge is sometimes useful, but can also be distracting, as the writer may be making a different point. Check the text carefully.*)

4 What point is the writer making about mass extinction?
   A Its likelihood has been exaggerated by some theorists.
   B It will mainly affect the big mammal groups.
   C It will destroy many small and unknown species.
   D It can only be prevented if we can identify species.

(HINT: *Three of these answers are partly true, but contain details which are incorrect or are not a true reflection of what the writer is saying. To find the correct answer you need to be aware of the details that make the other answers wrong.*)

5 The general tone of the article is
   A concerned.
   B objective.
   C critical.
   D hopeful.

(HINT: *Here you need to think about the overall impression given of the writer's attitude to the topic. Remember that you are evaluating the writer's attitude, not your own, and that the question asks about the general tone.*)

6 The writer's main message is that people should
   A preserve habitats.
   B make use of natural materials.
   C protect endangered insects.
   D identify species.

(HINT: *For this question you need to be able to infer the writer's main message. You need to look at the text as a whole, not just one part.*)

2 Discuss the following questions.

1 The writer argues that 'Biodiversity is [...] a matter of naked human self-interest' and cites two examples of potential benefits to people. What other examples could you give to support his point?

2 How far do you agree that the only reason for conserving disappearing species is their usefulness to us? What other reasons could you suggest?

3 A major cause of the 'great extinction' referred to is the pressure of the growing human population on space and land. How far do you consider this problem to be one that can be solved? What are the problems associated with attempts to curb population growth?

Vocabulary

1 Style and register

You may find it useful to refer to the table on page 57 for the following exercises.

1 Find words and phrases in the text on page 94 which mean the same as the words in italics in the following sentences. Are the words in the text formal, informal or literary?

1 The fish is so big that you couldn't miss it if you were *searching* for it.
2 How could such a large creature *quietly disappear* without being missed? *(two expressions)*
3 Carl Linneaus began the task of recording and classifying species, and other natural historians *followed his lead*.
4 When the researchers reached 50,000, they realised that *according to these calculations*, the total number of species might be far greater than they had expected.
5 Nature's *biggest advantage* is diversity.
6 Scientists calculated that if humans had to pay for the services they received free from nature – pollination, crop pest control *and suchlike* – the bill would be enormous.
7 *Rough estimates* provide evidence that many animals, plants and birds are seriously endangered.
8 The *outcome* of this rapid loss of species *could be extremely serious* for the planet.

2 Does the writer use a consistently personal or impersonal tone? Look for use of the first person, appeal to the reader, and use of rhetorical questions (questions the writer answers himself).

3 Where do you think the text is taken from?

2 Word formation

1 Find the following words in the text. What part of speech (noun, verb or adjective) is each word in the text? What other forms of the word are possible?

1 grow (introduction)   5 verge (para. 4)
2 habitation (para. 1)   6 precision (para. 4)
3 diversity (para. 3)   7 maintain (para. 5)
4 nutrients (para. 3)   8 exploitable (para. 5)

2 Use an appropriate form of each word to complete the sentences below.

1 It is difficult to make .... measurements of the numbers of endangered species.
2 It should be possible to .... the riches of nature without destroying it in the process.
3 Millions of different creatures contribute to the long-term .... of our ecosystem.
4 Most parts of Europe were once .... by wolves and bears.
5 The gradual .... of species is a process which has occurred over millions of years.
6 Their claim that we shall soon have classified all existing species .... on the ridiculous.
7 Warm, damp conditions may encourage the .... of harmful bacteria.
8 Young children need .... food if they are to grow up strong and healthy.

3 Fixed phrases: prepositional

Fixed prepositional phrases may be tested in Paper 1, Section A, and in Paper 3, for example in Question 4 (key word transformations). Look out for such phrases in your reading and make a note of them.

1 Rewrite the following sentences using the phrase in brackets. Make all the necessary changes to the rest of the sentence. Remember that if a verb follows a preposition, it will always be in the *-ing* form.

1 Half of all the creatures on the planet are about to become extinct. (on the verge of)
2 The bear has been wiped out in most countries of the European Union other than France and Spain. (with the exception of)
3 The government is setting up more nature reserves to try and save the remnant populations of these animals. (in the hope of)
4 He got the job because he had had so much experience with animals. (on the strength of)
5 The government does not understand what ordinary citizens need or want. (out of tune with)
6 With her husband's help, she came to be recognised as a leading talent in her field. (under the guidance of)

2 Now rewrite these sentences. This time you only have the key word.

1 Fair-skinned people are more likely to get skin cancer from over-exposure to the sun. (risk)
2 The charity appeal raised a lot of money. (response)
3 The police suspected that he had broken into the building and arrested him. (suspicion)
4 High production rates are often achieved only when the quality of the work is reduced. (expense)
5 Mary was short and plump, and was very different from her mother, who was tall and willowy. (contrast)
6 The medal was awarded to the retiring mayor for his services to the town. (recognition)

Listening: sentence completion

1   Read the following headlines. What do you think the problem is?

END OF A WAY OF LIFE

COD WARS INTENSIFY

What happened to all the fish?

2   You will hear a radio documentary about fishing. Before you listen, read the gapped sentences below. What do you think the progamme will focus on?

The fishermen's catch is made up of ....(1)

Since 1992 ....(2) has been almost completely forbidden.

The distant-water fleets used ....(3) to find the areas where the fish were breeding.

One effect of the new methods of fishing was that the ....(4) were damaged.

Another effect was that they were destroying the ....(5) of the people.

Fish farming does not help ....(6) to return to their original levels.

The people of Bristol Bay, Alaska, are protecting their salmon-fishing industry with a scheme involving ....(7) the fish.

The aim of the scheme is to allow enough fish to swim upstream and ....(8).

Mark and his two colleagues send information to ....(9).

At the end of an 'opening' the fishing boats are allowed to ....(10).

3   Now listen and complete the sentences with a word or short phrase. Your answers must fit the grammatical structure of the sentence.

4   Listen again to complete and check your answers. Finally, check that what you have written is grammatically correct and that you haven't made any spelling mistakes.

5   Discuss this question.

What does the report you have just heard suggest about our ability to reverse the pattern of extinctions of the last 1,000 years?

6   Say it again
Re-express the following sentences from the Listening text beginning with the words given.

1   Imposing fishing limits around the islands did no good.
    Fishing limits ....
2   The local people have come up with an answer to the problem.
    The problem ....
3   The fishing boats let the salmon pass.
    The salmon are ....
4   What we do is count the fish.
    It's our ....

Grammar plus: conditionals (2)

1 Hypothetical conditions

These include conditions which are unreal now or in the past, or unlikely to happen in the future. The result does not always happen in the same time period as the condition.

Read the examples below and underline the verb forms in each clause. Which sentences have:

a) a present/future time reference in the *if* clause, with a result in the present/future?

b) a past time reference in the *if* clause, with a result in the past?

c) a universal time reference in the *if* clause, with a result in the past?

d) a past time reference in the *if* clause, with a result in the present?

1 If government fishing quotas had been observed, fish stocks would not have collapsed.

2 If humans had to pay for the services they received free from nature, the bill would be $2.9 billion annually. (text, p. 94)

3 If efforts hadn't been made to protect wild salmon stocks at Bristol Bay, Alaska, the salmon industry would no longer exist today.

4 If mankind were less shortsighted, we would not have done so much damage to the environment.

5 More species might have become extinct if environmental groups were not so active.

► Grammar reference p. 209

2

1 Think of as many **present** results as you can for each of the following past conditions.

1 If the sea had not been over-fished, ...
   *... stocks **would still be abundant**.*
   *... species which feed on fish **would not be threatened**.*

2 If the car had not been invented, ...

3 If I'd been born ten years earlier, ...

4 If it hadn't been for my parents, I ....

2 Think of as many **past** results as you can for each of the following present unreal conditions.

1 If species such as the panda or elephant were less appealing, ...
   *... less effort **would have been** put into saving them.*
   *... they **might have become** extinct by now.*

2 If people had a greater awareness of environmental problems, we wouldn't have ....

3 If I were Prime Minister/President of my country, I would have ....

4 If I were rich, ...

3 Open conditions

These describe events that are a real possibility, already or in the future. Various verb forms are possible, and time references can be mixed, as with hypothetical conditions.

1 Underline the verb forms in each clause in the following sentences and complete the notes.

1 If something the size of a Barndoor *could* slip away without being missed, the fate of little-known species *is likely to be* worse. (could + future)

2 If you stand on the tip of Cape Bonavista, Newfoundland today, you can look out on the remnants of the richest fishery on earth.
   (present + ...)

3 If the world's waters are pure for humans to drink but contain no fish, then we haven't really solved our environmental problems.
   (........................ + ...)

4 If we are to avoid the catastrophic effects of global warming, we must take action now.
   (........................ + ...)

5 In the past, if men didn't find animals to kill, they went hungry.
   (........................ + ...)

6 If it will help, I will join an environmental group.
   (........................ + ...)

► Grammar reference p. 209

2 Which of the completions a)-c) are grammatically possible? Tick all the possible options.

1 If people continue to hunt tigers,
   a) they will have become extinct in 10 years.
   b) our children may never see one.
   c) they must have died out by now.

2 If prehistoric tribes chose to settle in villages,
   a) they would have been able to grow crops.
   b) they couldn't survive by hunting alone.
   c) they needed to domesticate animals.

3 If he went to the meeting yesterday,
   a) we'll hear all about it tomorrow.
   b) he had heard the news.
   c) he's probably still considering what to do.

4 If you'll bring some food to the party,
   a) I can do the rest.
   b) you'll have done your share.
   c) I'll bring something to drink.

5 If you're going to make a fuss,
   a) we won't do it.
   b) we've done something about it.
   c) we'd better not do it.

4 Inverted conditionals

1 Read the following sentences. Which of the versions in each group a) sounds more formal b) makes the event sound more unlikely?

1 a) If you see a rhino, ...
   b) If you should see a rhino, ...
   c) Should you see a rhino, ...
   ... run for your life
2 a) If we had only realised the danger, ...
   b) Had we only realised the danger, ...
   ... we would never have gone there.
3 a) If you study the proposals carefully, ...
   b) If you were to study the proposals carefully, ...
   c) Were you to study the proposals carefully, ...
   ... you might notice some technical problems.

▶ Grammar reference p. 210

2 Finish each of the following sentences in such a way that it is as similar as possible in meaning to the sentence printed before it.

1 If the regulations had been imposed earlier, they might have been more effective.
   Had ....
2 I would think carefully before dismissing him, if I were in your place.
   Were ....
3 If we had been warned, would we have acted differently?
   Had ....
4 Governments might decide to work together, in which case the laws would be more effective.
   Should ....
5 The only thing that prevented me from seeing her again was that I had lost her address.
   Had ....
6 The police will have to be informed if he has lost his passport.
   Should ....

5 Implied conditions

The following sentences illustrate other ways of expressing conditions. Rewrite the sentences using *if*.

1 Destroy the processes of nature, and you can expect untold damage to the world we inhabit.
2 Suppose we could see into the future, would that shock us into changing our behaviour?
3 Had it not been for the weather, it would have been a wonderful trip.
4 But for his intervention, the situation would have got much worse.
5 Assuming that you are reasonably fit, you should be able to go on the walk.
6 You shouldn't have any problems, provided you've got the instruction booklet.
7 I hope they take credit cards – otherwise I'll have to find a bank.
8 Don't move an inch, or I'll shoot!
9 Without government intervention, unemployment will continue to rise.

▶ Grammar reference p. 210

Watch Out! *in case*

1 Species should be preserved today, not tomorrow – *in case* there is no tomorrow.
2 Break the glass *in case* of emergency.

What is the meaning of *in case* in these sentences? Can the sentences be rewritten with *if*?

---

6 Use of English: gapped sentences
Fill each of the blanks in the following sentences with a suitable word or phrase.

1 We should get there in an hour, ... the traffic isn't too heavy.
2 He probably won't bother to wear a suit, always .... he comes to the wedding at all.
3 If it .... the bad weather, we'd have made a lot more money.
4 Relief organisations are organising stores of food .... the crops fail.
5 Mankind will continue to exploit the environment .... progress is seen as acquiring more and more consumer goods.
6 I would have gone with them .... that I had to get this report finished.
7 If .... study these proposals carefully, you would find they don't really make sense.
8 Affected countries should take preventive measures now; .... tourism could have devastating effects on the environment.

7 Imagine you had the power to introduce three laws that would help the environment. What would they be?

Listening: note-taking

1 Read the information and answer the questions below.

The WWF (World Wide Fund For Nature) and Greenpeace are well-known environmental campaign groups in the UK. The WWF was established as the World Wildlife Fund in 1961 to raise funds from the public for conservation of particular species, for example the Giant Panda, and habitats. Greenpeace is an international environmental pressure group, operating a policy of non-violent direct action supported by scientific research.

1 What similar environmental campaign groups exist in your country? What are their aims? What kind of activities are they involved in?

2 Are you a member of such a group? Why/Why not?

2 You will hear an interview in which David Cranshaw, who is an active member of an environmental campaign group, talks about the achievements of such groups. Before you listen, look through the notes below.

Effects of environmental campaign groups:

- *In business and industry*
- *encouraging companies to be accountable*
  e.g. by monitoring use of ....(1)
- *encouraging ....(2) to provide*
  financial incentives for change.
- *Working with ....(3)*
- *encouraging consideration of environmental issues e.g.*
  ...(4) proposals in Cheshire
- *Working with general public*
- *raising awareness of need for ....(5)*
- *Evidence of change:*
- *more people buying ....(6)*
- *refusal to buy ....(7)*
- *individual activities such as:*
  - *recycling*
  - *buying smaller cars*
  - *using cotton nappies*
  - *...(8)*
- *Important because:*
- *could have big effect if everyone took part*
- *encourage people to consider ....(9)*

 3 Now listen and complete the notes. Remember that you only have to write a few words in each space.

 4 Listen again and complete and check your answers.

5 Say it again

Re-express the following sentences from the Listening text, using the words given.

1 We've made far more progress than anyone would have predicted.
We've achieved ....

2 There's certainly been an increase in accountability from businesses.
Businesses ....

3 Environmental groups are building bridges between governments and people.
The gap ....

4 People's choices of what to buy and what not to buy can carry weight.
.... difference.

6 Vocabulary: verb-noun collocations

1 Complete the phrases below using verbs from the box.

follow	identify	make	monitor
provide	raise	take	

1 .... a real difference
2 .... air quality
3 .... financial support
4 .... key targets
5 .... more environmentally aware policies
6 .... public awareness
7 .... some responsibility

2 Think about some environmental issues in your country and write four sentences using some of the collocations above.

► Exam Maximiser Gold

Speaking: selection and discussion

1   Selection

1   Work in pairs. Look at this list of practical measures which individuals can take to help preserve the environment and the world's natural resources. Discuss what each measure can achieve, and choose the five measures you feel are the most effective in helping the environment. Add at least one more idea of your own to the list.

- recycle paper
- travel by public transport
- use lead-free petrol
- refuse to accept plastic packaging
- insist on organically produced food
- turn off the lights when you leave a room
- don't use disposable products
- ride a bicycle
- use natural ventilation instead of air conditioning
- don't use disposable nappies for babies

2   Now discuss how easy or difficult the measures above would be to bring into your life. For example:

A: If we recycle paper, fewer trees will have to be cut down, so it seems like a good idea to me.
B: Yes, but on the other hand, most paper is made from trees that are specially grown for the purpose. Recycling paper isn't going to save the rainforests.
A: So you think it's not so important?
B: Not really. I'd say that travelling by public transport is probably the most effective thing we can do …

2   Discussion

Work with a different partner. Read the statement below.

'It's not enough to make small changes in the way we live – what's needed is a major change in lifestyle if we are to protect the planet.'

Decide how far you agree with the statement. What changes do you think can be made by a) individuals b) individual countries c) groups of countries? Think about the following points:

- transport
- energy
- the workplace
- shopping, buying and selling
- farming and agriculture
- the home

Writing: formal letter (3)

Read the following message from the Policy and Campaigns Director of Friends of the Earth, another environmental campaign group. Choose one of the suggested topics and write a letter. Look back at Units 4 and 5 for guidance on how to write a formal letter.

TAKE ACTION!

Think of the impact of hundreds of thousands of people demanding of their MP (Member of Parliament) that the food they eat is free from poisonous chemicals. Or switching their custom to the more environmentally friendly energy producers. The effect would be enormous, as those with political and financial power felt the force of democratic and consumer action. And there are plenty of opportunities to take action in this way.

One major source of damage to our countryside is the leaching of pesticides and other chemicals from farms into our waterways. Recent research has shown that these chemicals remain within the fruit and vegetables that we consume. Why not write to your MP or local council and let your local supplier know that you don't want to eat fruit laden with toxic residues?

All governments have signed up to measures which will help to minimise climate change, including commitments to cut carbon dioxide emissions. Why not write to your MP, MEP (Member of the European Parliament) or even to the US President, asking them to support policy measures that would enable these targets to be achieved? Say that you particularly support measures to increase energy efficiency and generation from renewable resources, alongside traffic reduction measures and increased public transport.

 Write a letter!

 Personal action

 Telephone call

 Send a fax

 Send an E-mail

Use of English: cloze

1 Look at the picture. Do you know anything about the bird that's illustrated? Why do you think it is important?

2 Read the following passage to see if your ideas were right.

America's big bird is back

The American bald eagle is top of a list of recovering species which are likely either to be (1) .... off the endangered register in the next two years, or downgraded (2) ....'threatened' status. More than 1,130 animals and plants are listed (3) .... the US Fish and Wildlife Service (4) .... endangered or threatened, making (5) .... illegal to kill or harm them. Recently, the list has been growing by (6) .... average of 85 new species each year. (7) .... now, few species had been removed from the register and when they (8) .... it was usually because (9) .... had finally become extinct.

As America's national bird, the bald eagle has been protected (10) .... various ways since 1940. The eagle, (11) .... is not really bald but looks it because of the white feathers on its head, is (12) .... only in North America. It (13) .... on the national coat of arms and on (14) .... sorts of everyday items, including the dollar bill, and has been the (15) .... of attention in the argument (16) .... the best way to protect endangered species. Its numbers had been reduced to (17) .... than 500 by the (18) .... of pesticides that affected (19) .... reproductive system, but (20) .... are now more than 5,000 nesting pairs in the continental US and the numbers are growing at 10 per cent a year.

3 Fill each of the numbered blanks in the passage with one suitable word.

4 Discuss and justify your answers with a partner. For example:

'Number 1 can't be "removed" because it's followed by "off".'
'Number 2 must be a dependent preposition after "downgraded".'

5 Discuss these questions.

1 Do you know of any other species that have been saved from extinction? How was this done?
2 What do you think is the best way to protect endangered species? Think about:
  • captive breeding programmes in zoos and aquariums
  • creating wildlife reserves
  • fund-raising for organisations such as WWF, dedicated to saving wildlife
  • banning pesticides and encouraging traditional methods of farming
  • encouraging tourism in countries with endangered wildlife habitats
  • political campaigns.

Writing: discursive composition (1)

In Paper 2 you may be asked to write a composition in which you present an argument. Depending on how the task is worded, you may need to:

• present both sides of an argument in a balanced discussion
• present one point of view, giving supporting evidence.

In this section you will see the best way to plan your writing and organise your ideas for presenting a balanced discussion.

1   You need to understand exactly what the question is asking you to write about. Look at the following writing task and underline the key words. Then answer the questions below.

> Protecting the environment is the most important problem facing the world today. Discuss. (About 350 words.)

1   Should you:
   a) write about all the different ways of protecting the environment?
   b) omit the environment and only write about the other problems facing the world today?
   c) discuss whether the environment or a different problem(s) is the most important in the world today?
2   What problems would you include in your answer to the question?

2

1   Read the following composition, which was written in answer to the task. What issues does the writer discuss? Would you have selected the same problems to write about?

2   Now answer these questions.

1   What is the purpose of the introduction? How has the writer attempted to draw the reader into the discussion?
2   In what order are the issues introduced?
3   Underline the linking expressions used in paragraphs 2, 3 and 4. Which organisational pattern has the writer used?
   a) a list of specific examples
   b) contrasting and conceding points
4   What is the writer's opinion about these issues in paragraphs 2, 3 and 4? How important does he/she consider them to be?
5   In what way(s) is the issue of the environment different, according to the writer?
6   The writer has discussed the issue that he/she considers most important last. What is the reason for this?
7   What is the purpose of the conclusion?

A

The modern world faces many major problems to which there are no easy solutions. These include unemployment, health, over-population and of course the environment. All have a bearing on all our lives, but is the environment really the most important?

If people are unemployed, they are unable to earn money and it is a fact of life that without an income it is difficult to live. Of course, work provides more than financial support; it gives people self-esteem and pride. However, technological developments and other factors mean that the job market is shrinking world-wide and young people have reduced prospects for work. Although this is certainly a major threat to people's well-being, it needs to be addressed by individual governments rather than globally.

Health is clearly an important concern that affects both individuals and the planet as a whole. Even though many illnesses have been eradicated, others remain a threat, and the overuse of antibiotics has led to the development of resistant strains of virus. However, on the whole, general health is improving, and in the developing countries medical aid programmes are already working towards creating a healthier population.

Over-population has implications for the entire planet and improved general health means that people are living longer. However, as with health, there are already programmes in place implementing measures to deal with not only a rising population, but an ageing population.

So what about the environment? There are urgent issues that need to be faced, including global warming, pollution and species loss. Unlike the other issues discussed, there is no clearly discernible global move to deal with these problems. Also, unlike the other issues, changes in the environment have a direct impact on the whole planet. Climate change and destruction of ecosystems could endanger all life on the planet if not dealt with quickly and at an international level.

In conclusion, other problems primarily affect only the quality of life, whereas environmental issues affect the actual existence of life itself. It is clear, therefore, that protecting the environment is the most important problem facing the world today.

3 Now read the following extracts from another composition written in answer to the same task. In what way is the organisation of the composition different?

B

There are many important issues facing the world today, including unemployment, health and overpopulation. Whether these issues are more important than environmental problems is debatable.

The growth in unemployment is a serious problem world-wide. It has partly been caused by improvements in technology as well as changing economic factors, which together mean that the job market is shrinking. While unemployment can of course have a devastating effect on the quality of life of individuals, an environmental issue such as the burning of fossil fuels is potentially more serious. It has resulted in global warming, causing climate change which could threaten the existence of entire nations. Is full employment worth this risk?

From this it must be clear that protecting the environment is the most important issue facing the world today. We ignore it at our peril. If we look after the houses we live in as individuals, why do we not take care of the larger house we all share?

4

1 Read composition A again, and complete the following outline in note form.

> **Introduction**
> Statement of topic: *The world faces many problems.*
> Plan of development: *Unemployment, health, over-population, environment.*
>
> **First supporting paragraph**
> Issue 1: *Unemployment*
> Details: *Need work to live, for self-esteem; but local issue, not global.*
>
> **Second supporting paragraph**
> Issue 2: ....
> Details: ....
>
> **Third supporting paragraph**
> Issue 3: ....
> Details: ....
>
> **Fourth supporting paragraph**
> Issue 4: ....
> Details: ....
>
> **Closing paragraph**
> Conclusion: ....

2 Now use information from composition A and your own ideas to complete the following outline of composition B.

> **Introduction**
> Statement of topic: *Many important issues facing world today.*
> Plan of development: *Unemployment, health, over-population.*
>
> **First supporting paragraph**
> Issue 1: *Unemployment*
> Details: ....
> Environmental issue 1: ....
>
> **Second supporting paragraph**
> Issue 2: ....
> Details: ....
> Environmental issue 2: ....
> *(e.g. skin cancer caused by depletion of the ozone layer)*
>
> **Third supporting paragraph**
> Issue 3: ....
> Details: ....
> Environmental issue 3: ....
>
> **Closing paragraph**
> Conclusion: ....

3 Both approaches are acceptable for an exam answer. However, one is more focused and more complex than the other. Decide which one, and give your reasons.

5

1 Read the task below and underline the key words. Decide what the question requires you to write.

> Generally, the future for the planet looks bright. Those who argue otherwise are only being pessimistic about the state of the environment. Discuss. (About 350 words.)

2 Jot down some ideas. What issues do you want to raise? What supporting evidence can you think of?

3 Decide on the approach you want to take and write an outline.

6 Now write your composition, making sure that you support your ideas with plenty of evidence.

7 Exchange your composition with a partner. Evaluate each other's work. Use your partner's comments to help you improve your composition.

► Exam Maximiser

1 Rewrite the following sentences beginning with *If*. Make any changes necessary.

1 They built that chemical factory and our local river is now polluted.
2 Environmental scientists tested the water so people realised how dangerous it was.
3 The scientists published the results of their tests and prevented people from becoming ill.
4 The authorities might have ignored pollution hazards, had they seen the chance of creating jobs.
5 With authorities who refuse to investigate, it's up to us to find out the truth.
6 Clean up the environment and most people will agree it improves their quality of life.

2 Choose the word or phrase which best completes each sentence.

1 Many animals are threatened with extinction as their traditional .... disappears.
   A ecosystem   B environment
   C nature   D habitat

2 Some species are in .... of becoming extinct.
   A risk   B danger   C verge   D brink

3 Naturalists are still battling to save endangered species, ... it may be too late for some of them.
   A as if   B in case   C even though
   D just as

4 Without financial aid, small farms like this one will soon be a .... of the past.
   A thing   B token   C sign   D feature

5 Do you think our message is .... through to the people who most need to hear it?
   A putting   B reaching   C getting
   D going

3 Fill each of the blanks with a suitable word or phrase.

1 Pollutants .... forms are often released into the sea.
2 What is acceptable in one country doesn't always turn .... acceptable elsewhere.
3 Many small species may disappear .... had time to classify them.
4 If we are to conserve rare animals, the habitats that support .... be conserved.
5 Had .... warned me, I would have made a terrible mistake.
6 Without the support they received from local businesses, the campaigners .... their case.

4 Talk about the photo.

1 Describe the photo and the situation.
2 How does it relate to the topic of the unit?
3 How important do you think are the issues raised?
4 How effective do you think the photo is? Why?

Vocabulary: sport

1 Describe the activities shown in each photo. In what ways are the people involved taking risks?

2

1 Look at the lists of factors below. Choose the factors which are most and least important for each of the activities shown in the photos, giving reasons.

skill	**mental qualities**
muscular control	strong nerves
sense of balance	courage
co-ordination	determination
sense of timing	self-control
	trust
	sensitivity

technology	**fitness**
specialised	regular training
equipment and	special diet
clothing	individual fitness
back-up support	programme
safety checks	gene traits
	individual body
	chemistry

2 Can you add any other factors which may be important?

3 Read the headline of the article opposite and look at the accompanying photo and caption. What do you think 'THE EDGE' refers to? Read the article to find out.

4

1 Find **one** phrase from the article which illustrates each of the following ideas.

- the skill of the windsurfer, e.g. '...*he swoops down the front of the wave*'
- the nerve of the windsurfer
- the quality of the technology and equipment involved

2 Match each of the verbs in the box below to one of the following subjects. Then check your answers by referring to the text.

a) the windsurfer   b) the sail   c) the sea

heaves	powers	accelerates
catapults	hums	leans
rises	snaps	spins
swoops	twists	splashes

3 Which verb(s) in the box suggest(s):

1 very rapid, powerful movement?
2 an upward movement?
3 a circular movement?
4 movement accompanied by sound?

WINDSURFING THE EDGE

Rocking gently on his board a thousand yards out from shore on the blue-grey waters of the Pacific, Rich Foster is waiting for a wave. Or rather, the wave. Then the sea slowly heaves itself skyward, rising into a mountain of water. Foster leans well back into his harness and as his sail snaps into a tight aerodynamic curve, the wind's energy surges down through his body and into the shark-like board below.

To gain momentum, he swoops down the front of the wave, the nose of the board slicing through the water, and then turns back to power up the steepening cliff. The sail hums with energy as man and board accelerate through the foamy wave-crest and catapult skyward. Day-Glo sail and board form a pyrotechnic display against the blue sky.

Foster spins and twists in the air, a quick barrel-roll before board and rider splash down safely into the sea to wait for the next wave. Once again he's escaped being thrown into the craggy embrace of the many rocks fringing this Hawaiian beach. For this is windsurfing at the edge: the edge of your skill, the edge of your nerve, and the cutting edge of technology.

Catapulted by wind and wave, a windsurfer experiences the thrill of staying in control aboard one of the most high-tech machines there is.

---

5   Work with a partner.

1   Choose one of the photos you discussed in Exercise 1. Use some of the verbs in the box below to help you describe more accurately the type of movement or activity involved.

dive	drive	flash	grasp	hurtle
leap	plummet	shoot	spin	strike
sweep	swerve	wheel	whirl	strain

2   Write a caption for your photo similar to the one used with the picture of the windsurfer. Use these prompts to help you.

Photo 1: nerves/to the limit/racing cyclist/into a corner/last lap/gruelling race

Photo 2: heart pound/striker/swerve round defender/shoot into net/best goal season

Photo 3: grasp partner/under arms/lift/whirl round/fast spin

6   Interview a partner about his/her attitudes to sport and risk, using these questions as a guide.

1   What is your favourite sport either as a spectator or participant?

2   What skills and training does it need? Is any special equipment required? Which of the factors in Exercise 2 are most important?

3   What do you think are the main benefits of sport?
   • builds team spirit
   • provides the chance of fame and fortune
   • builds confidence
   • promotes health and fitness

4   What do you think is the attraction of sports that are physically dangerous?

5   What drives some people to push themselves to 'the edge' of their skill and nerve?

4 When assessing the narrative composition, one of the things examiners look for is range and appropriacy of vocabulary. In the story you have read, the writer chooses words and expressions that help the reader visualise the setting and the situation.

Find the words or phrases the writer uses to:

1 emphasise the idea of speed and the need for quick reactions. (para. 2)
2 suggest that Jim reacted quickly to the officials. (para. 3)
3 emphasise the idea of total concentration. (para. 3)
4 show that Jim had practised the start many times. (para. 3)
5 show that Jim thought very briefly that it might be too dangerous. (para. 3)
6 indicate that Jim knew the course well. (para. 4)
7 suggest Jim reacted on instinct to correct the mistake. (para. 4)
8 suggest that something was hit very hard. (para. 4)
9 suggest uncontrolled movement on a slippery surface. (para. 4)

5 The narrative composition is also assessed on range and appropriacy of sentence structure.

1 Rewrite the following sentences using a participle (-ing) clause.

1 Jim stood with his team-mates at the top of the bobsled run and reflected on the words of his first coach.
2 He'd pointed to the bobsled and said, 'This will hurtle you down a mile of terror.'
3 He heard the officials call his team to the starting line and snapped back to the present.
4 Jim slithered helplessly down the course and saw the shadow of the sled above him.

2 Now compare your answers with the original version on page 117. What is the effect of using participle clauses?

3 Most of the sentences in the story are quite short, with no more than one subordinate clause. Why do you think this is?

6 Read the following writing task. Use the prompts below to help you plan and organise your story.

Write a story entitled 'The Game'.
(About 350 words.)

- **General topic**
1 What is the game? Is it a type of sport or some other kind of game?
- **Plot**
2 Is the game taking place now, or is it over?
3 Who is involved?
4 What happens?
5 What will your ending be? For example, does anyone learn anything from the game?
- **Structure**
6 Use the same structure as the model composition (see Exercise 2). This will give you practice in using the flashback technique.
- **A powerful ending**
7 Read the final lines of this story, written by three different students. Which do you think is the most effective? Why? What is wrong with the other endings?

A *Finally, when the game was over, she went to the restaurant and had a lovely evening.*

B *Shrugging his shoulders, he left the room. After all, it was only a game.*

C *She knew that she shouldn't play games because they were a waste of time.*

7 Now write your story.

8 Exchange your story with other students. Decide whose story:

- is the most exciting
- is the saddest
- is the most gripping
- creates the most vivid impression of the main character(s).

Exam Strategy

To score high marks in the narrative composition, DO make sure your story:
- relates clearly to the title given (or the first/last line provided).
- captures the reader's interest from the start, e.g. begins with an incident rather than explanations.
- has a coherent structure that builds up to a dramatic ending.

DON'T
- start writing without knowing what your ending will be.
- include too many details – you will run out of time in the exam.

▶ Exam Maximiser

1 Complete each of the following sentences with one of the words from the box below.

aback	away	between	behind	down
for	in	of	on	through	to	up

1 If everyone's ready, I think it's time we got .... to some serious practice.
2 He found there was a strong correlation .... diet and stamina.
3 She was somewhat taken .... by the team's reaction to her speech.
4 He was advised to take .... a less strenuous sport after his accident.
5 A bout of flu meant I had fallen .... in my training schedule.
6 We roped .... our parents to help and the sports pavilion was soon as good as new.
7 No one should remain in ignorance .... the dangers such activities may hold.
8 Is it right to expect the manager to take .... extra responsibilities at such a critical time?
9 I've tried persuasion and punishment, but I just don't seem to be able to get .... to him.
10 Tests reveal that some players have recourse .... drugs to enhance their performance.
11 They really shouldn't be allowed to get .... with such behaviour.
12 He was too young to be eligible .... the full marathon, but won the junior one easily.

2 Finish each of the following sentences in such a way that it is as similar as possible in meaning to the sentence printed before it.

1 This is the sort of thing that makes life worth living.
It's things ....
2 His refusal to take the test is what proves he must have something to hide.
The very ....
3 The kids were motivated, and on top of that, they were having fun.
Besides ....
4 She was so disappointed that she refused to speak to the press.
Such was ....
5 They had such bad weather that the match had to be abandoned.
So ....
6 Although I had no reason to trust him, I did.
There ....

3 For each of the sentences below, write a new sentence as similar as possible in meaning to the original sentence, but using the word given. This word must not be altered in any way.

1 The only reason he competes is to make money. **purely**
....
2 I'm completely against using drugs to improve how well I perform. **enhancing**
....
3 It is totally unnecessary for players to return to the changing rooms. **whatsoever**
....
4 We've done absolutely everything we can to make allowances for you, but this is asking too much! **bent**
....
5 The rules have been altered because there are so many young players joining the club. **account**
....
6 I wasn't at all surprised when that team won the cup. **slightest**
....
7 After yet another defeat, the runner resigned from the team feeling completely desperate. **utter**
....
8 Ther's only one thing which can guarantee success in sport and that's regular training. **key**
....

4 Read the passages below. Decide where they may have been taken from and how they link with the general theme of the unit. What do they say about the importance of sport in the lives of those who take part?

1. When my youngest turned out to be a natural athlete, I was unprepared for the thrill his sporting achievements gave me. For a start, his skills brought him instant friends. Bouncing his basketball with bravura precision, he has only to walk on to an outdoor court in an unfamiliar town and other boys hail him. He's popular, he's confident, and his success at sports seems to contribute to his success in other school activities.

2. My parents could not appreciate what climbing meant to me. I had tried to explain it, and had been careful to emphasise the seriousness of it. If something were to happen to me, I wanted them to understand that I had accepted this possibility. Above all I disliked the idea that they might think it a waste of a life and never understand the truth – that for me it was the most life-enhancing thing I had ever experienced, that the very nature of the pursuit made me and my climbing friends the characters we were.

The mind's eye

Speaking

1

1   Close your eyes and try to recall in detail the events of the last dream you can remember. Why do you remember it? Have you had the same dream more than once? How did it make you feel?

2   Work with a partner. Can you identify some typical features of dreams? For example:

- The events don't follow any logical sequence.
- You can do things that you can't do in real life.

2   Now discuss the following general statements about dreams. Which ones do you agree/disagree with? Can you give examples to support any of the statements?

'Dreams are just random thoughts and memories which don't have any special meaning.'

'Our dreams are symbolic – the things we dream about have special meanings which can be interpreted.'

'When we dream, our unconscious mind is working out the day's unresolved problems.'

Reading: literary text (comprehension)

The third text in Paper 1 is usually a literary extract, and the questions may focus on aspects such as the development of the narrative, the writer's use of language, the description of setting, and characters. In Papers 2 and 5 you can choose to write and talk about the set book. While in-depth literary analysis is not required, an ability to appreciate various elements of a text is expected. The exercises in this section will help you develop these skills.

1   The following passage is an extract from a novel, and describes a dream and how it affected the dreamer. Read the passage carefully to find out what happened in the dream.

The dream came to her again, but this time it was different. Cassie no longer tried to run, allowed herself instead to drift, as though carried by some invisible, intangible force towards Tan's Hill.

The woman waited, blue dress swirling around her, arms outstretched as if welcoming her. Cassie turned from the Greenway and began to climb the hill. This time she didn't fight to reach the top. She seemed able, by sheer force of will, to rise easily and effortlessly up the slope. In her head, she could hear a voice calling to her. 'Cassie! Caa-ssie!'

For an instant Cassie tried to hurry, felt the resistance return and forced herself to relax, to give in to the strange current drifting her slowly towards her destination. She could see the woman clearly now, though she stood with her back to Cassie, face turned away. Cassie approached, reached out towards her. 'I'm here.' The woman turned, outstretched arms ready to embrace, fingers extended as though she couldn't move from that spot, couldn't quite reach out far enough to draw Cassie to her.

'Cassie …' The voice was soft, whispering inside her head. Cassie reached out again, longing to touch, to make that last effort to contact, but her feet seemed to be sliding backwards. Looking down, she saw her body, her legs being extended, stretched, as though something were pulling her down from the hill, but her will to be there kept her hands reaching, her upper body still and untouched. For a moment, Cassie found herself

2   Without looking back at the text, say which details of the story you remember most vividly. What words or expressions can you remember that contributed to the effect of these parts of the story?

3   Discuss these questions. Read the extract again if necessary.

1   Who could the woman be? What does she want from Cassie?
2   What are the main emotions conveyed by the story? For example: fear, loss, sadness, joy.
3   What type of novel do you think the extract is from?
   a) romantic fiction   b) a children's novel
   c) a thriller   d) a ghost story for adults
4   Would you like to read it? Why/Why not?
5   Have you any ideas how the story might continue?

examining this strange phenomenon. Some part of herself knew she was dreaming, wondered which particular cartoon this ridiculous effect was from. Some other part of her mind railed against the distraction it offered, ordered her to look back at this strange woman, reach out that little bit further, hold tight.

5 A slight gasp made her turn. She stared horrified as the woman, mouth open now in some parody of a scream, hands thrown abruptly above her head, was sucked down, swallowed whole and alive into the hill itself.

6 There were seconds when Cassie could not act; she fell forward as though drawn by the other's momentum. Then, as though someone at the other end of herself, that part where her feet disappeared down the hill, had given a sudden jerk, she felt herself retracting rapidly, body and legs compressing, squashing back into their original form. Cassie hung on, trying to dig her fingers into the grassy slope, but there was no purchase. The dew-dampened grass came away in her hands. Her nails dug into the earth, only to be torn away again by the urgent pulling on her ankles.

7 Cassie woke with a sudden jolt as though falling from a great height. She lay still, trying not to waken Fergus, then on a sudden impulse, held her hands in front of her face, inspecting them closely. Somehow, she was not surprised to find still-damp mud caked beneath her fingernails.

4 Now answer these questions, which focus on details of the text and use of language.

1 What differences between Cassie's previous dream and this are indicated in the first two paragraphs?
2 Which two words in paragraph 3 continue the idea of 'an invisible force' in paragraph 1?
3 What detail about the woman's voice in paragraph 4 supports the idea that this is a dream?
4 In paragraph 4, Cassie is aware of two things at the same time. Explain what they are.
5 Why does the writer mention cartoons in paragraph 4?
6 What does 'it' refer to in the last sentence of paragraph 4?
7 What is suggested by the verbs 'sucked down ... swallowed' in paragraph 5?
8 Find three words in paragraph 6 which continue the image of the cartoon-like movements introduced in paragraph 4.

9 Explain in your own words the meaning of the phrase 'but there was no purchase' in paragraph 6.
10 What are the implications of the final sentence? What earlier detail in the narrative does it refer back to?

5 There may be words in the extract that you don't know but would like to understand and learn.

1 Use context clues to help you work out a synonym or definition for the following words.

1 intangible (para. 1)
(CLUE: *If you can't see it, do you think you can touch it?*)
2 (force of) will (para. 2)
(CLUE: *Look for another occurrence in paragraph 4.*)
3 to long (para. 4)
(CLUE: *What does paragraph 3 tell you about Cassie's attitude to the woman?*)
4 to rail (para. 4)
(CLUE: *What does the preposition* against *suggest?*)
5 parody (para. 5)
(CLUE: *Can we hear the woman?*)
6 momentum (para. 6)
(CLUE: *What has happened to the woman that could draw Cassie towards her?*)

2 What other words are new to you? Can you work out their meaning or do you need to use a dictionary?

6 The writer makes a number of comparisons introduced by *as if/as though* to describe the events in the dream, for example:

* *She allowed herself to drift **as though carried** by some invisible force.* (para. 1)

1 How many more examples can you find? Underline them. What is their effect?

2 In the example, the subject and auxiliary verb have been deliberately omitted from the clause. Can you put them back in? What form will the verbs be in? Do the same with the other examples where subjects and auxiliary verbs have been omitted.

7 Work with a partner. Underline all the verbs and nouns of movement in the passage. Then categorise them into groups, e.g. involuntary / violent / sudden movement.

8 Write a paragraph describing a dream – it could be one you've had, or you could make it up. Your dream should convey one of the following:

* fear   * loss   * peace   * freedom

Grammar plus: verb patterns (-ing and infinitive)

> When two verbs follow one another, the second verb may be an infinitive with *to*, a bare infinitive (without *to*) or a gerund. Sometimes the first verb can or must have an object.

1 How much do you know?

1 Fill in the gaps using the correct form(s) of the verb in brackets. In which sentences are two alternative forms possible? Does a change of form affect the meaning or not?

1 In her dream, Cassie began .... the hill. (climb)
2 She longed .... the woman standing at the top. (touch)
3 A part of her mind ordered her .... tight. (hold)
4 She found herself .... this strange phenomenon. (examine)
5 She tried .... her fingers into the grassy slope. (dig)
6 A slight gasp made her .... (turn)
7 She saw the hill .... the woman. (swallow up)
8 For days afterwards, she kept .... the dream. (remember)
9 She didn't look forward to the dream .... (come back)

2 Add the verbs from sentences 1–9 to column 2 of the table below, next to the appropriate pattern.

PATTERNS	EXAMPLES
1 Verb + *to* infinitive	agree, decide, fail, hope, refuse
2 Verb + *-ing* (gerund)	admit, deny, finish
3 Verb + *to* infinitive **or** *-ing*	
a) little change in meaning	like, prefer / continue
b) a change in meaning	dread, remember, forget, go on, mean
4 Verb + object + bare infinitive	let
5 Verb (+ object) + *to* infinitive	choose, expect, intend, want
6 Verb + object + *to* infinitive	compel, force, consider/ imagine, know
7 Verb (+ object or genitive) + *-ing* (gerund)	anticipate, dislike, enjoy, risk, insist on
8 Verb + object + *-ing* (participle)	observe / imagine
9 Verb + object + bare infinitive or *-ing* with some change in meaning	feel, hear, see

▶ Grammar reference pp. 211-212

As you do the exercises below, add the verbs you meet to the table.

2 Verb + infinitive

Verbs followed by an infinitive often refer forward to the future. Continuous, passive and perfect forms of the infinitive are all possible, e.g.:

He pretended **to be working**.
She expects **to be promoted** soon.
I hope **to have finished** this by tomorrow.

Rewrite the following sentences using an appropriate infinitive form.

1 I hope that I will make a million by the time I'm 30.
2 It seems that he has put on weight. (He ...)
3 She resolved that they would never take advantage of her.
4 They pretended that they had not met before.
5 It just happens that I was passing by when the police arrived. (I ...)
6 It appears that he is living off his inheritance. (He ...)

3 Verb + -ing form

Verbs followed by an *-ing* form often look back to an action or state before the main verb. Passive and perfect *-ing* forms are possible. A perfect *-ing* form is used to emphasise that one action happened before another and may be replaced by a *that*-clause + perfect tense, e.g.:

She remembered **having had** the dream before.
She denied **having been followed**.
She remembered **that she had had** the dream before.

Rewrite the following sentences using an *-ing* form or *that*-clause. Which sentence can't be rewritten using an *-ing* form without adding an extra word? Why?

1 The man denied having been anywhere near the scene of the crime.
2 I admitted that I had forgotten to lock the door behind me.
3 I often regret not having been made to study History.
4 Did I ever mention that I worked on a ship once upon a time?
5 I remembered that I had seen her at the party the previous weekend.
6 I remembered that she had been at the party.

4   Adding an object

Choose the correct option or options to complete each sentence. More than one is possible. Think about these questions.

- Which group of verbs never/sometimes/ always takes an object before the second verb? (*Look at the examples in the table in Exercise 1.*)
- Which group of verbs can be followed by a *that*-clause?
- When do you have to use a *that*-clause rather than an infinitive?

1   I hope
   a) to go soon.
   b) him to go soon.
   c) that he and I will go soon.
   d) to have gone by tomorrow.

2   I want
   a) to see that film.
   b) him to see that film.
   c) that I will see that film.
   d) that he sees that film.

3   He promised
   a) to finish it.
   b) me to finish it.
   c) me that he would finish it.
   d) that his secretary would finish it.

4   The robbers told
   a) everyone to lie down.
   b) that they would shoot.
   c) us that we were hostages.
   d) we had to keep quiet.

5   We have applied
   a) for her to be transferred.
   b) for to transfer her.
   c) her to be transferred.
   d) that they will transfer her.

6   The doctor advised
   a) her to stay in bed.
   b) staying in bed.
   c) her staying in bed.
   d) her that she should stay in bed.

7   We heard
   a) the orchestra to play as we arrived.
   b) the orchestra playing as we arrived.
   c) the orchestra play several new pieces.
   d) that the orchestra played several new pieces.

8   I appreciate
   a) your inviting me.
   b) you inviting me.
   c) that you invited me.
   d) it that you invited me.

5   Rewrite the following sentences using the words given in brackets.

1   They pushed the car, but it still wouldn't start. (tried) ....

2   He did not inform us that he had a criminal record. (failed) ....

3   After achieving fame as a singer, she then made a career in films. (went on)
....

4   I don't have any recollection of hearing him speak at the meeting. (remember) ....

5   I wish I had learned how to drive as a teenager. (regret) ....

6   They claimed not to have been avoiding us at all. (deny) ....

7   I would never have allowed him to be seen wearing those clothes. (let) ....

8   I was very unhappy that I was made to wear the same clothes as my little sister. (hated)
....

6   Use of English: sentence transformations

Finish each of the following sentences so that it is as similar as possible in meaning to the one printed before it.

1   They thought she was the best candidate for the job.
   She was felt ....

2   The fact that he had been to prison counted against him.
   His ....

3   The gardener will water the plants while I'm away.
   I've arranged for ....

4   They didn't think that he was intending to stay long.
   He ....

5   He wished that the holidays would arrive.
   He longed ....

6   Her advice was that I should be more careful.
   She ....

7   They now believe that the cause of the problem was lack of communication.
   Lack of communication ....

8   It's inconceivable that he would consent to do such a thing.
   His ....

Exam Focus

Paper 4 Listening (sentence completion)

One of the tasks in Paper 4 involves completing sentences with information from the text. The sentences summarise the main ideas in the text. You need to listen for and understand:

- the relation between main ideas and details
- the opinions and attitudes of the speaker(s).

You only need to write a word or short phrase for each answer. The sentence you must complete will probably not contain exactly the same words as the original passage, but you may use words from the passage to complete your answer.

See Unit 3, page 40, for a recommended procedure for Listening tasks. Remember, your answers must fit the grammar and be spelled correctly.

1 Look at the photos. What do you know about the American actor Christopher Reeve?

2 You will hear an extract from Christopher Reeve's autobiography, about a man in a situation similar to his own. For questions 1–10, complete the sentences with a word or short phrase.

In Reeve's film, a paralysed man _____ **1** that he can go sailing.

Gradually, his night-time sailing trips come to seem _____ **2** to him.

In the mornings, the nurse thinks _____ **3** is her fault.

His wife notices that he is becoming less _____ **4**

_____ **5** watches him sailing at night.

The hero decides to escape by sailing until _____ **6**

But thoughts of _____ **7** make him turn back.

He gives _____ **8** to the other man.

Finally, he has _____ **9** on which to build his life.

Reeve's own story was different because he _____ **10** by his family much earlier on.

3 To analyse your answers, look at the extracts from the tapescript and answer the questions on page 220.

Exam Strategy

- Before you listen, read through all the sentences.
- Look at the words before and after the gap, and decide what kind of information is missing.
- Write only a short word or phrase in the gap.
- Check and complete your answers on the second listening.
- Check that your answers fit the grammar of the sentence and are spelled correctly.

▶ Exam Maximiser

Grammar plus: emphasis (4) (cleft sentences)

- *It was sailing **that** he loved most in the world.*
- ***What** his family and friends were most afraid of **was** that he would leave them.*
- ***What** he was tempted to do **was** to sail away and never return.*
- ***All** he wanted to do **was** to be in his boat, sailing down the path of the moon.*

1 Cleft sentences with *It + be*

This structure can be used to emphasise almost any element of a sentence. It often implies a contrast with a previous statement.

1 Rewrite the following sentence to emphasise the different parts.

Rick took his cousin out for a meal last night.

1 It was *Rick* that *took his cousin out*, (not Steve).
2 It was .... that .... , (not his girlfriend).
3 It was .... that .... , (not for a drink).
4 It was .... that .... , (not the night before last).

2 Which part of the sentence **can't** be emphasised using this structure?

3 Re-express these sentences using standard word order. Which part of the sentence has been emphasised?

1 It was sailing that he loved most in the world.
2 It was in December that we first met.
3 It's my sister who does most of the cooking in the family.
4 It's learning about a new culture that's the most important thing for me.

▶ Grammar reference p. 212

> **Watch Out!** *modals in cleft sentences*
>
> Stewart can't have won the race.
> a) It can't / couldn't have been Stewart that won the race.
> b) It was Stewart that can't have won the race.
>
> Which of the alternatives is better, a) or b)?

2 Cleft sentences with *What* and *all*

This structure can focus on the object, the verb, or on the whole sentence.

1 Rewrite the following sentences without using a cleft structure.

1 Football is what he really loves.
2 What is happening nowadays is that everyone is trying to do more work in less time.
3 What they're doing now is trying to find a cheap solution.
4 What we've never done is ask the children what they think.
5 What I am enjoying is the social life.
6 All he wanted was to have a car of his own. (*Use 'just'*)

2 In which of the sentences 1–6 above is the cleft structure focusing on:

a) the object: Sentences ......, ... and ......
b) the verb: Sentences ...... and ......
c) the whole phrase: Sentence ......

3 Rewrite the following sentence in five different ways.

Scientists are looking for a cure for the common cold.

 Grammar reference p. 212

> **Watch Out!**
>
> 1   What she did was feel afraid. ✗
> 2   What she did was phone the police. ✓
>
> What types of verbs **can't** be used in this structure?

3 Other ways of introducing cleft sentences

We may use a general word such as *person, thing, reason,* to introduce a cleft sentence e.g.:

*The only **person who** knows the answer is John.*
*The **reason (why)** I came was to meet Sarah.*

Complete the following sentences by writing a suitable general word in each gap. Use the context to help you decide what word is needed.

1 The .... where I saw him first was in a crowded restaurant.
2 The .... who introduced us was his girlfriend at the time.
3 The .... that I noticed first was his beautiful smile.
4 The next .... that I saw him was a year later, on January 31.
5 The .... I remember the date so well is because he asked me to marry him.

4 Complete the sentences below, giving true information. Then take turns to read your sentences to a partner, giving a reason for or explanation of each statement.

1 What I most enjoy is ...
2 What really annoys me is when ...
3 All I want to do when ...
4 It's ... that make me feel really ...
5 ... is playing computer games.
6 The place where I'd like to be right now is ...
7 The reason ... is to pass the Proficiency exam.

5 Use of English: sentence transformations

Finish each of the following sentences in such a way that it is as similar as possible in meaning to the sentence printed before it.

1 You couldn't have seen Mary in the park.
It ....

2 He first thought of becoming a writer when he won a prize at school.
What ....

3 They had never considered leaving their money to Philip.
The last ....

4 She only ever wanted to learn how to play the drums.
All ....

5 Classes have got larger in many schools.
What has ....

6 She paints watercolour pictures of flowers as a hobby.
What she ....

7 She felt very nervous because of the large number of people.
What ....

8 I'm more worried by the expense of the journey than by the time it takes.
It's not ....

Use of English: cloze

1 Look at the photograph and discuss the following questions.

1 What are these people doing?
2 How do you think they do it?
3 Can you give any other examples of people performing feats which appear physically impossible?

2 Look through the passage but don't try to fill in the gaps yet.

1 Underline the topic sentence. How does this relate to the title?

2 The rest of the passage gives supporting evidence for the topic sentence. Three sets of examples are given. Underline them in the text. One sentence later in the passage tells you what these cases all have in common. Find this sentence and underline it.

Mind over matter

The control that our mind can have over the physical processes of our body has been well documented. In a large (1) .... of cases, people have shown that they are able to use (2) .... power of their imagination to produce measurable physical changes (3) .... their bodies. One man could change the (4) .... of two areas of skin on the palm (5) .... his hand, simultaneously making (6) .... hotter and the other colder. He did this by picturing one part of his hand being burned by a hot flame and the other part being (7) .... by ice. Another man could (8) .... or lower his heart beat rate by imagining (9) .... running for a train or lying in bed. He could also (10) .... the pupils of his eyes larger or smaller by visualising varying degrees of light. He could even use (11) .... imagination to control pain (12) .... he was at the dentist by visualising the pain (13) .... an orange-red thread that he could make smaller and smaller (14) .... it disappeared completely. It has been shown that it is possible to walk barefoot over red hot coals (15) .... suffering any injury, once those involved have been trained to (16) .... the right mental state. In all these cases, the people involved do (17) .... try to change the physical processes of their bodies directly, (18) .... aim instead to create a situation in (19) .... minds that will produce the required (20) ....

3 Fill each of the numbered blanks in the passage with one suitable word. Then read the completed text again to check that it makes sense.

4 Compare and justify your answers with a partner.

Vocabulary: expressions with *come*

1   Word formation

1   Read the text below. What is it about?

So can our minds be used to help us to achieve less physical goals such as (1) .... shyness or achieving success in business? Of course they can! It's (2) .... itself. What you have to do at the (3) .... is first define what you want to achieve and then imagine the situation in which your (4) .... has been achieved. It comes down to this. Once you can (5) .... having achieved your goal, your (6) .... mind accepts that the goal is possible, and it can then work out (7) .... ways and means by which you can get there in reality. This process can throw up (8) .... solutions that the rational mind would never have come up with.

1 COME	**2** SIMPLE	**3** SET
4 OBJECT	**5** VISUAL	**6** CONSCIOUS
7 VARY	**8** EXPECT	

2   Complete the text with the correct form of the words given in capitals. You may need to add a prefix and / or an appropriate ending.

3   Work with a partner. Discuss how the technique described in the passage could be helpful in the following situations.

- overcoming exam nerves
- learning to overcome a particular fear, e.g. of insects, or the dark
- dealing with an important interview

2   Three-word phrasal verbs with come

Read the following examples of phrasal verbs from the text in Exercise 1. Notice that each verb is followed by two particles.

- *It **comes down to** this.*
- *... solutions that the rational mind would never have **come up with**.*

Fill in the missing particles in the following sentences.

1   I can't come .... a better explanation for how people can walk on hot coals.
2   In the interview she came .... cool, calm and collected.
3   Now you've said that, I'm starting to come .... your way of thinking.
4   I feel really ill – I must be coming .... flu.
5   What it comes .... is a straight choice – a well-paid but stressful job, or a badly-paid job with no stress.

6   The President came .... heavy criticism when he admitted not having told the truth.
7   Those who claim to have special mental powers may come .... considerable prejudice and opposition.
8   My membership comes .... renewal next April.
9   She came .... a really stupid remark in the middle of the meeting.
10   If I eat crab, I come .... a rash.

3   Use of English: key word transformations

1   Rewrite the sentences using the word given. Do not change this word in any way. In each case this involves making a phrase with *come*. Use the patterns *verb + preposition / particle + noun* or *verb + adjective*.

1   In Britain, people become adults when they are 18. **age**
....

2   Everything worked out well in the end. **right**
....

3   The hero finally accepted his situation. **terms**
....

4   The game didn't start getting exciting until the second half. **life**
....

5   I think you should tell the truth about the incident. **clean**
....

6   Just use whatever is available. **hand**
....

7   The ball rolled down the slope and stopped just in front of him. **rest**
....

8   In spite of his efforts, his plans failed. **nothing**
....

2   Which of the fixed phrases above are neutral, and which are colloquial?

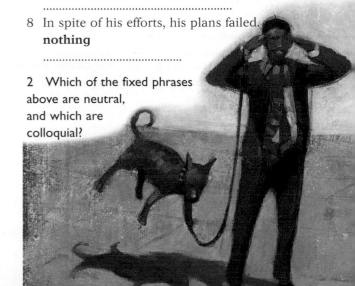

Reading: literary text

1 You are going to read a passage about a man who takes his mentally and physically disabled daughter to a faith-healer. First, read through the extract and answer the following question.

What is your impression of Miss Whittaker?

a) She is a dangerous woman with strong powers.

b) She is a sincere woman with real but limited powers.

c) She is a convincing fraud with no real powers.

She waits for me to move away and then goes to the bed and strokes Hilary's hair. Immediately the child quietens and begins to gurgle softly.

'What a pretty little girl,' Miss Whittaker murmurs. 'What a pretty pink ribbon Mummy has put in your hair. What pretty clothes. Someone's mummy and daddy think a lot of them, don't they? Someone's a very lucky little girl.'

Curiously, she is right. We do think a lot of her.

I sit in the chair watching the woman's squat back. Hilary is lying quite still and calm, despite the strange place, the strange voice. This is very unusual. A good sign. So, do I sense the faintest ray of hope? It's quickly quelled. How can this woman even know what's wrong with my daughter?

Kneeling on a cushion, Miss Whittaker runs her small podgy hands the length of the child's body, letting them slide lightly over her clothes. Minutes pass. She has stopped talking now, her hands move back and forth, not hypnotically or even rhythmically, but more with a questing motion, stopping here and there, hovering, moving back, coming quietly to rest: on her head for a full minute, above her knees, her ankles, which below her socks, I know, are fierce with scars. Hilary lies still, eyes blindly open, breathing soft. She doesn't even move when a plump hand covers her face, gently pressing the eyelids. Leaning over her, Miss Whittaker blows very lightly on her forehead. Then repeats the whole rigmarole.

I watch, biting a nail. Fifteen minutes. It's hard keeping still, frankly. I fidget. I feel tense. It's farcical. For of course, now I'm here, I don't expect anything. In the end I would have done a lot better by myself and Hilary if I'd gone to St James's Park. Shirley* would think I'd lost my marbles.

Another ten minutes before at last Miss Whittaker rises slowly to her feet, then sits on the bed and strokes Hilary's hair in what is now an entirely normal way. Immediately the child begins to smile and gurgle again.

'Poor little lovey.' Then she turns to me. She says: 'Well, apart from some small irritation or infection which I may have been able to help, your child is really perfectly healthy, Mr Crawley, and beautifully, beautifully innocent. Don't you see how her smiles shine?'

What? Is the 'session' over? Is that her verdict? But she holds up a hand to stop my protest. 'As for the question of what she is, I mean the form in which she was sent into this world, I'm afraid it is far, far beyond my humble powers to alter that.'

After a moment's awkward silence in this dimly-lit room, I decide the best thing to do is cut my losses. Only £12.50 after all. A joke. I stand up to go, reaching for my wallet.

She smiles her sad smile, so similar to any sympathetic, middle-class smile an older woman might give you waiting in a long queue at a supermarket or post office. And she says calmly:

'Perhaps I could help you, though, Mr Crawley.'

'I'm sorry, I beg your pardon.'

'Perhaps I could help you more than your child.'

Shirley is the narrator's wife.

2 Read the passage again and choose the best option, **A, B, C** or **D** to answer the questions or finish the statements below.

1 Miss Whittaker realises that the little girl's parents
   A are overprotective towards their child.
   B have a disturbing effect on their child.
   C can't forget about their child.
   D care about their child.

2 By her movements over the child's body, Miss Whittaker is trying
   A to stop the child's pain.
   B to sense where there may be a problem.
   C to send the child to sleep.
   D to build up the child's confidence in her.

3 What does the man feel as he watches Miss
   Whittaker?
   A He is nervous about the effect she is having on
       the child.
   B He is worried that his wife does not
       know where he is.
   C He is sure that whatever she does will make no
       real difference to the child.
   D He is relieved that the child does not have any
       major problems after all.

4 After her examination of the child, Miss Whittaker
   suggests that the child's disability
   A should not be seen as a problem.
   B is not as serious as her parents thought.
   C has not affected her mental powers.
   D needs specialist treatment.

5 The narrator decides
   A he won't pay the full price for the consultation.
   B Miss Whittaker isn't serious in her comments.
   C Miss Whittaker is only pretending to be
       sympathetic.
   D he'll accept he's wasted his money.

6 What is the effect of the visit?
   A The child is miraculously cured.
   B The child is cured, but there are side effects.
   C There is no real change in the child's condition.
   D The child no longer has problems, but the father
       suffers as a result.

3 Discuss the following questions about the passage.

1 In what ways do you think the narrator might have
   needed help?
2 Do you think he was right to go to the faith-healer?
   Why / Why not?

Vocabulary: words with similar meaning

1

1 Read the following definitions from the Longman
Dictionary of Contemporary English. What are the main
differences in meaning between the verbs *heal, cure* and
treat?

> **heal** *v* 1 [I] if a wound or a broken bone heals, the flesh,
> skin, bone etc grows back together and becomes healthy
> again: *It took three months for my arm to heal properly.*
> 2 [T] to cure someone who is ill or make a wound heal.

> **cure**¹ *v* [T] 1 to make someone who is ill well again: *The
> doctors did everything they could to cure her, but she died
> three months later.* 2 to make an illness disappear
> completely, usually by medical treatment: *an operation to
> cure a hernia problem.*

> **treat**¹ *v* [T]
> 3 ▶ MEDICAL ◀ to try to cure an illness or injury by using
> drugs, hospital care, operations, etc.: *Nowadays malaria
> can be treated with drugs.*

2 Now use one of the verbs in the appropriate form to
complete each of the sentences below.

1 At first Colin was .... for influenza, but then
   they found he actually had malaria.
2 Some types of cancer can now be completely ....
   if the disease is detected early enough.
3 I cut myself last week and it still hasn't .... – I'd
   better see a doctor.

2 Work in groups of three. Choose one box each, **A**,
B or **C**. Using your dictionary to help you, write an
explanation or definition of the words and expressions in
your box. Then discuss your explanations together and
decide what the main differences are between your words.

A	B	C
1 an illusion	an illustration	a hallucination
2 a faith healer	a witch doctor	a charlatan
3 a vision	a dream	an ideal
4 romanticism	escapism	idealism
5 his imagination ran riot	he had a fertile imagination	he built castles in the air

3

1 Choose the word, **A**, **B**, **C** or **D** that best completes each sentence.

1 Many people are .... about the idea of faith-healing.
   A mistrustful **B** incredulous
   C hesitating **D** sceptical

2 The idea that positive thinking can help to overcome physical illness should not be dismissed as a ....
   A fancy **B** myth **C** fable **D** legend

3 For some people, the chance of a cure remains .... thinking.
   A inventive **B** hopeful **C** wishful
   D creative

2 What's **your** opinion on this issue?

4 What do you know about other types of cure which don't depend on conventional medicine, such as:

- acupuncture?
- homeopathy?
- aromatherapy?
- hypnosis?

Would you ever be prepared to try any of these yourself?

Speaking: discussion

In Part 3 of the Speaking test, you may be asked to discuss a list of items and react to them in some way. In the task below, you have to relate the items to your own feelings.

1 Which of the factors below do you think have the greatest effect on you, either physically or mentally? Discuss each one and say how it can change the way you feel.

- diet
- leisure
- relationships
- environment
- exercise

Can you add any other factors to the list?

2 Imagine that you could create an ideal environment for a new baby to grow up in. Which factors would you consider to be the most important and why?

Grammar plus: *do, give, have, make, take* + noun phrase

> English often uses general verbs such as *do, give, have, make* and *take* followed by a noun phrase to replace a verbal construction, e.g.:
> She smiled sadly. → She **gave** a sad smile.
> He works very little. → He **does** very little work.
> He napped. → He **took** a nap.
>
> This structure may be less formal than the use of the related verb, e.g.:
> I'll think about it. → I'll **have** a think about it.
>
> In some cases there may be a slight difference in meaning, e.g.:
> a) She chatted with him briefly. (incomplete)
> b) She had a brief chat with him. (completed activity)

1 Rewrite the following sentences, using *do, give, have, make* or *take* + noun phrase. Make any other changes necessary.

1 She glanced at him fleetingly as she left.
2 I drank some water.
3 Let's rest for an hour.
4 He kicked the dog viciously.
5 I had to lecture to a group of 500 students.
6 She kissed him tenderly.
7 Who will volunteer to wash up?
8 In time, Peter recovered fully from his illness.
9 She affected him strangely. (*Be careful with the spelling.*)
10 Then Marie suggested something unusual.

2 Read the following story. Replace the verbs in italics using a *verb + noun* construction, as in Exercise 1.

Zoe (1) *frowned* worriedly. It was late at night, she was alone, and someone was following her. She could hear the footsteps coming closer as she walked down the dark street. She (2) *looked* behind her quickly and as she did so, the man who was following her turned his head away. 'He doesn't want me to see his face,' she thought in terror.

She started to run, and then (3) *cried out* as she tripped and felt herself falling. The next moment he had caught her up and was bending over her. She looked up and realised that she knew him – she'd met him at the club and (4) *danced* with him a couple of times that evening.

'I'm sorry,' he said. 'It's me, Philip. It was stupid of me. I wanted to see you got home safely. I didn't want to frighten you.'

Zoe was more concerned about her ankle. She (5) *groaned* as she tried to stand. 'I've twisted my ankle,' she said. 'You'd better try to find a taxi. And I'd like to (6) *suggest* something – if you want to see people home safely, it's not a bad idea to ask them first.'

Writing: descriptive composition (3)

For the descriptive composition in Paper 2, you may be asked to write about an event or a situation that has affected your life, saying how or why It has affected you. This involves **narrat**ing events and **describ**ing their effects, giving reasons.

1   Read the following writing task. How many parts does it have?

> Describe a challenge you faced as a child and how you met it. Explain how this experience has affected you. (About 350 words.)

Can you think of any challenges you faced as a child that you could write about?

2

1   Read the introduction to the following composition, which was written in answer to the task.

1   What was the challenge that the girl faced?
2   Underline the sentence which introduces the topic of the composition.

> *I had a happy childhood with plenty of friends and a loving family. I even enjoyed school work. However, I had one phobia that I couldn't overcome – I was terrified of heights.*

2   Read paragraph 2, ignoring the instructions in brackets. Then answer the questions below.

> *It started when I was about five years old and it was totally irrational. For some reason my mind told me that being high was dangerous, and no matter how much I tried to persuade myself otherwise, I couldn't overcome the fear. When the rational side of my mind said 'Don't be stupid,' the irrational side would say 'Don't ignore the danger!' Whenever I was asked to do anything which involved heights I felt absolutely terrified. (Give details of how you felt.) Looking down, I felt as though I was going to fall. The fear affected my whole life. I couldn't stand on a ladder. I couldn't use escalators. (Explain how you felt when you tried. Use 'without -ing'.) I couldn't even visit anyone who lived in a flat higher than the second floor. (Describe how you felt when you did. Use 'without -ing'.)*

1   What is the main idea of paragraph 2? Underline the topic sentence.
2   The paragraph would be more effective if it had more supporting detail. Look at the instructions in brackets. What details could you add?
3   What is the effect of the direct speech in this paragraph?

3   Read the next paragraph, ignoring the instructions.

> *One day when I was about 12, I decided that I was going to overcome this fear. What I decided to do was attack the phobia in stages. I started by visualising myself managing in situations that normally caused the panic. For example, (describe the situation/s you visualised). The next step was the real thing. (Describe a real situation you deliberately faced.) It took time, and I had various setbacks. (Describe a setback.) However, gradually I got better and better. Once my mind realised that I was actually safe in these situations, it stopped telling me to be afraid.*

1   What is the main idea of this paragraph? Underline the topic sentence.
2   Look at the instructions in brackets. What details could you add?

4   Read the last paragraph, ignoring the gaps.

> *Now I can .... without .... I can .... without .... It has improved my confidence, because I overcame the difficulty alone, and although I will never be completely happy with heights, I can at least live with them.*

1   Underline the main conclusion.
2   Now decide on suitable information to fill in the gaps. The paragraph should link back to earlier ideas in the composition.

3

1   Write the composition out, incorporating all the additional ideas you have thought of.

2   Exchange your completed composition with a partner. Do you find the added detail convincing? Does it improve the composition?

4   Read the following writing task.

> Describe a success you have had in your life, how you achieved it and what its effect on you has been. (About 350 words.)

Plan what you are going to write, following the structure of the composition in Exercise 2.

5   Now write your composition. Include:

- plenty of supporting detail
- reference to feelings and reactions
- vocabulary that conveys these feelings vividly
- emphatic structures such as cleft sentences, inversion and intensifying expressions.

1 Find and correct the errors in the following sentences.

1 All the students denied to have written the note.
2 There's nothing you can do which will make me to change my mind.
3 If you're caught driving without a licence, you risk to be heavily fined.
4 They were quite wrong to assume us all being in agreement with their proposals.
5 We were delighted when our school was chosen testing the new software.
6 I'm so upset that they all heard you to be rude me.
7 I had expected having heard from the selection committee by now.
8 The worried father had refused believing the doctor until he was shown the test results.
9 If you so dislike that I am in charge, you'd better ask to work with another group.
10 She absolutely dreaded to tell her father what had happened.

2 Choose the word or phrase which best completes each sentence.

1 My father .... us a long lecture on how we should behave when we had visitors.
   A offered   B said   C told   D gave

2 It is known that depriving people of sleep may cause ....
   A illustrations B illusions C hallucinations D visions

3 When his membership came .... renewal, he was startled to see how much the cost had risen.
   A in for   B up for   C round to
   D up against

4 I'm afraid I have only a .... memory of the incident.
   A vague   B rough   C poor   D dull

5 I doubt whether he ever .... any intention of marrying her.
   A had   B made   C kept   D felt

6 She .... fleetingly at the brochure and put it down again.
   A glared   B glanced   C stared   D gazed

3 Fill each of the blanks with a suitable word or phrase.

1 Almost anyone can do this, once .... trained to achieve the right attitude.
2 If he pretends not .... any payment, show him the receipt.
3 All we'd hoped .... a little encouragement.
4 All she cares .... making money.
5 It wasn't my brother .... me what you had done, actually.
6 I really regret .... told you what was going on, so you could have taken part.
7 It .... me you saw that evening, but I rather doubt it.
8 Understanding .... that child needs, not punishment.
9 What the students should have .... make an appointment with the principal.
10 The .... I lived as a child has been pulled down.
11 The thing we really wanted to know .... they had hidden the gold.
12 The .... remembered him was that he'd asked me several difficult questions.

4 Talk about the photo.

1 Describe the photo and the situation.
2 How does it relate to the topic of the unit?
3 How important do you think it is to control stress and mental pressures in the world today? Can you make any suggestions for ways of doing this?

The world of work

Speaking: photographs / ranking

1 Work with a partner.

1 Choose one photo each to talk about. Say where you think the photo was taken. Describe the situation and the people.

2 Discuss together the different aspects of work and attitudes to work illustrated by the two photos you have chosen. Think about:

- the relationship between work and home life
- the different values of old and modern lifestyles.

3 Report back to the class and share your ideas about all the photos.

2 Look at the following list of factors you might consider when choosing a job. Select five and rank them in order of importance for you. Compare your ideas with a partner and discuss the reasons for your choices.

- job security
- independence
- income
- status
- job satisfaction/self-fulfilment
- social life
- future prospects

3 Do you think work means the same thing in different cultures? Think of other countries that you have read about, seen in films or visited. Do you think other factors might be more important than those you discussed in Exercise 2?

Paper 3 Use of English (Section B, comprehension)

The comprehension questions in this section test your understanding of the language and ideas of a text. You don't always need to write full sentences for your answers. Sometimes you are asked to express the ideas from the text in your own words in order to show that you have understood them. Some questions only carry one mark, but when you are asked for more than one piece of information, two or even three marks may be allocated.

Always check to make sure that you have answered all parts of the question. You should also check for grammar errors, although these will only be penalised if they make your answer unclear.

Here is a procedure you can follow.

- Read the title to predict what the passage is about.
- Skim the passage quickly to decide what type of text it is, and to check your predictions.
- Read the questions.
- Read the text again quickly and mark any lines you notice that answer a question.
- Go through the text carefully and answer the questions.
- If you can't find the answer to a question, then leave it and go on. The answers follow the order of the text, so once you have found the next answer, it will be easier to find the preceding one.

1 The following extract describes a traditional craft which is still carried out by village people in Indonesia. The writer is a visitor who is travelling round Indonesia with a friend. She is taken to a village by the local priest, Bollen, who is very conscious of the value of these crafts to the tourist industry. Read the passage, then answer the questions which follow it. Follow the procedure recommended above.

The ikat weavers of Flores, Indonesia

We went to visit him at the seminary, as we had heard that the nearby village produced weavings. Bollen confirmed this and, giving the signal to one of his domestic staff, said, 'In fact, I believe they are doing so just now.' The servant sped

5 off and Bollen took us on a long circuitous route, presumably giving the weavers time to set up their spinning wheels and looms. On seeing us, six women just happened to start performing simultaneously all the complex steps necessary to produce an *ikat*. One was crushing the seeds out of raw

10 cotton on an old-fashioned mangle, another spinning it into thread on a wheel which was turned by foot, while, on a frame, the long threads were being bound with coconut fibres to produce the desired pattern. An older woman with several ivory bracelets on both wrists was in charge of the

15 dyeing process. She was stirring a pot over a fire, in which threads were undergoing coloration from a red dye made from special roots. Nearby, other pots contained blue, yellow and green dyes, which were made from indigo flowers, seed pods and green leaves.

20 *Ikat* means 'to tie', and *ikat* cloths are fashioned by binding the warp threads tightly with grass or palm leaves to create a dye-resistant pattern. Sometimes the patterns are recorded, but more often than not, the weaver knows by heart which areas and individual threads need to be bound. Gazing

25 incredulously at the sea of tiny knots stretched on the wooden frame before us, it was hard to imagine the skill

(a) Explain in your own words why Bollen took the writer on a 'circuitous route' to the seminary. (line 5)

(b) What do the words 'just happened to start performing simultaneously' (line 7) suggest about the writer's attitude to the situation?

(c) What were 'the long threads' (line 12) made of?

(d) What are the functions of the wheel and the frame?

(e) What does the word 'fashioned' mean in this context (line 20) and why does the writer use it here?

(f) In your own words, explain why the writer was 'gazing incredulously'. (line 24)

(g) What is the weavers' attitude to chemical dyes? What reason is suggested for this?

(h) Explain exactly why it is important that 'certain rules must be obeyed'. (line 35)

(i) What does 'this' refer to in line 40?

involved in tying the knots precisely and evenly enough to form the intricate patterns, let alone doing it from memory.

After they are bound, the threads are dyed. Cheap, easy-to-use chemical dyes are widely available in Indonesia now, but though they are often used to make textiles to sell, most weavers refuse to use them for cloths that will be kept in their own families. The dyeing process is often a closely guarded secret, surrounded by superstitions and taboos. To ensure success, certain rules must be obeyed. In some parts of Indonesia, for example, the enclosure where the blue dyeing is done is absolutely off-limits to men.

The process of binding and dyeing can take months — even years — depending on the richness of the colour desired. Once this is finished, the actual weaving begins. Throughout Indonesia, the 'back loom' is the one most commonly used. A young woman sat at one of these, bracing her feet against a tree and controlling the tension of the threads by leaning backwards or forwards against a back brace. Every few seconds she would raise the warp threads with a long slender piece of ebony and then slip the shuttle containing the weft threads through. It was slow, painstaking work. An *ikat* woven in this way can take weeks, whereas a factory-made cloth can be finished in a matter of hours.

The finished sarongs had wonderfully rich colours and elaborate, mostly geometrical designs which, we were told, were very private to their creators and passed down through the generations. Nowadays only the old village women are said to know what they really mean. Most motifs have developed from animist beliefs, and revolve around fertility symbols, hence the recurring symbols of man and woman, animals, birds and flowers.

(j)   How does the text suggest that the back loom is physically difficult to manipulate?

(k)   What does 'they' refer to in line 54?

(l)   Which two different aspects of ikat production does the writer suggest have special significance to the people who make them?

Exam Strategy

This text contains a number of specialised technical words. From the context you should be able to deduce that they are all objects or processes connected with the process of spinning cotton and weaving cloth, but you don't need to understand the words to answer the questions. In the exam, you won't be tested on the meaning of specialised vocabulary.

2   **Look back at the questions and your answers. For which questions did you have to do the following?**

1   paraphrase the words of the text
2   quote the words of the text directly to support your answer
3   explain the meaning of a word in the context
4   find an answer stated directly in the text
5   find an answer implied in the text
6   interpret the writer's attitude
7   identify what words like *it* and *this* refer to
8   include more than one point in your answer

3   **Summary**

1   Read the summary question. Underline the key words.

> In a paragraph of 60–80 words describe the aspects of the work that struck the writer as significant or interesting, and say why.

2   Find the information you need in the passage and make notes in your own words, following the order of the paragraph.

- Remember that what the writer thought was 'significant' may include positive or negative features. You don't have to describe exactly how the cloth was produced.
- Use the paragraph divisions to help you. Each paragraph stresses one aspect of the work (either positive or negative) which impressed the writer. Check your answer to Exercise 1 **(b)** for help with paragraph 1.
- Make brief notes on these general points only.

3   Write the paragraph. Use verbs like *realised/was struck by/was impressed by/learned*, and appropriate linking words, particularly to signal the contrast between positive and negative ideas.

4   Check and edit your summary. See Exam Focus Units 2 and 8 (pages 29 and 115) for help with general techniques in summary writing.

Grammar check: position of adjectives

1 Read the following information about the position of adjectives and do the exercises that follow.

---

1 Most adjectives can occur in two positions:
  a) **in front of** a noun, e.g.:
    Bollen took us on a long circuitous route.
  b) **after** a noun and verb such as *be / get / become* or *seem / look / feel*, e.g.:
    The route Bollen took us on was long and circuitous.

2 However, some adjectives can only be used in one or other of these positions.
  a) Adjectives used only before a noun include:
    former (wife), *upper* (storey), *lone* (parent), *actual* (reason), *utter* (disbelief), (a) *mere* (trifle), *coastal* (town), *indoor* (pool), *southern* (climes)
  b) Adjectives used only after a noun and verb include: *afraid, ill, bound to, devoid of*

---

1 The adjectives below are limited to one position, either before or after a noun. Decide which group each adjective belongs to.

---

alive	ill	asleep	coastal	former	mere
inside	glad	outdoor	earthen	unable	
unwell	western	neighbouring	alone		

---

2 What can you say about the position of adjectives:

- beginning with the letter *a*?
- with related adverbs? e.g. *outdoor/outdoors*
- that are derived from nouns? e.g. *coastal*
- that function as intensifiers? e.g. *main*
- followed by a preposition or infinitive? e.g. *able*

► Grammar reference p. 212

2 Choose the best word to complete each of the following sentences.

1 The *frightened/afraid* children didn't panic.
2 When it rains the children have to play *indoor/indoors*.
3 She seems to be a very *contented/content* baby.
4 The *unwell/sick* animal was taken to the vet.
5 Countries in the *south/southern* hemisphere have their winter in July and August.
6 His arguments seemed very *convincing/convinced*.
7 The difference in appearance between the twins was *mere/minute*.
8 We have done our best to contact any *living/alive* relatives.

3 We can use some adjectives before and after nouns, but with a change of meaning.

1 Compare these pairs of sentences. What does the adjective in italics mean in each case?

1 a) The *late* President will be remembered for the economic reforms he instigated.
  b) The measures taken are certainly welcome, but they have been introduced too *late*.
2 a) The heroines of nineteenth-century novels often seem very prim and *proper* in comparison with those of today.
  b) How do you expect me to do this job if I don't have the *proper* tools?
3 a) In the *present* circumstances, I feel that we have no option but to cancel the meeting.
  b) I made a note of all those *present* at the meeting.
4 a) I have asked to see all those *responsible* for the disturbances last night in my office.
  b) He can hardly be said to be a *responsible* member of society.
5 a) The new film had an extremely *involved* plot which was very difficult to follow.
  b) The people *involved* in the incident have been asked to appear at a disciplinary hearing.

2 What can you say about the adjectives in **3b**, **4a** and **5b**?

4 Order of adjectives before a noun
Do you know the rules for adjective order? Add the adjective in brackets in the appropriate place in the clause.

1 a hand-fired clay pot (black)
2 a tough cardboard box (storage)
3 a good-value metal bangle (adjustable)
4 a wooden ornament (charming)
5 a hand-made ceramic ornament (Peruvian)
6 a 100% silk scarf (long)
7 ceramic fridge magnets (miniature)
8 six hand-painted wooden animals (adorable)
9 a carved wooden photo frame (simple)
10 a simple hand-woven double sheet (100% cotton)

► Grammar reference p. 212

5   *and* or comma to link adjectives

1   Match the rules in the box to the examples below.

> 1   When several adjectives **follow** a noun they are usually linked by commas plus *and*.
>
> 2   When several adjectives **precede** a noun, commas or *and* are **not** generally used.
>
> However:
>
> 3   *and* must be used to link adjectives which refer to colours and different parts of the same thing.
>
> 4   a comma or *and* may be used to link gradeable adjectives, especially those describing personal opinions and qualities.

a) It was an interesting and memorable visit.

b) The route Bollen took us on was long, slow and circuitous.

c) The women were weaving blue and white *ikat* cloths.

d) I bought a traditional hand-woven *ikat* cloth.

e) It had a lively, attractive design.

2   Read the descriptions of items in a mail-order catalogue which sells traditional handicrafts from around the world. Add *and* or commas to the underlined phrases where necessary, using the rules above to help you. You will sometimes find that two ways of linking are possible.

1

This eye-opening puzzle shows the world in its true proportions and makes an interesting gift which can be mailed easily in its <u>sturdy tube container</u>. With <u>simple complicated</u> sections for different abilities plus guide map inside. Completed jigsaw 84 x 59 cm.

2

Ornate antique style wooden jewellery box with <u>front pull-out drawer</u> and <u>4.5cm deep inner compartment</u> under the <u>hinged handcarved lid</u>. From Indonesia. 22 x 13 x 13cm.

3

This <u>watchful wooden mask</u> is handcrafted by a master carver from Foase in the Ashanti region of Ghana. Its story is "I don't move about but I see a lot going on around me so be careful as to what you do and say whenever I am around." 22 cm diameter.

4

<u>100% cotton cushion covers</u> from India in <u>bold black white designs</u> with plain backs. Available in two designs. Each cover 41 x 41cm. Dry clean only.

5

A delightful gift to show your affection, this Thai necklace of <u>traditional design sterling silver beads</u> comes in its own <u>handmade paper-covered gift box</u>. With antique finish. 42cm long.

6

Intricately carved in Indonesia, these <u>sterling silver garnet drop earrings</u> give a <u>smart finishing touch</u> to an evening outfit. With silver hooks. 1.5cm long.

3   Work in pairs. You are preparing your own mail-order mini-catalogue. Make a list of items – traditional or modern – that are produced in your country which you think will sell well abroad. Write similar captions for the illustrations that will go in the catalogue.

Listening: sentence completion

1 Look at the advertisement below, produced by a charity dedicated to the needs of children around the world. What point is the advertisement making?

Andrew is 12.
He practises football every evening.

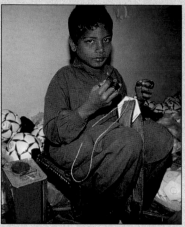

Ali is 12.
He sews footballs every day.

2 You will hear an interview with Joanne Waters, who works for a children's charity. Before you listen, read the sentences below and try to predict what kind of information is missing.

On her fact-finding trip Joanne was investigating the problem of
....(1)

Children may be employed to ....(2)

It's important to consider ....(3) before taking action.

If this type of work were banned, these children might have to work
....(4)

Joanne's charity is aiming to ....(5) gradually.

The charity started investigating work conditions by
....(6) about their work.

The children felt that two advantages of the work they were doing was that it was ....(7) and it could be done at home.

The charity wants to begin by banning ....(8) jobs.

Joanne also recommends checking children's...(9) regularly.

Children would not need to work if ....(10) earned more money.

3 Now listen and complete the sentences with a word or short phrase. Then check and complete your answers on the second listening.

4 Discuss these questions.

1 How far you agree with the following statement in the light of the information you heard in the interview?

'Consumers should boycott all products whose manufacture has involved the use of child labour.'

2 Can you think of any arguments to **justify** young children working, apart from the need to make money?

5 In the interview, the speaker said: 'If children don't need to work, they can have the sort of life we think of as a child's life'.

1 What do you think the basic ingredients of a child's life should be?
2 If you were drawing up a list of children's rights to be applied internationally, what would you include?

Vocabulary: adverb + adjective collocation

> Adverbs are often used to intensify the meaning of adjectives, for example:
>
> A: **Very hot** today, isn't it?
> B: Yes, **absolutely boiling**.
>
> The adverb you can use depends on the type of adjective that follows it.

1   Which of the sets of adverbs 1–3 below can you use to intensify the adjectives in groups **A**, **B** and **C**? Can you explain the reason for your answer?

1   very / extremely / exceedingly / incredibly
2   fairly / moderately / rather / relatively
3   absolutely / completely / totally

A   terrified / amazed / exhausted / ruined

B   large / important / old / happy

C   perfect / frozen / extinct

▶ Grammar reference p. 213

Watch Out! *quite* ◀

1   The film was *quite* good.
2   The film was *quite* marvellous.

What's the difference in meaning?

---

2   Some intensifiers collocate strongly with particular adjectives. Complete the sentences using intensifiers from the box.

| deeply   closely   entirely   highly   widely   wildly |

1   The whereabouts of the exiled president remains a .... guarded secret.
2   English language newspapers are not .... available outside the main tourist centres.
3   The company employs a team of .... skilled designers.
4   I was .... moved by the experience of visiting the refugee camp.
5   We were not .... convinced by his arguments.
6   His description of the accident is .... exaggerated – it was far less dangerous than he suggests.

3   Work in pairs. Take turns to ask and answer the following questions. Use an adverb from box A and an adjective from box B in your answers.

Say what you think of:

- a film / play you have seen recently
- a well-known personality at home and / or abroad
- the public transport system in your country
- your first job / the worst job you have ever done
- your first day at secondary school
- the education system in your country.

A | deadly   extremely   fantastically   hopelessly
utterly   relatively   totally   incredibly

B | boring   conceited   competitive   dull
confusing   heavy-handed   enjoyable   funny
good-looking   (in)efficient   rich   successful

4   Re-express the following sentences using the intensifier given in brackets, so that they mean almost the same. You will need to change the adjective used in the original sentence, and you may need to make other changes as a result.

1   I was very pleased to be able to see the weaving. (absolutely)
2   Men were not allowed to go into the dyeing area at all. (totally)
3   The weavers were very clever at their job. (highly)
4   The weather could not have been better. (absolutely).
5   They had no idea where they were. (completely)
6   I found the film absolutely terrifying. (extremely)
7   I was absolutely amazed when I heard I'd passed the exam. (exceedingly)
8   When her boyfriend left her she was extremely unhappy. (utterly)

▶ Exam Maximiser

Vocabulary: adjective + noun collocation

1   In the following sentences, only two of the three adjectives collocate with the noun. Cross out the adjective that doesn't collocate.

1   The *high / large / increasing* incidence of heart disease may be due to poor diet.
2   The pass rate in the exam is *higher / lower / smaller* in some areas than in others.
3   A *large / considerable / big* number of companies are reducing their workforces.
4   Tourism is the most *major / important / significant* source of income in the area.
5   Our *entire / full / whole* stock of winter clothes is on sale.

6 We have invested *expanding/even greater/ever-increasing* sums of money in improving our equipment.

7 A *high/considerable/rising* ratio of pupils to teachers is bound to lead to falling standards in education.

8 This town has a *larger/greater/higher* proportion of older residents than its neighbour.

9 Counterfeit goods are being produced in *large/enormous/grand* quantities.

10 The submersible is able to descend to *great/deep/enormous* depths.

2 Choose the word which best completes each sentence.

1 There has been a massive increase in the .... of traffic passing through the city centre.
A volume **B** density **C** extent **D** rate

2 There is only likely to be a .... margin of error in these calculations.
A thin **B** lean **C** narrow **D** minute

3 These policies are to a .... extent responsible for the region's economic decline.
A great **B** wide **C** broad **D** complete

4 Many goods are considerably cheaper if you buy them in ....
A numbers **B** quantities **C** bulk **D** volume

5 There is a .... degree of uncertainty concerning their future plans.
A great **B** high **C** large **D** big

6 The new MD only joined the company yesterday, so at the moment she's an .... quantity.
A unrevealed **B** unfamiliar **C** untested **D** unknown

7 We are importing consumer goods in greater .... than ever before.
A proportions **B** quantities **C** ratios **D** numbers

8 Our work .... has increased to an unacceptable level.
A amount **B** quantity **C** ratio **D** load

Use of English: cloze

1 Look at the list below. Which would you be prepared to do as part of your job? Rank them in order of acceptability. Are there any that you would not do?

- spend hours commuting to and from work
- spend a lot of time travelling overseas
- move to live in another country
- work unsociable hours
- work in conditions where you are physically at risk
- work overtime regularly without extra pay
- live away from your family
- bring work home in the evenings and at weekends

2 Read the following text, ignoring the gaps. Answer the questions.

1 Why is Tadao Masuda unusual?
2 Would you agree with his final statement?

The long journey home

So you think you have one of the most evil commuting journeys known to mankind? You travel for an hour, maybe an hour and a half, to work. You change trains, you fight (1) .... crowds, down tunnels and up escalators and you (2) .... at work crumpled and sweaty and wrung out (3) .... face the day.

Well, it (4) .... be a whole lot worse. (5) .... a passing thought for Tadao Masuda. At (6) .... glance he does not particularly (7) .... out in the crowds of blue-suited office workers who swarm into central Tokyo from the suburbs (8) .... morning. Not, that is, (9) .... you learn that not only (10) .... he travel for three and a quarter hours to get to work but he then spends another three and a quarter hours travelling home again.

"Well, I can't (11) .... that I actually enjoy my commuting, (12) .... then again I don't feel it is time (13) .... ," he says. "People who go out drinking after work or just sleep later in the morning are using their time (14) .... constructively than me. It (15) .... me the chance to have private time for my own thoughts, with (16) .... interruptions. Also, coming home in the evenings, I find that (17) .... many problems there were at work during the day, I have always forgotten (18) .... by the time I get home. It's my way of getting (19) .... of stress. In fact, to (20) .... you the truth, I regard myself as rather a lucky man."

3 Now fill each of the numbered blanks in the passage with one suitable word. Then discuss and justify your answers with a partner.

▶ Exam Maximiser

Vocabulary: work

1 Read the following text. In each numbered line there is a word or phrase used wrongly. Find them and correct them. Be prepared to explain why they are inappropriate.

The boss from hell

Before I went for my interview for the job with Cramer and Blake

1 Services, I talked to a few people and found out some informations

2 about the company. This strategy worked very effective as it gave the

3 impression that I was keen and committal and I was offered the job

4 by the personnel manager in the spot.

5 I was very delighted at first, but I soon discovered that my new

6 boss, Tom, worked totally hard, spending all his time in the office and

7 never leaving before 8 p.m. He expected the same grade of commitment

8 from his employees — the workload he expected every and each one of us

9 to carry was deeply unreasonable. He accused anyone who didn't work

10 overtime regularly of not making their fair share and letting the team down.

11 I decided to put up to the situation without complaining for a while

12 but lastly I felt I had to confront Tom. I told him I wasn't prepared to

13 work so hard for such a low salary. Tom said that I had large potential

14 and could easily get to the top if I was prepared to have an effort.

15 However, he thoroughly refused to reduce my workload and so in the

16 end I decided to hand out my resignation.

17 Just a week later I got another job in Cramer and Blake's main

18 competitors. Now I'm earning twice as high as my old boss, and my

19 job's twice as interesting. I work exactly as long hours — but I'm glad I

20 moved. I haven't got to the top yet — but I'm far on the way!

2 Read the text again and discuss the following questions.

1 What problems did the narrator have with her job?
2 Do you think her boss should have tried harder to keep her?

3

1 Work with a partner. Take turns to read the following statements to each other. Your partner should respond with an appropriate idiomatic expression from the list below. There are two possible responses in each case and four that are not appropriate at all.

1 I've just started a fantastic job with an advertising agency – the money's great too.
'You must be over the moon!'

2 It's a job that is very unpredictable – it means I often have to think quickly.

3 The fly in the ointment is – my boss works all hours. He never leaves the office before 8 p.m.

4 It wouldn't matter so much, but he expects all of us to do the same.

5 And there's another manager who's always ordering people about and setting us totally unreasonable deadlines.

6 I really like the job, but the workload is a problem. What do you think I should do?

a) He has no right to work you so hard.
b) Well, you could grin and bear it for the sake of the money.
c) So he won't play ball.
d) You must be thrilled to bits.
e) Everyone has to pull their weight.
f) You've got to be able to think on your feet.
g) A real slave-driver!
h) Someone who likes to throw his weight around, huh?
i) You must be over the moon! ✔
j) He's a workaholic, then?
k) It's all in a day's work.
l) You could try making a fuss and standing up for your rights – it could work wonders.
m) So you've really got to be on the ball.
n) He's obviously driving himself too hard.
o) Obviously a good team player.
p) It's hard to work with someone breathing down your neck, isn't it?

2 Check the meaning of the expressions you didn't use and suggest a context for them.

Grammar check: future forms

1

1   Read the text below. What main point is the writer making about the workplace of the future?

The workplace of the future

Forget science fiction, future workplaces could resemble images from centuries past.

Ask any IT or telecommunications firm what the office of the future is going to be like and you are likely to get a realistic but fairly short-sighted answer, mainly because they need to sell the products at their disposal now. However, ask a crystal-gazing professor and he or she will have a wider grasp of the concept.

Professor Jeremy Myerson, who runs a 'Tomorrow's office' course at de Montfort University predicts: 'Thanks to modern technology, we will have gone back to a more natural pre-industrial, pre-modern way of life by the mid-21st century. The modern office is inflexible, structured and encased by technology. But as communication equipment shrinks, everything we need to send or receive can be carried around in something as small as a Filofax*. Open-plan,

desktop and computer-linked systems will become things of the past. And going to work in these weird buildings that we call offices will seem as quaint as chucking sewage into the street.'

One leading IT services provider believes that we will become less and less dependent on the office concept itself. Technology will have disposed of cables and offices. Like our ancestors, we will be making all those important business transactions in coffee houses. Twenty years on, we won't need vast numbers of people working in large offices, so we can move back to the coffee table to do our business. What we all need to ask ourselves though is: will we want to work office-less, will we be able to take on the sociological implications, whatever they might be?

Filofax: a pocket-sized ring binder with a diary, notepad, address list, etc. Often used by business people.

2   Underline all the examples you can find of verb forms referring to the future. Which form is used:

a) to make a general prediction?
b) to indicate certainty on the part of the speaker?
c) for a repeated activity around a point in the future?
d) for an action that will be finished before a point of time in the future?
e) for an action that will fairly certainly take place?
f) to indicate future ability?

▶   Grammar reference p.213

3   How would you answer the question in the last paragraph of the article? What are the possible 'sociological implications' referred to?

2   *will / be going to*
Fill in the gaps with the correct form of *will* or *be going to*. Can you add any uses to the list in Exercise 1?

1   It seems inevitable that the nature of office work .... be changed by recent developments in technology.
2   My husband hates commuting, so he .... apply for a new job nearer home.
3   It's nine o'clock already! I .... late for work.
4   Since everyone appears to be here, I .... ask the Divisional Manager to give his report.

3   *will be doing / will have done / will have been doing*
1   Fill in the gaps with the correct form of the verb in brackets. Can you add any more uses to the list in Exercise 1?

1   Things we take for granted like note-books and typewriters .... (most likely disappear) by the middle of the 21st century.
2   Maybe in fifty years time we .... (spend) our days entirely at home.
3   However, people .... (travel) to work for a few more years yet.
4   My plane arrives at 11.00 a.m. tomorrow. You'll be able to recognise me easily – I .... (carry) a red briefcase.
5   By the end of this month, we .... (work) on this project for 10 years.

2   Which time expressions are used with which tense forms? Group them into categories.

4   Write five sentences making predictions about your partner without talking to him/her. Use the phrases in the box and a future tense. Then read out your predictions to your partner. Does he/she agree?

> this weekend   by this time next year
> in a couple of years   in ten years' time
> by the time you are fifty   quite soon

5 Other ways of referring to the future

1 Underline the ways of referring to the future used in the following sentences.

1 Guidelines for improved working conditions are to be introduced shortly.
2 I was wondering if you might like to buy a ticket for the school concert.
3 She looks as if she's on the point of losing her temper.
4 The committee is due to meet tomorrow.
5 Were you thinking of staying for a week? We can offer a special rate.

2 Which of the sentences above suggests:

a) a polite question about future plans?
b) a formal arrangement?
c) something which should happen because a time has been fixed for it?
d) something which may not have been planned, but is going to happen almost immediately?
e) a polite and rather tentative request?

6 Use of English: gapped sentences

Fill each of the gaps with a suitable word or phrase.

1 By next April Jenny .... to Mike for ten years.
2 According to the doctor, Mandy is ....
   .... to have the baby a week tomorrow.
3 We were .... you might be interested in signing our petition.
4 I was on .... giving up on him when he finally showed up.
5 This time next week I ....
   my new job.
6 Will you .... Tessa to the office party, or Bob?
7 New regulations concerning company cars .... introduced by the government, according to reports.
8 If we win the election, we ....
   all this campaigning in vain.

7 Tenses in time clauses

• *As communication equipment **shrinks**, everything we need to send or receive **can be carried around** in something as small as a Filofax.* (text, p. 142)

1 Read the following examples and complete the chart below, to show what tenses can be used in complex sentences referring to the future.

1 I'll start work as soon as I finish university.
2 After I've finished university, I plan to go abroad to work.
3 I have always forgotten my problems by the time I get home. (cloze text, p. 140)
4 I envy you going on holiday – while we're working our fingers to the bone, you'll be lying on a beach somewhere.
5 By the time he retires, he'll have been working for the company for 30 years.
6 I'll do it when I can find the time.

MAIN CLAUSE	LINK WORD	SUBORDINATE CLAUSE
future simple	*as soon as*	*present simple*

2 Fill in the gaps in the following paragraph with an appropriate verb form.

Kate and Mickey are doing a four-year degree course in fashion design and marketing. As soon as they (1) .... qualified, they (2) .... to set up their own company, designing and making children's clothes. When they (3) .... into business, they (4) .... from home and sell the clothes by mail order. However, once they (5) .... to make a profit they (6) .... to their own premises and take on extra staff. Later on, as their business (7) ...., they (8) .... into producing clothes for babies and toddlers. With luck and hard work, they (9) .... have their own factory and a chain of shops all over Europe by the time they (10) .... thirty.

8 Interview a partner about his/her career plans. Ask questions like these.

1 What do you plan to do once you have qualified?
2 Where do you see yourself in 10 years time?
3 What do you hope to have achieved in your career by the time you are 30 / 40 / 50?

Writing: report (2)

1 In this section, you are going to write a report. Which three of the following are **not** features of report writing? Cross them out.

A report:
- deals with facts
- includes interviews and direct quotes
- is written for a particular purpose
- may contain recommendations for action
- normally uses headings for each section
- uses adjectives for dramatic effect
- is written in an impersonal, formal style
- uses set phrases and passive forms
- uses irony and other stylistic effects such as rhetorical questions.

2 Read the task. What is your report going to be about? What information do you have to include?

> You have been asked to help your college to improve its facilities for helping college leavers with career advice. Write a report for the new careers officer on any facilities that exist at present, assess their usefulness and make recommendations for ways in which they could be improved. (About 300 words.)

3 Discuss the following points in groups. If you are already in work, think back to the school or college you attended.

1 Does your school or college
   a) offer a careers advice service? How helpful is it?
   b) arrange work experience opportunities for the students in local companies or organisations?
2 What opportunities do you have to discuss the world of work with working people, or with former students who are now working?
3 Do you know where to find out information about job opportunities? What information do you think you might find helpful when you make your choices?

4 Listen to a former student talking about her problems in finding work and what could have helped her make better choices. As you listen, answer the questions below by writing notes.

1 Why did the speaker have an unsatisfying job after leaving school?

2 What does she think would have helped her and why?
3 What three recommendations does she make for her college?

5 Using your own ideas or ideas from the Listening text, write an outline for your report using headings suggested by the task. Remember to add an introductory section giving background information (see Unit 6, page 90). The sections may be of different lengths; if there are few existing facilities, then your section for recommendations will be longer.

6 Read the three possible introductions to the report below.

1 Which one do you think is the best? Why?

A

> I think it's absolutely terrible that there isn't any solid information to help us make career choices — there's nothing to give us exciting ideas and I haven't a clue how to go about finding out what to do. So what can the school do to help? It's a big problem,' say the teachers, 'But it's nothing to do with us.'

B

> There are many more opportunities available for accessing data and data banks now than in the past, and I think the school should make full use of these. Why not use the information that's there? After all, someone put it there! So this report will describe interviews with different people giving their opinions and then try to assess the best way forward – if there is one.

C

> There are about 200 school leavers each year who should be given the best possible advice on their future careers. This means that they need well-presented, clear, up-to-date information on opportunities open to them. This report will examine existing facilities, assess the best way of improving them, and make recommendations for future action.

2 Can you find examples of features not usually included in reports in the two introductions you rejected?

7 In the middle section of the report you will have to assess the value of current facilities. Read the notes below and turn them into full sentences, using appropriate connecting words and phrases.

1 *Only 2 computers available to students, usually being used: v. frustrating for other students.*

2 *Not many books in library; out of date, so not v. helpful.*

3 *Librarian v. knowledgeable: tries to help, provides good service, but v. busy, not always available.*

4 *Reps. from local companies visit, give information: vital, helps us to learn about real life.*

5 *Weekly sessions after school run by a teacher: inconvenient, few students go. Has potential: better if time changed.*

8

1 The sentences below come from the Listening text in Exercise 4. Underline the linking expressions. How do they connect the ideas?

1 I had no help at all and as a result I ended up in a dead-end job.
2 My friend said that in this way she found out about opportunities that she had no idea existed.

2 Combine these sentences in as many ways as you can. Use a subordinate or relative clause, or an appropriate linking expression.

1 Setting up connections with local firms enables students to learn about work. They make fewer mistakes when they come to choosing their career.
2 I feel that the best way forward is to set up a formal system for advice. This makes the scheme an integral part of the school curriculum.
3 There is no opportunity for students to talk about their ambitions. They never have a fair chance to realise them.
4 My friend found career information in her library. She could make a reasoned choice.
5 Students should be able to visit a company they are interested in. They get a good idea of what the job entails.

3 In which sections of the report could the ideas in the sentences above be used?

9 Look at the pairs of sentences below, which could form part of the final section of the report. Which one is most appropriate for this type of writing? Why?

1 a) The school has to make changes to the current library set-up.
   b) The school should look at ways of changing the current library layout.
2 a) If the computers were linked to a job information database, this could provide a major resource for school leavers.
   b) If we could all get into a job information database on the computers, we'd be able to use it as a resource.
3 a) I think they've got to present everything really clearly, with ways of getting in touch with possible employers.
   b) The information should be presented as clearly and simply as possible, preferably with instructions on ways of contacting potential employers.

10 Now write your report.

> ### Exam Strategy
>
> When you write a report, remember:
> DO
> • keep your points clear and concise: your target reader is busy.
> • use headings to organise the information and make it easy for the reader to follow.
> • use a neutral to formal register, and use it consistently.
> DON'T
> • begin and end your report like a formal letter.

1 Choose the word or phrase which best completes each sentence.

1 For most teachers, ... satisfaction is more important than a high salary.
   A job   B work   C career   D employment

2 The crowd remained totally silent, ... held by a strange spell.
   A just as   B even if   C as though   D even though

3 He claimed he just .... to be passing the house, but I doubt that.
   A occurred   B noticed   C happened   D found

4 The doors were decorated with .... carved wooden panels.
   A intimately B intrinsically C implicitly
   D intricately

5 Do you expect there will be a lot of .... to the project from the local community?
   A rejections   B disapproval   C disagreement
   D objections

6 As a .... parent, my main concern is balancing the needs of a small child with the need to earn a living.
   A solo   B single   C sole   D solitary

7 By the time we got home, we were .... frozen and starving hungry.
   A extremely B very C absolutely D exceedingly

8 She says that unfortunately, in the .... circumstances, she cannot afford to help us.
   A ongoing B contemporary C actual D present

9 The recipe is a .... guarded secret, handed down from one generation to the next.
   A closely   B tightly   C deeply   D nearly

10 The queue .... forward very slowly as the officials checked the fans' tickets for forgeries.
   A wormed   B inched   C waved   D measured

11 We do have rules about dress, but they aren't .... by many students these days.
   A attended B remarked C observed D conducted

12 In the corner stood an ancient wardrobe, painted with a .... of trees and birds.
   A motif   B theme   C subject   D matter

13 The car park was screened .... from the hotel by a tall hedge.
   A off   B away   C out   D around

14 Has someone been .... with the sound system again?
   A fingering B tampering C mucking D poking

15 The firm pays low wages, ... because employees sometimes receive tips from visitors.
   A believably   B expectantly   C credibly
   D presumably

16 Her work has shown a .... improvement since her return from holiday.
   A marked   B measured   C noted   D counted

17 The builder claimed he had been .... down by his suppliers, who had failed to deliver on time.
   A broken   B let   C put   D pulled

18 The city centre has been much quieter since the market place was ....
   A prioritised   B tranquillised   C pedestrianised
   D industrialised

19 We look forward to the bank holiday as an opportunity to .... our batteries before the busy season.
   A recharge   B revive   C relive   D reinforce

20 The needs of local residents have been .... for far too long.
   A rejected   B distracted   C negated
   D neglected

21 He is the kind of person .... whom you can depend for good advice.
   A from   B with   C of   D on

22 The house felt cold .... the central heating had been on for hours.
   A even though   B as though   C even if
   D just as

23 Few people will be .... by the changes that the government plans to make.
   A unattended   B unturned   C unaffected
   D unimpaired

24 If you don't .... up for yourself in this place, no-one else will do it for you.
   A put   B get   C work   D stand

25 Local roads and pavements are .... in need of repair.
   A urgently   B extremely   C absolutely
   D rapidly

2 Finish each of the following sentences in such a way that it is as similar as possible in meaning to the sentence printed before it.

1 Both the doctors I consulted were confident of curing me.
I consulted ....

2 The manager wrote a long ungrammatical report.
The report ....

3 Why no one checked the man's story is what amazes me.
The thing ....

4 If Cathy hadn't been so mean, we'd have had a really good time.
But ....

5 The boys clearly intended to make trouble when they entered the hotel.
The boys were ....

6 The coastal villages in this region are the most affluent.
The villages ....

7 We might be asked to stay the night, in which case I'll phone to let you know.
Should ....

8 We cannot guarantee accommodation until we receive a deposit.
A deposit ....

9 It was clear that Michael knew about the theft, because he didn't ask any questions.
The very ....

10 We discovered the visitors had eaten all the food we'd bought.
We discovered that all ....

3 Fill each of the blanks with a suitable word or phrase.

1 We were .... you might perhaps prefer a larger room.

2 We soon got used .... watched as we worked.

3 What happened .... the rope broke and the boat was carried away.

4 That's a subject .... I know absolutely nothing.

5 If it wasn't you who took it, it .... one of your friends, because no one else came in here.

6 Were you thinking .... the bus, or would you like a walk?

7 I refuse to be held .... the actions of other people.

8 No-one .... least surprised to hear they planned to get married.

9 Everyone gets fed up with a colleague who .... weight when there's a lot of work to do.

10 I'm sure you .... once you've had a rest.

4 For each of the sentences below, write a new sentence as similar as possible in meaning to the original sentence, but using the word given. This word must not be altered in any way.

1 You can buy these gadgets almost anywhere nowadays. **widely**
....

2 I have every confidence in your ability to run the business without help. **confident**
....

3 The girl was about to leave when her boyfriend finally entered the cafe. **point**
....

4 When I get home, I'm going to have a shower straightaway. **soon**
....

5 The motorcyclist rounded the corner at a quite unbelievable speed. **which**
....

6 The town centre features an old hospital, imaginatively converted into flats. **been**
....

7 I firmly believe him to be the rudest person I know. **without**
....

8 The weather was so appalling that we came home early. **such**
....

9 His charming manners deceived several people, including me. **taken**
....

10 All that's involved is signing a few papers. **just**
....

The monster in the machine

Speaking

1 Look at the photos.

1 In pairs or groups, choose two of the examples of technology illustrated, and think of as many ways as you can in which:

- they make life easier or more pleasant
- they may be dangerous to individuals or to the environment
- they may develop in the future.

2 Without the technology we take for granted, how would everyday life be different? Think of a normal day, and describe how it would change if you had to manage without any help from technology.

2 Which of the following qualities do humans share with animals such as dogs, horses and chimpanzees?

- intelligence
- feelings and emotions
- creativity
- a moral sense

Which of these qualities do you think a computer might have in the future?

Listening: note-taking

1

1 The study of cybernetics, which includes artificial intelligence and robotics, now forms an important part of academic research. You will hear a radio talk about current technological developments in this area and their implications for the future. Before you listen to the first part of the talk, read through the questions below to get an idea of the content of the talk.

1 What is the first level at which technology affects our lives? Give one example.

....

2 What is the second level at which technology affects our lives? Give two examples.

....

3 What is the 'sinister' aspect of the 'march of the machines'?

....

4 Give two examples of ways in which computers may collect information about you.

....

5 What is this information needed for?

....

6 How might computers develop in the future?

....

 2 Now listen to the first part of the recording and give brief answers to the questions above. You don't need to write complete sentences. Listen again if you need to.

2   The following sentences summarise some of the information from the Listening. In each sentence, only two of the three verbs given are possible. Cross out the verb which is inappropriate.

1   Nowadays, computers can *work/function/manage* independently of humans.
2   Computers can *operate/store/run* machinery and data bases.
3   They can *manage/monitor/supervise* manufacturing processes.
4   They can *calculate/store/hold* information in data banks.
5   They can *have/do/perform* increasingly complex calculations.

3   Discuss these questions.

1   What other examples can you give of things that used to be done by people but are now done by computers?
2   Do you agree that this is a dangerous trend? Why/Why not?

4   In the second part of the talk, the speaker goes on to describe two possible future scenarios. Read through the notes below. What differences can you find between the two scenarios?

Scenario 1

Machines
– have (1)..
– make decisions based on (2).., not emotions

People
– treated like animals, exploited by machines
– bred to (3)..
– adapted to do specific jobs eg labouring, fighting or (4)..
– have unnecessary parts of their (5).. removed
– only survive to the age of about (6)..

Scenario 2

People in control but technology can (7).. for itself.

More gadgets, e.g.: implanted microchips
– act as translators
– provide information and replace (8)..

Robots
– do everything in the home
– come in (9)..

Clothes
– can adapt to (10)..
– (11)..

Cars
– create less pollution
– are less (12).. as driven by robots on smart* roads

Other new gadgets – small and (13)..
e.g. shirt-button sized object which is a combined telephone and (14)..

5   Now listen and complete the notes using a word or short phrase. Then listen again to check and complete your answers.

6   Discuss these questions.

1   What ideas do the two scenarios share?
2   Which scenario do you think is most likely? What current trends support each one?
3   Which of the gadgets mentioned do you think are most/least likely to actually be developed? Why? Think about the difference between what is technologically possible and what is useful – what people actually want and need for work and leisure.
4   Can you think of any other gadgets that have already been invented but haven't caught on, e.g. wristwatch TVs, videophones?

smart: able to remember and store formation

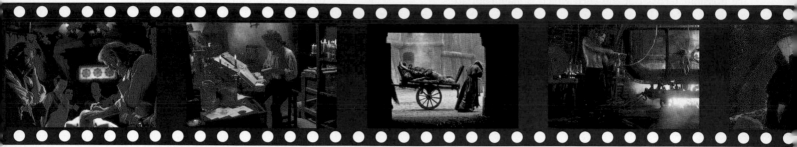

1 What do you know about Frankenstein? Try this quiz.

1 The story of *Frankenstein* was written by
 a) a Hollywood screenwriter.
 b) a 19th-century woman novelist.

2 Frankenstein was
 a) a monster.
 b) a scientist.

3 The monster was made from
 a) parts of dead bodies.
 b) pieces of spare machinery.

4 In the story the monster is
 a) initially good, but becomes evil.
 b) initially evil, but learns humanity.

5 The story explores
 a) the effects of being rejected.
 b) the distinction between man
  and machine.

2 Now read paragraphs 1 and 2 of the passage to check your answers.

3 Read the rest of the passage and decide which of the following titles best reflects the main idea in it.

A Could the story of Frankenstein's monster come true?

B Could computers threaten humanity?

C Could a computer have a soul?

Exam Strategy

Unlike the reading passages in Paper 1, the comprehension passage in Paper 3, Section B, always has a title. Remember to read it first, as it can help you identify the main focus of the passage.

O N E of the high points in Mary Shelley's gothic novel *Frankenstein* is when the tragic creature cobbled together from cadavers comes face to face with its human creator Victor Frankenstein, the real monster of the story. The creature, tired of
5 constant rejection, has committed murder. Yet when it first became conscious it was not evil. "Believe me," it says in anguish, "I was benevolent; my soul glowed with love and humanity."

This heart-rending declaration exposes a paradox about the hapless creature. Frankenstein built his creation from spare parts,
10 so in one sense it is just a machine. Yet the creature "instinctively understands himself as human, something more than a machine". Shelley's story raised the question of whether or not something manufactured would have a soul – that mysterious entity which is the very essence of humanness, the thing that
15 links us irrevocably to God.

Nearly two centuries later the same question has surfaced again. And today the question is being asked not of some fictional creature, but of machines in various states of creation that promise to have human-like senses and to be conscious, at
20 least in some form. Theologians and computer scientists are starting to wonder if any of these machines might ever be said to have a soul. If so, would such a soul be like a human being's, or something altogether different?

Opinions tend to fall between two extremes. On the one hand,
25 many people want to draw an unbreachable divide between humans and machines, insisting that however smart a computer might become it could never have a soul. On the other hand, many artificial intelligence researchers insist that humans are just complex machines, so why wouldn't a silicon-based machine also
30 have a soul? In the future, as machines become more like humans, the distinction between them could become blurred.

Artificial intelligence researchers are already dabbling with computers that could become "conscious" of themselves and their surroundings. One of the most ambitious of these projects
5 is Cog, a talking robot designed in human form that will be capable of exploring the world through sight, sound and touch. The project team hopes that Cog will be able to discover the world the way a human baby does, and will thus come to understand things as a child does. Eventually, they argue, it's
10 surely going to be able to say, "I'm afraid," or "I'm bored," and mean it. And if Cog does say such things — and mean them — then is it so far-fetched to wonder if it would have a soul?

Yet how would we tell if a computer developed a soul? It might not be enough for a machine to look, behave and think like a
15 human. It might also involve a more complex definition, such as the possession of a sense of moral responsibility, or sense of self. Of course, a sense of moral responsibility could be programmed into a computer. But what if a silicon-based being were to develop a morality of its own — its own conscience? This might
20 be different from the human variety. Take death, for example. A computer with a backup tape might not see death as a big deal. Think about how different life would be if we had backup tapes. Alternatively, a computer could be "cloned", so many examples of the same "being" could exist. What would that do to the
25 machine's conception of itself and others?

Stories such as *Frankenstein* suggest that the things we humans create are often more than the sum of their parts. Many people imagine that if we built something, we would know all about it. But this is not necessarily so. From Shelley's *19th-century*
30 monster to today's real-life robots, complex entities have a habit of taking on a life of their own.

4   Read the passage again carefully and answer the following questions.

1   Which words in paragraph 1 suggest that the monster was not made very skilfully?
2   Explain exactly why the monster is 'in anguish'. (line 6)
3   What is the 'paradox' referred to in paragraph 2, line 8?
4   Explain the meaning of 'surfaced' in line 16.
5   Explain in your own words the reasoning put forward by researchers who believe that computers could have a soul.
6   Why is the Cog project described as 'ambitious'? (line 34)
7   Explain the significance of the phrase 'and mean it'. (line 40)
8   How does the writer illustrate the idea that a computer's sense of right and wrong might be different from a human's?
9   Explain the meaning of 'cloned' as it is used in line 53.
10   What does the writer mean by the expression 'more than the sum of their parts'? (line 57)
11   What is the writer's overall conclusion about the machines we create?

5   Find words or expressions in the text which fit these definitions from the Longman *Dictionary of Contemporary English*.

Paragraph 2
1   *adj* making you feel great pity
2   *n* [C] something that exists as a single and complete unit
3   *adv* in a way that cannot be changed or stopped
Paragraph 4
4   *adj* **1** ►CLEVER◄ *especially AmE*
5   *adj* **2** difficult to understand or deal with
6   *v* **1** [I] to do something in a way that is not very serious
7   *adj* extremely unlikely to be true or to happen
Paragraph 5
8   *n* **1** [C, V] a general idea of what something is like, or a general understanding of something

6   Discuss these questions.

1   In books you have read or films you have seen about monsters, extra-terrestrials or robots, have they mainly been portrayed as:
a) more intelligent than humans or less intelligent?
b) threatening humans or being threatened by them?
c) having the same morality as humans or a different one?

2   Can you suggest any reasons why this is so?

7   Explain in a paragraph of 60–80 words how the Cog project could make the difference between humans and machines less clear. (See Exam Focus Units 2 and 8 for guidance.)

► Exam Maximiser

Use of English: cloze

1 Read through the following text quickly without filling in any gaps. Find answers to these questions.

1 What social problem is mentioned in the first paragraph?
2 How can the 'robot room' help?

Although there is a strong tradition in Japan of children taking care of their elderly parents, an increasing number of women are now continuing to work after they marry. This (1) .... that no-one is left at home to (2) .... after the sick and elderly.

Japanese scientists have begun work (3) .... a robotic room (4) .... occupants need never lift a (5) .... , since their every need is (6) .... for by a series of devices controlled by a central computer that allows them to interact with one (7) ....

The room holds a bed (8) .... contains over two hundred small pressure sensors monitored (9) .... a computer. (10) .... allows a record to be (11) .... of the position and movement of the person in the bed. Above the bed, five video cameras are constantly (12) .... on the patient to ensure that he or she is moving and breathing.

As well as (13) .... a watch over the patient's condition, the room provides other

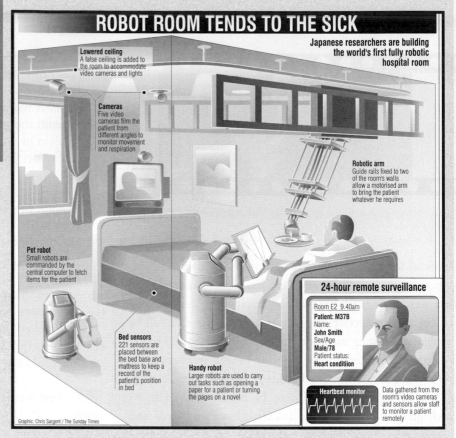

ROBOT ROOM TENDS TO THE SICK

Japanese researchers are building the world's first fully robotic hospital room

Lowered ceiling A false ceiling is added to the room to accommodate video cameras and lights

Cameras Five video cameras film the patient from different angles to monitor movement and respiration

Robotic arm Guide rails fixed to two of the room's walls allow a motorised arm to bring the patient whatever he requires

Pet robot Small robots are commanded by the central computer to fetch items for the patient

Bed sensors 221 sensors are placed between the bed base and mattress to keep a record of the patient's position in bed

Handy robot Larger robots are used to carry out tasks such as opening a paper for a patient or turning the pages on a novel

24-hour remote surveillance

Room E2 9.40am
Patient: M37B
Name: John Smith
Sex/Age
Male/78
Patient status: Heart conditiion

Heartbeat monitor Data gathered from the room's video cameras and sensors allow staff to monitor a patient remotely

Graphic: Chris Sargent / The Sunday Times

(14) .... of help. If the patient wants to watch television, he (15) .... only to point at it and the television will turn (16) .... on.

A robotic arm can pick up (17) .... the patient is pointing at and bring them to his bedside. In addition, small 'pet' robots are now (18) .... developed to carry smaller items and keep the person company.

(19) .... , the team warns that several years of research are still needed (20) .... the robotic room could be trusted to guard our loved ones.

2 Now fill each of the numbered blanks in the passage with one suitable word.

3 Discuss these questions.

1 In many countries, the population is ageing rapidly, with a growing proportion of elderly people. What problems is this likely to cause?
2 Is this an issue in your country? If so, what solutions are being discussed to deal with the problem?
3 How would you ideally like to spend your old age?

4 **Vocabulary:** idiomatic expressions

1 The following idiomatic expressions involving parts of the body are usually used only in the negative. Match each one to the appropriate explanation below.

1 He didn't move a muscle.
2 He didn't turn a hair.
3 He didn't lift a finger to help.
4 He didn't put a foot wrong.
5 He didn't have a leg to stand on.

a) He didn't make any mistakes.
b) He didn't do anything.
c) He remained totally still.
d) He stayed completely calm.
e) He had no proof or evidence.

2 Think of situations when each expression above would be appropriate, for example:

Number 1: He's a spy or a thief. He was in someone's else's room when they came back unexpectedly – he hid behind the curtains and didn't move a muscle so as not to be discovered.'

Grammar check: reflexive verbs

- *... the television will turn itself on.*
  (cloze text, p. 152)

1   Which of the following sentences contain incorrect uses of reflexive pronouns? Put a cross next to them. How does the use of reflexive pronouns compare with your language?

1   The monster created by Frankenstein regarded itself as human.
2   Forbes got up, showered himself and went down to breakfast.
3   As they approached the gloomy old house, the door slowly opened itself.
4   She prides herself on her immaculate apartment.
5   Shall I make ourselves a cup of coffee?
6   This is no time to lose control! Pull yourself together!
7   Hearing footsteps on the stairs, I quickly hid myself behind the curtains.
8   The bad weather spoiled their plans for a picnic, so they had to content themselves with a meal in a restaurant.
9   You'll wear yourself out if you carry on working 70 hours a week.
10   He finds it hard to concentrate himself on his work.
11   The girls devoted themselves to looking after their sick mother.
12   Why don't you resign yourself to the fact you're never going to be a famous inventor?

2   Look at these pairs of sentences. What's the difference in meaning when the verb is used with a reflexive pronoun?

1 a) Genetic differences may explain why some people develop cancer.
 b) That's not what I meant. I probably haven't explained myself very clearly.
2 a) She sat down to compose a letter of complaint to the holiday company.
 b) She was so angry that she needed to compose herself before she could start writing the letter.
3 a) New technology is being applied to almost every industrial process.
 b) You will never do well if you don't apply yourself at school.
4 a) He dedicated his first book to his wife.
 b) He has dedicated himself to helping the poor.
5 a) I'm perfectly willing to lend you the money.
 b) His new novel lends itself perfectly to being made into a film.

6 a) There's not much to distinguish her from the other students in terms of ability.
 b) She distinguished herself by achieving the highest sales in the company.
7 a) He said he wouldn't mind helping me with my tax return if I needed it.
 b) He didn't mean to snap her head off, but he just couldn't help himself.
8 a) That coat suits you down to the ground.
 b) A: 'I think I'd rather not go out tonight.'
   B: 'Suit yourself.'
9 a) I'm sorry about last night – I behaved like a child.
 b) Did the children behave themselves while I was away?
10 a) The family were finally reconciled after years of silence following the argument.
 b) He reconciled himself to the idea of moving to another town.

3   **Use of English:** key word transformations
For each of the sentences below, write a new sentence as similar as possible in meaning to the original sentence, but using the word given. This word must not be altered in any way.

1   She told us to take whatever was in the fridge if we were hungry. **help**
....
2   They don't need to make a final decision yet. **commit**
....
3   She expected him to do particularly well in the final exams. **excel**
....
4   I consider it to be my fault that we lost the game. **blame**
....
5   The government is anxious not to get involved in the affair, which could damage its credibility. **distance**
....
6   It can be very hard to get used to a completely different culture and lifestyle. **adapt**
....
7   You have to insist on your rights or you will end up being exploited. **assert**
....
8   He is successful in everything despite never seeming to make any effort. **exert**
....
9   After years of silence, she finally made it up with her family. **reconciled**
....
10   It's obvious she doesn't love you, so why continue to pretend she does? **deceive**
....

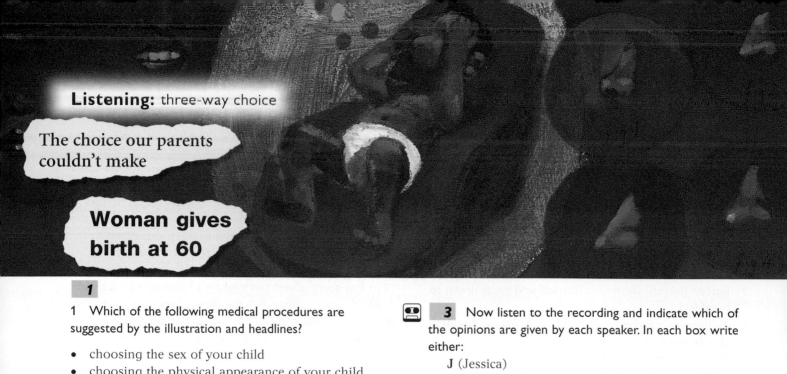

The choice our parents couldn't make

Woman gives birth at 60

1

1 Which of the following medical procedures are suggested by the illustration and headlines?

- choosing the sex of your child
- choosing the physical appearance of your child
- fertility treatment for older women
- cosmetic surgery
- allowing a child to be conceived after the death of one or both of the parents
- allowing a child to be created with identical characteristics to another person

2 Some of the medical procedures listed above are already possible, and some are likely to be possible in the near future. Do you think that they should:

a) never be allowed?
b) be allowed in special circumstances?
c) be generally available to those who want them?

2 You will hear two friends, Jessica and Will, discussing a television documentary about medical advances. Before you listen, look through the list of opinions below. Which of the topics from Exercise 1 do you expect to be discussed in the conversation? Are there any additional topics that were not listed?

1	Cosmetic surgery can be acceptable at any age.	1
2	Children's toys may establish false standards of beauty.	2
3	Cosmetic surgery can make people look unnatural.	3
4	People should be allowed to pay for cosmetic if they want to.	4
5	Cosmetic surgery should be regulated.	5
6	It's acceptable for older women to be given fertility treatment.	6
7	Multiple births may lead to problems for the children and families.	7
8	It is unwise for scientists to explore the possibility of men giving birth.	8

3 Now listen to the recording and indicate which of the opinions are given by each speaker. In each box write either:

    J (Jessica)
or **W** (Will)
or **B** (both Jessica and Will)

Then listen again to check and complete your answers.

4 To get the answers to Questions 4 and 5 of the Listening right, you had to interpret the speakers' intonation patterns correctly. You need to be aware of the effect of intonation patterns in the exam.

Listen again to these extracts from the recording and notice the intonation used in the underlined phrases. Answer the questions below.

1 **Will:** But how can you legislate – if it can be done, the medical profession will do it eventually and people will pay for it.
    Jessica: <u>So if people pay, it must be all right.</u>
    Will: Well, why not?

Is Jessica
a) agreeing with Will?
b) checking that she has understood?
c) contradicting him?
How can you tell?

2 **Jessica:** But it must be possible to develop some sort of criteria for what's necessary and what's just ... vanity?
    Will: <u>Must it?</u>

What is the real meaning of Will's reply?

5 Discuss this question.

How far do you agree that the developments discussed in the Listening are 'flying in the face of nature'?

Grammar check: future forms with modal verbs

1   Read the examples below and decide whether the modal auxiliary verb suggests:

a) a fairly certain prediction.
b) a future possibility.
c) an implied condition.
d) a strong suggestion.

1   I don't think that cosmetic surgery *should* be completely forbidden.
2   I *will* probably go bald early, like my father did.
3   It *could/may/might* even happen before I'm thirty if I'm really unlucky.
4   In that case, I *might/may* have a hair transplant.
5   However, I *would* never wear a toupee.

2   In the following extract, an expert predicts what he thinks will be possible in the field of medicine in the year 2020. Complete the sentences using the verbs in brackets with an appropriate modal verb in the correct tense.

I think 'spare-part surgery' using animal organs (1) *may well have become* (well/become) a routine procedure for transplants by 2020. Current concerns about animal organs transmitting diseases to humans are likely (2) .... (resolve) by then. Of course, any transplants of animal organs that took place (3) .... (need/precede) by very careful tests to make sure the organ did not contain harmful micro-organisms.

By that time, however, instead of using animal organs, people who know they may need transplants in the future (4) .... (have) themselves (5) .... (clone) instead. Their clone's organs (6) .... (use) as spare parts for transplant surgery. Many people see this as a horrendous development which (7) .... (not allow) to happen. But history shows us that once technological developments become possible they (8) .... (always take up) by people in the long run, however much we may try to prevent this.

3   Discuss these questions.

1   What 'horrendous' consequences do you think cloning humans could have?
2   What justification could be given for human cloning other than its use in spare-part surgery? What benefits could it bring in future?

▶   Grammar reference p. 214

Vocabulary: idiomatic expressions

1   The expressions in the following sentences all contain verbs or phrases to do with holding, touching or moving in some way. Fill in the gaps using words from the box in the correct form.

blow	grasp	grip	hit	hold
move	pinch	push	put	squeeze

1   I can't .... my finger on exactly why, but I just don't trust her somehow.
2   His failure to get promoted was a severe .... to his pride.
3   She has a good .... of abstract concepts.
4   The country people in that area .... fast to their traditional way of life.
5   The story was so sad, it .... me to tears.
6   The loss of his job has .... him very hard – he feels he's lost his identity.
7   The doctor's very busy today, but if it's really urgent I'll try to .... you in.
8   We're a bit .... for time – you'd better get a move on or we'll be late.
9   Try to get a .... on yourself – you won't help by getting upset.
10   I haven't got much time but I can fit your appointment in at a ....

2   Use of English: key word transformations

• *It's really **flying in the face of nature**.* (Listening text)

For each of the sentences below, write a new sentence as similar as possible in meaning to the original sentence, but using the word given. This word must not be altered in any way. In this exercise the new sentence will include a collocation or idiom with the words *nature / natural / naturally*.

1   The north of the country is rich in raw materials such as coal and iron. **resources**
2   The explosion wasn't due to any human cause. **disaster**
3   The detective refused to believe that the victim had died as a result of illness. **causes**
4   If you've got a minor illness, it's best to let your body cure itself. **course**
5   She's not bad-looking but she spends a fortune trying to look even better. **improve**
6   She seems to be able to learn languages without really trying. **come**
7   I got her to help by pointing out it was a good thing to do. **appealing**
8   Most people automatically fasten the seatbelt when they get into a car. **second**

Reading: non-fiction

1

1 The following are all positive qualities which parents may wish their children to have. Which four would you wish for a child of yours? Rank these four in order of importance. What others would you add to the list?

- beauty
- good health
- a calm and friendly personality
- energy and determination
- a brilliant scientific mind
- physical strength and co-ordination
- originality and creativity

2 Discuss the four qualities you chose with a partner. Do you think these qualities are:

- inherited from one or both parents?
- fostered by a stable family background?
- developed through a good education?
- enhanced by a healthy environment?
- encouraged by difficult circumstances?
- related to national background?

2

The passage below is from a book for the general reader by Lee Silver, a Professor of Genetics at Princeton University, USA. In the book the author discusses possible future uses of genetic engineering.

Read the extract and answer the following questions.

1 What is the main idea stated in the introductory paragraph?
2 What general uses for genetic engineering does the writer suggest in the next two paragraphs?
3 How does the first sentence of paragraph 3 link back to paragraph 2? What is the previous 'frontier' described?
4 Paragraph 4 refers to genetic enhancements. What enhancements are mentioned in paragraph 3?
5 What is the main idea of paragraph 5?
6 Which words introduce the contrast in focus between paragraphs 5 and 6?

3

The questions below focus on the details and implications of the passage. Choose the best option, **A**, **B**, **C** or **D**, to answer the questions.

1 According to the writer, what has been 'left to chance in the past'? (para. 1)
  A The qualities and characteristics that children inherit.
  B The social and environmental factors affecting children.

1 If we now know enough to be able to make changes in the genetic material that parents hand on to their children, why not seize this power? Why not control what has been left to chance in the past? Social and environmental influences already control many other aspects of our children's lives and identities. Can we really reject positive genetic influences on the next generation's minds and bodies when we accept the rights of parents to benefit their children in every other way?

2 It seems to me inevitable that genetic engineering will eventually be used. It will probably begin in a way that is most ethically acceptable to the largest portion of society, to prevent babies inheriting conditions that have a severe impact on the quality of life, such as deafness or blindness. The number of parents needing or desiring this service might be tiny, but their experience would help to ease society's fears, and geneticists could then begin to expand their services to prevent the inheritance of genes leading to other disorders such as asthma, heart disease, and various forms of cancer.

3 A further frontier will be the mind and the senses. Here, genetic engineering could have enormous benefits. Alcohol addiction could be eliminated, along with tendencies toward mental disease. People's senses of sight and hearing could be improved, allowing for new dimensions in art and music. And when our understanding of brain development has advanced, geneticists will be able to give parents the chance to choose intellectual gifts for their children as well.

4 Are there any limits to what can be accomplished with genetic enhancements? Some experts say there are boundaries beyond which we cannot go. But humans have a tendency to prove the experts wrong. One way to identify types of human enhancements that lie in the realm of possibility – no matter how outlandish they may seem today – is to consider what already exists in the living world. If

  C The genetic information passed on to children.
  D The ways in which parents may benefit their children.

2 Genetic engineering may first be applied to conditions affecting children because
  A very few people would regard this as immoral.
  B it could benefit a large proportion of society.
  C a lot is already known about these conditions.
  D these are life-threatening disorders.

3 Once people have started to accept genetic engineering,
  A it could be used to cure mental illness.
  B musicians and artists could improve their techniques.
  C its use will be limited to improving intellectual powers.
  D parents could select talents for their offspring.

another living creature already has a particular attribute, then we can work out its genetic basis and eventually we should be able to make it available to humans. For example, we could provide humans with a greatly enhanced sense of smell like that of dogs and other mammals, and the ability to "see" objects in complete darkness through a biological sonar system like the one that allows bats to find their way in the dark.

In the longer term, it might be possible to identify the genetic information which allows creatures to live under extreme conditions here on earth – like the microscopic bacteria that live in scalding hot water around volcanic vents on the ocean floor, far removed from light and free oxygen, and other creatures that are genetically adapted to thrive in subzero temperatures in the Arctic. One day it may even be possible to incorporate photosynthetic units into human embryos so that humans could receive energy directly from the sun, just like plants. Such genetic gifts could allow these genetically modified humans to survive on other planets in the solar system, where they could in turn use genetic engineering to further enhance the ability of their own children to survive on their chosen worlds.

In the short term, though, most genetic enhancements will surely be much more mundane. They will provide little fixes to all of the naturally occurring genetic defects that shorten the lives of so many people. They will enrich physical and cognitive attributes in small ways. But as the years go by over the next two centuries, the number and variety of possible genetic extensions to the basic human genome* will rise dramatically – like the additions to computer operating systems that occurred during the 1980s and 1990s. Extensions that were once unimaginable will become indispensable – to those parents who are able to afford them.

*The total of all the genes that are found in one living thing

4   Looking further into the future, the writer suggests that human attributes
   A   could be transferred to other living creatures.
   B   could be improved with genetic information from other creatures.
   C   should not be interfered with beyond certain limits.
   D   can only be enhanced with characteristics from other humans.

5   He suggests that genetic engineering may ultimately allow humans to
   A   live under the ocean.
   B   reproduce with creatures from other planets.
   C   produce energy by using the sun.
   D   live and reproduce in inhospitable conditions.

6   In the final paragraph he implies that genetic engineering
   A   should only be used to deal with genetic defects.
   B   may not be used to benefit everyone equally.
   C   cannot be developed without sophisticated computer programmes.
   D   will be taken for granted by everyone one day.

7   Is the writer generally
   A   enthusiastic about future developments in genetic engineering?
   B   suspicious of the implications of future developments?
   C   anticipating rapid developments in the near future?
   D   bored by the mundane advances already achieved?

4   Discuss this question.

Which specific developments discussed in the text do you consider acceptable, and which are unacceptable or incredible?

5   **Vocabulary:** word formation
1   Look at the following words from the text. What part of speech (noun, verb or adjective) is each word in the text? What other forms of the word are possible?

1	genetic (para. 1)	7	tendency (para. 4)
2	ethically (para. 2)	8	attribute (para. 4)
3	inheriting (para. 2)	9	provide (para. 4)
4	expand (para. 2)	10	modified (para. 5)
5	addiction (para. 3)	11	enhancements (para. 6)
6	intellectual (para. 3)	12	defects (para. 6)

2   Use an appropriate form of six of the words above to complete the sentences below.

1   Governments should make .... for controlling developments in genetic engineering.
2   Some people are very wary of the kind of genetic .... being made to food nowadays.
3   If .... genes are inherited, these may cause problems either in childhood or later on.
4   Once I start eating chocolate I can't stop – I find it's really ....
5   The new novel is an .... version of a short story he wrote years ago.
6   I think it's very .... to use animals in experiments to test cosmetics.

3 Read the following writing task.

> Recent scientific advances have allowed us to modify many natural processes. Discuss some of the ways in which you feel this benefits both the individual and society as a whole. (About 350 words.)

Jot down some ideas in answer to these questions.

1 What natural processes can now be modified? (Use ideas from this unit and Units 7 and 8, or from your own general knowledge.)
2 How does this benefit individuals?
3 How does this benefit society?

4

1 Read the two opening paragraphs below. Which one relates best to the writing task in Exercise 3 and states the main idea of the composition most clearly?

A There have been so many scientific advances over the last decade that it is difficult to remember them all, but the most dramatic have been connected with changing nature. Scientists can now do this in many ways, and the effects of this, both good and bad, can be seen everywhere in society.

B There have been many scientific advances over the last decade, but the most dramatic are related to our increasing ability to modify nature. Developments in the fields of medical science, agriculture and diet have brought a wide range of benefits for both individuals and society.

2 The supporting paragraphs of your composition should reflect the plan of development given in the introduction. (See Unit 7, p. 104.) How many supporting paragraphs would you write following on from Introduction B above?

5

1 Read the following sentences. What topic areas do they relate to?

1 There are more chemical sprays being used. Crops have fewer diseases.
2 People live longer but still age in appearance. Many want plastic surgery to improve their looks.
3 Hereditary illness may be eradicated. This would mean that the population would be healthier.
4 People in the UK want organic food. The idea of genetically modified food is frightening.
5 A baby's capabilities can be enhanced before birth. The baby may be very clever.

6 Because of improved farming methods, food is safer. There is more of it.

2 Combine each pair of sentences above using a word or phrase from the box and making any other changes necessary. There may be more than one possible answer.

because	as a result	if
so that	accordingly	furthermore

6 You may want to discuss the statement in the writing task briefly in your conclusion, to show that you are aware of the alternative point of view, but your conclusion should always finish by supporting the statement. Choose the best conclusion for the writing task in Exercise 3.

A All in all, it is clear that there have been so many advances in scientific knowledge that we can change nature in almost every area of our lives. Who knows what the future will bring?

B To sum up, scientists' ability to make nature work for them has had clear benefits. Of course some people do question the ethics of certain experiments, and others demand to know just how far we are prepared to go with scientific change. Nevertheless, the benefits to both individuals and the whole of society outweigh these concerns.

C In conclusion, the problems would seem to be enormous. What right do we have to think that we can tamper with nature in this way? The road the scientists are travelling is a dangerous one, and society should be on its guard.

7 Write your outline for the task, using the notes you made in Exercise 3.

8 Now write your composition. When you have finished, evaluate and edit your work.

Exam Strategy

To write a good discursive composition:
- plan before you write.
- don't include too many points, or you may go over the word limit.
- state your plan of development in your introduction.
- deal with each topic in a separate paragraph.
- include specific evidence for all your points.
- use linking devices to signal the relationship of ideas within and between paragraphs.
- use a fairly formal style, avoiding colloquial language.

► Exam Maximiser **Gold**

1 Complete the following sentences by writing **one** word in each of the spaces.

1 Although our computer systems can communicate and even .... with one another without our involvement, we do .... all their operations continuously.

2 Genetic engineering may one day .... inherited disorders, and perhaps even produce genetically .... human beings.

3 Our grandparents would never have dreamed of owning the domestic .... we now take for ....

4 My brother-in-law, who's very keen on conserving the world's natural .... , has built a bicycle out of .... parts from the rubbish dump.

5 Opinion is divided as to whether awarding the research scholarship to one so young offers a wonderful .... , or establishes a dangerous ....

2 Rewrite the following sentences using a verb + reflexive pronoun and making any necessary changes.

1 By bedtime the children had become so tired running around the garden that they fell asleep immediately.

2 Once her children had started school, the scientist could spend all her time and energy on her research.

3 After failing my test three times, I had almost accepted the idea that I would never get a driving licence.

4 The architect doesn't think this barn would be suitable for conversion into holiday flats.

5 In an unexciting match, my brother stood out from the rest of the players because he scored the only goal.

6 The unfortunate clerk was called in to the manager's office and requested to give a reason for his actions.

7 If you have to deal with a difficult customer, it's important to control the situation without appearing rude.

8 I'm trying to lose weight, but when I see a chocolate biscuit I just lose control.

9 If you'd only try a bit harder, you could be a very good player.

10 Although the employees criticised their boss in private, they refused to give a definite opinion in public.

3 Fill each of the blanks with a suitable word or phrase.

1 We may miss the last bus, but .... case we can always get a taxi.

2 All the time he was here, he never lifted .... help around the house.

3 No doubt he .... as indispensable, but unfortunately for him, his employer doesn't.

4 If savings .... , the accountants will find ways to make them.

5 You must be mistaken – Jack .... such a dreadful lie.

6 Experience .... once people become used to a dishwasher, they find it hard to do without one.

7 We asked all the students, but no one could .... light on the matter.

8 In view of the conditions .... this research was done, the results are excellent.

9 It's no use .... nature, she's just a really selfish person.

10 We've knocked down the wall .... result we now get more light on the terrace.

11 When the door opened, I found myself face .... the professor.

4 Talk about the photo.

1 Describe the photo and the situation.

2 How does it relate to the topic of the unit?

3 What does it suggest about the world today? How do you react to this idea?

12 The last frontier

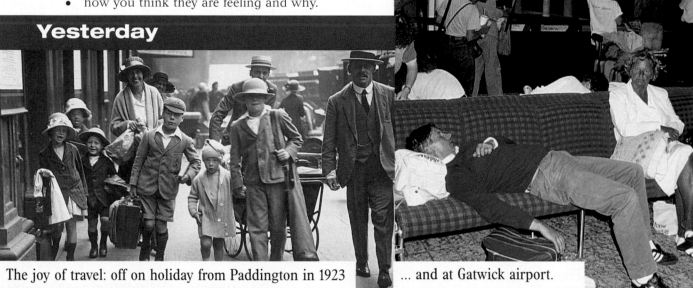

Today

Speaking: photos/discussion

1 Look at the two photographs. Describe and compare the people and the situations. Say:

- what sort of places the people might be travelling to
- how you think they are feeling and why.

Yesterday

The joy of travel: off on holiday from Paddington in 1923

... and at Gatwick airport.

2 Discuss what the two pictures suggest about the way holiday travel has changed over the last century. Do you think travelling has become:

- safer or more dangerous?
- easier or more difficult?
- more or less comfortable?

2 How far do you agree with this statement?

'Travel abroad is no longer the adventure it used to be. Mass tourism has destroyed the adventure of foreign travel.'

Think about these points.

- increased speed and ease of travel
- popularity of organised adventure holidays
- increasing interest in travel to exotic or remote places

3 Read the extract from the Longman *Dictionary of Contemporary English* below.

tourism *n* [U] the business of providing things for people to do, places for them to stay, etc while they are on holiday.

Now consider the following types of tourism and answer the questions below.

- green, or eco-tourism
- heritage tourism
- space tourism
- virtual tourism

1 What sort of things might people do in the types of tourism listed above, and where might they stay?
2 What sort of people might be interested in each of these types of tourism?
3 What are the advantages and disadvantages of each type for a) the environment b) the inhabitants of the place visited c) the tourist?
4 Which type of holiday would you prefer? Why?

Reading: non-fiction

1   You have won a prize of a two-week holiday in Antarctica. How would you feel?

a) disappointed – you'd rather stay in a luxury hotel in your own country
b) horrified – won't it be cold, uncomfortable and dangerous?
c) concerned – is nowhere safe from tourism?
d) thrilled – you'll be able to visit a place few other people have ever set foot in

2   Now read through the following text to get a general idea of the content. Does it make you change your view of Antarctica?

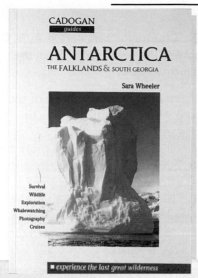

WELCOME TO THE WORLD'S LONELIEST TOURIST SPOT

W Magazine

1 GUIDE BOOKS TO ANTARCTICA? The notion that the last wilderness is being colonised by tourists tends to provoke the kind of shock-horror reaction associated with tabloid headlines. Is nothing sacred? Apparently not. Thirty years ago, not a single tourist visited Antarctica. Now, as many as 10,000 tourists visit it each year. What next? Package holidays at the South Pole?

2 The idea of mass tourism on the ice is shocking, of course, because Antarctica is a powerful symbol of the uncorrupted earth – the planet before we mucked it up. It is a blank in time, the last wilderness and the only geographical symbol of innocence left unless we set up colonies in space.

3 The dangerous implications of tourism in Antarctica, however, have been exaggerated. 10,000 people aren't actually all that many on a continent one and a half times the size of Europe. In addition, almost all tourists arrive on cruise ships and spend only a few hours on the continent itself. There is no accommodation available to holidaymakers on the ice, so they are obliged to return to their cruise ships in inflatable dinghies to sleep in heated cabins. Nor are there shops or food or water in Antarctica. Antarctic tourism is now well-policed and all reputable organisations adhere to the environmental regulations of the Antarctic Treaty and the guidelines laid down by IAATO, the International Association of Antarctica Tour Operators. Whilst it is essential to maintain strict control over all visitors to the sepulchral wastes, the reality is that the vast majority of the continent has never seen a Nikon and probably never will.

4 This doesn't mean that Antarctica has not developed a human culture of its own. No: despite the fact that it has no indigenous population, since the first man stepped onto the continent in about 1821, explorers, scientists, base workers and mountaineers have come to the ice and given it a history. At the beginning they lived only in tents, or in the cramped quarters of their ships, or in prefabricated huts they had brought from home. Now, life in the tiny clusters of human life on the continent is rather more sophisticated. McMurdo, the largest of the three American bases in Antarctica, resembles a small Alaskan mining town. It has roads, three-story buildings, the ill-matched architecture of a utilitarian institution and a summer population of more than a thousand people.

5 As many as 200 research camps function in Antarctica in the summer, and about thirty remain manned during the winter. They belong to a variety of national programmes, and each country transports its culture to the bottom of the world. I ate Antarctica's best food at the Italian station, Terra Nova Bay, had sweet, syrupy dumplings with the Chinese at Great Wall and drank vodka at the Russian base at Bellinghausen.

6 But none of these people were tourists, and their overall impact on the continent of Antarctica was minimal. To return to the point I made at the beginning about the alarming rise of Antarctic tourism, people often ask me if I am afraid that some entrepreneurial spirit is going to arrive on the ice to start building huge hotels and shopping malls. The reality is that Antarctica is different from Spain or Greece or Thailand. Even if someone is prepared to contravene the Antarctic treaty, there are still the almost intractable problems of building and operating a service industry in a place where there is no running water, a place where each barrel of oil has to be transported many hundreds of miles across the worst seas on the planet and which is shrouded in darkness for five months of the year. And despite the complicated politics of the Antarctic treaty, on the continent itself there is no concept of ownership. In the end, neither tourism nor tourist guides can taint the majesty of Antarctica.

3 Choose the best option, **A, B, C** or **D**, to answer the questions or finish the statements below.

1 What are the implications of the appearance of guide books to Antarctica?
   A They will attract even more tourists.
   B They may encourage the wrong type of tourist.
   C They are an indication of the growth of tourism.
   D They give an exaggerated idea of the dangers.

2 The writer sees Antarctica as symbolic because it is
   A untouched by man.
   B unspoiled.
   C timeless.
   D empty.

3 The writer suggests that tourists visiting Antarctica
   A travel in comfortable conditions.
   B may be disappointed by how little they actually see.
   C are not aware of its history and culture.
   D have little effect on the environment.

4 People working in Antarctica
   A are causing more damage than tourists.
   B have developed their own lifestyle.
   C travel over most of the continent.
   D have to adapt their culture to the new environment.

5 The buildings at the American base in McMurdo
   A are not well suited to the environment.
   B are not attractive, but are practical.
   C are sophisticated and comfortable.
   D are typically American.

6 How does the writer feel about the changes that are taking place in Antarctica?
   A She is generally positive about them.
   B She feels they have led to unrealistic expectations.
   C She is very concerned about their effects.
   D She accepts they are necessary.

4 Read the text again to find the answers to the following questions, which focus on the language and style of the passage.

1 What expression does the writer use in paragraph 1 of the text to suggest the language used by tabloid newspapers? How does the style of the first paragraph reinforce this suggestion?

2 Find three expressions the writer uses in paragraph 2 to emphasise the fact that Antarctica is mostly untouched and has not been spoiled by human greed. Which of these expressions is colloquial?

3 What image of the uninhabited area is created by the expression 'sepulchral wastes' (para. 3)? Find an expression in the last paragraph which continues this image.

4 Paragraph 4 describes the living conditions of the people on Antarctica. What words and phrases emphasise the difference between the wide open spaces of the Antarctic and the conditions in the human settlements?

5 Which expression in paragraph 6 reinforces the idea of the inaccessibility of Antarctica?

5 Discuss these questions.

1 The extract refers to 'the environmental regulations of the Antarctic Treaty and the guidelines laid down by the International Association of Antarctica Tour Operators'. What sort of controls do you think might be specified by these agreements?

2 Look back at your answer to Exercise 1. After reading the article, would you modify your views? How?

3 Which isolated place would you most like to visit? Why?

164

► Exam Maximiser Gold

Vocabulary: exam practice

1   Multiple-choice questions

1   Choose the word or phrase which best completes each sentence below. The words you need all occurred in the Reading passage on page 163.

1   Tim was so keen on travel that he set .... his own travel agency.
A off   B down   C up   D out

2   Tourist organisations have to .... to certain regulations.
A maintain   B follow   C adhere   D abide

3   The police maintained .... control over the crowds at the demonstration.
A strict   B severe   C strong   D stern

4   .... it is essential to regulate the tourist industry, the fact remains that this is very difficult to organise.
A Whilst   B Since   C So   D When

5   In the distance I could see a .... of low farm buildings.
A batch   B gathering   C clump   D cluster

6   When operating internationally, it is vital not to .... treaty agreements.
A contradict   B contrive   C contravene   D concede

7   At peak times we have to .... the information desk twenty-four hours a day.
A work   B man   C maintain   D keep

8   Some people have no .... of what responsible tourism means.
A concept   B theory   C outline   D thesis

9   Providing services for people in isolated areas can be an .... problem.
A impractical   B intense   C inherent   D intractable

10   The .... majority of people will never visit Antarctica.
A big   B large   C vast   D huge

11   There are more opportunities .... to would-be adventurers than ever before.
A available   B ready   C convenient   D applicable

12   The whole area .... the surface of some strange planet.
A seems   B resembles   C appears   D assumes

13   Being quite tall, I tend to find the seating arrangements on most planes rather ....
A short   B cramped   C squashed   D narrow

14   The house was empty, its expensive furniture .... in white sheets to protect it from the dust.
A dressed   B lined   C enshrined   D shrouded

15   The accusation was never proved, but his reputation was .... forever.
A hurt   B tainted   C blurred   D dirtied

2   Look again at questions 1–5 above. Which question is testing:
a)   collocation?
b)   words of similar meanings?
c)   words with special grammatical patterns?
d)   connectors?
e)   phrasal verbs?

2   Use of English: key word transformations

For each of the sentences below, write a new sentence as similar as possible in meaning to the original sentence, but using the word given. This word must not be altered in any way.

1   There are at least 200 research camps in action in Antarctica in the summer.
function
....

2   No one came forward when they asked for volunteers to spend the winter in the base camp.
single
....

3   The new cruise ship is half as big again as the old one.
size
....

4   The tourists don't spend many hours on the land itself.
only
....

5   They told me that actually the situation is very different from what people think.
reality
....

6   The new plans for the Tourist Centre have been approved by the authorities.
met
....

7   Lack of accommodation may mean that tourists may have to share rooms.
obliged
....

8   Up to 1000 people visited the Information Centre last week.
many
....

Listening: note-taking

1 Look at the picture and discuss the questions below.

1 What is the picture illustrating and how realistic is it intended to be?
2 What sorts of activities might people really do on a holiday like this?
3 Why might they want to go on such a holiday?

2 You will hear an extract from a radio interview about the possibility of space tourism. Before you listen, look at the notes below. What can you predict about the content of the interview?

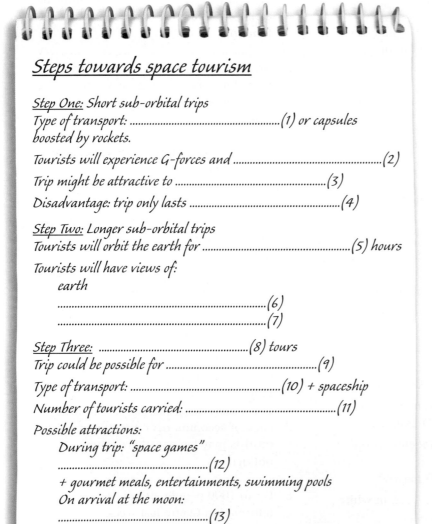

Steps towards space tourism

Step One: Short sub-orbital trips
Type of transport: ....(1) or capsules boosted by rockets.

Tourists will experience G-forces and ....(2)

Trip might be attractive to ....(3)

Disadvantage: trip only lasts ....(4)

Step Two: Longer sub-orbital trips
Tourists will orbit the earth for ....(5) hours

Tourists will have views of:
    earth
    ....(6)
    ....(7)

Step Three: ....(8) tours
Trip could be possible for ....(9)

Type of transport: ....(10) + spaceship

Number of tourists carried: ....(11)

Possible attractions:
    During trip: "space games"
    ....(12)
    + gourmet meals, entertainments, swimming pools
On arrival at the moon:
    ....(13)
    ....(14)

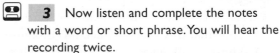
3 Now listen and complete the notes with a word or short phrase. You will hear the recording twice.

4 In the recording, the interviewer asked Richard Bennet:

1 who he thought would be interested in sub-orbital trips.
2 if he expected many people to be interested in these trips.
3 whether holidays on Mars were a possibility.
4 if tourists could go outside the spaceship during the journey to the moon.
5 what people would do when they arrived at the moon.

What were Richard Bennet's answers? Begin:

'He told her/said that …'

5 Say it again
Re-express these sentences from the Listening text using the key word given.

1 It's on the same lines as a holiday cruise. **very**
2 For some people, extended weightlessness might be difficult to handle. **coping**
3 If the spaceship broke down, which is unlikely, there would be no danger to passengers. **event**
4 The lifecraft have the capacity to return to earth on their own. **possible**

Grammar check: indirect speech

1   The writer of the extract below describes a difficult and dangerous journey in which he and two friends crossed the mountains from Afghanistan to Nuristan on foot. They were guided to the border by a young boy, who then left them.

1   Read through the text, ignoring the gaps for the moment, to get a general idea of the content. Then choose from the list below the best phrases or sentences to fill the gaps.

In front of us, the desolate beauty of Nuristan stretched out towards the majestic range of the Hindu Kush and freedom. It was late afternoon, the sun had dropped below the mountains and a sharp wind was picking up. (1) .... , but we had been walking for three or four hours already and there was still no sign of it. (2) .... but then (3) ....

An hour later we rounded a bend in the river and saw a thread of smoke drifting from between some large rocks at the bottom of a cliff. The fire belonged to a family from Khunduz (4) ....

We walked on until it grew dark. The moon was high in the sky by the time we came to the glow of a lamp hanging inside a tent. (5) .... (6) .... We had been travelling almost continuously for more than eighteen hours. As we sat drinking tea (7) .... I had already guessed the answer, and I was not disappointed.

"With a good horse – maybe an hour."

A   I asked one of them, out of idle interest, how far he thought it might be to the next village.
B   We briefly considered spending the night in one of the shelters
C   (we) decided to press on.
D   Some men invited us inside to share their meal and stay the night.
E   The boy had told us of a village an hour's journey over the pass into Nuristan
F   who told us that there was, indeed, a village another hour's walk down the river.
G   We accepted gratefully.

2   Rewrite the extracts **A–G**, beginning with the words given below. Don't change the original meaning. More than one answer may be possible.

A   ' .... ' I asked, out of idle interest.
B   We briefly wondered whether we ....
C   We agreed that ....
D   The men said, '........................ '
E   The boy had said that ....
F   'Oh, yes,' they said, ' .... '
G   We replied that .... (*Use the previous sentence in the text to help you.*)

2   Now discuss these questions with reference to Exercise 1.

1   What verbs do we use to introduce
    a) indirect statements?
    b) indirect questions?
2   What patterns follow these verbs in indirect speech?
3   What changes do we make to vocabulary and tenses?
4   When we report what someone said, do we always use their exact words?

▶   Grammar reference p. 214

3   Fill each of the blanks with a suitable word or phrase. In which sentences do you have a choice of tense?

1   I told you it didn't matter .... alone or brought someone along with you.
2   Jenny just wanted to check that we .... to the party tomorrow and that we know the address.
3   He claimed that his wallet .... by a pick-pocket, but in fact he'd just left it at home.
4   She told me I .... to go as she could manage on her own.
5   I wasn't able to confirm whether it .... be possible for me to attend the meeting.
6   I wish I .... gone with you, but I had to stay at home with the children.
7   She said she wished they .... insist on bringing their dog with them every time they came to visit her.
8   He said he might possibly come along if he .... time, but we shouldn't wait for him.

4 We can also report statements, orders and questions using a verb + *to*-infinitive or verb + *-ing*, with or without an object.

1 Match sentences 1–7 to the appropriate statements below.

1 'Don't stay any longer – it's dangerous.'
2 'Get out now!'
3 'It would be a good idea if you left now.'
4 'Don't forget to go.'
5 'Please, please, go!'
6 'Would you mind leaving now?'
7 'I've made plans for you to go.'

a) He ordered me to go.
b) He advised me to go.
c) He requested me to go.
d) He reminded me to go.
e) He intended me to go.
f) He pleaded with me to go.
g) He warned me not to stay.

2 In which of the reported statements a)–g) above could the object be omitted? How does this affect the meaning?

3 Read the following anecdote told by a tourist guide. Then fill in the gaps with an appropriate verb in the *-ing* form. Add any other words necessary. In some cases a preposition is needed.

The group of tourists suggested (1) .... for a meal together. I advised (2) .... at a small local restaurant, but they insisted (3) .... to an expensive restaurant in the middle of town. When we got there, they blamed (4) .... a parking space immediately outside, and grumbled (5) .... made to walk a few metres from the minibus to the restaurant. They protested (6) .... to wait for a table, and accused the waiter (7) .... them the wrong sort of wine. At the end of the evening, they congratulated (8) .... organised such an enjoyable outing.

5 When we report what people say, we often report the general meaning rather than the exact words. In this case, the reporting verb may carry much of the meaning of the original statement. Read the story again. What do you think the tourists' original words were?

6

1 We can use impersonal passive constructions with reporting verbs such as: *allege, believe, know, report, rumour, think* as in the following examples.

1 a) *It is said that* the Department of Tourism *is* very interested in this project.
   b) The Department of Tourism *is said to be* very interested in this project.
2 a) *It is reported that* tenders *have been invited* from several construction companies.
   b) Tenders *are reported to have been invited* from several construction companies.

2 Pattern b) is not possible with all verbs. Which of the sentences below are not possible?

1 a) It is not expected that the authorities will grant planning permission for the hotel.
   b) The authorities are not expected to grant planning permission for the hotel.
2 a It is feared that the authorities will refuse permission for the development.
   b) The authorities are feared to refuse permission for the development.
3 a) It is hoped that fines will discourage unruly holiday-makers.
   b) Fines are hoped to discourage unruly holiday-makers.

▶ Grammar reference p. 214

7 Read the report on the evening news programme below. Then complete the second, written version, using the passive and including patterns from Exercise 6.

' *To attract more tourists, the authorities are planning to build a new airport on the island. Most islanders expect the plans to go ahead, although there are fears that increased tourist numbers will lead to serious environmental problems. Some residents say that water supplies are insufficient to cope with large numbers of tourists, and no-one knows if there is sufficient electricity generating capacity to supply the new hotels that will be built. Others claim that tourism has already brought valuable revenue and employment to the island, and should be encouraged. There have been reassuring reports that the authorities are drawing up plans for strict control and monitoring of tourist developments.* '

Concern over new airport

A new airport (1) is .... for the island to attract more tourists. The plans are (2) .... go ahead, although it (3) .... could lead to serious environmental problems. Water supplies (4) .... to cope with large numbers of tourists, and it (5) .... there will be sufficient electricity generating capacity to supply the new hotels that are expected (6) .... On the other hand, it (7) .... tourism has already brought valuable revenue and employment to the island, and should be encouraged. Reassuringly, the authorities (8) .... plans for strict control and monitoring of tourist developments.

▶ Exam Maximiser Gold

Use of English: comprehension and summary

1 Read the title of the following passage.

1 What do you think the passage is about?

2 What arguments can you think of for and against tourism? Think of two arguments **for** and two **against**.

3 Read the passage through quite quickly to compare your ideas with the text.

2 Read the passage again carefully, then answer the questions which follow it (page 170).

Tourism on trial

International tourism is on trial, and the charge sheet is as long as it is damning. Mass tourism is associated with rising crime, begging and other social problems. It stands accused of imposing itself on some of the world's most fragile
5 ecosystems and of being a force for environmental destruction. Powerful international companies are charged with robbing local people of water and other precious natural resources, of forcing them from their homes, their lands and means of survival.

10 Tourists to the developing world behave badly. They disrespect their hosts by failing to observe dress codes and other cultural norms. Moreover, it is alleged, tourism works to promote dominant Western values at the expense of proud and ancient cultures. The trade is fixed by multinational
15 companies from the richest countries that cream off the lion's share of the profits, leaving little for local people, bar menial jobs. Those accusing the companies include charities and human rights groups, communities affected by tourism, and academics.

20 Such accusations are hard to reconcile with the defendant in the dock – the tourist industry which is, after all, the 'funshine' industry. It promises some of our happiest times – those two weeks in paradise that we spend the rest of the year longing and saving for.

25 The claim that developing countries do not benefit from tourism simply does not square with the facts. The industry creates over ten per cent of the world's income and provides employment for one in 25 people on earth. A fast-growing proportion of that trade is going to poorer countries – rather
30 than being a freeloader, the industry is throwing an economic lifeline to emerging nations. It is a quick, lead-free engine of wealth creation, driving fledgling economies and creating much-needed foreign exchange. The plea from the dock is unequivocal: 'not guilty'.

35 If charges were brought before a real court the case might well split the jury. The search for the truth means looking at a series of complex economic and social activities that cross many cultures and visit different destinations. Causal
40 relationships about the real effects of tourism are hard to establish. While some entire communities have been dispossessed, others have discovered business opportunities and valued waged employment.

Furthermore, even if international tourism is dominated
45 by multinational companies bent on exploiting the new frontiers of the developing world, this hardly distinguishes it from any other form of trade. So if tourism is not so different, why has it become one of the most talked about issues in development?

50 Tourism is different. It is different because there is an expectation that it should be a force for fair social change. The industry has billed itself as a place where cultures meet, a catalyst to international understanding and to the transfer of wealth from visitor to visited. Even those most sceptical about
55 the industry's track record in this field are up-beat about the development potential of tourism – if only it were regulated. Tourism is talked about precisely because there is still much to be won – and lost – from discussions that may shape its future. For the development of 'third world' tourism is
60 perhaps the most eloquent metaphor for the unjust world in which we live. Fuelled by the growing gaps in income and ever cheaper travel, tourism has become something the world's rich do to the world's poor. In the words of one Namibian school pupil, 'When I grow up I want to be a
65 tourist'.

If there is one truth about the effects of tourism, it is yet to be found. But the search for a more just and sustainable form of tourism is still a noble enterprise.

1 According to the writer, what three main charges are made against international tourism?

2 Explain in your own words two ways in which tourists often 'disrespect their hosts'. (line 11)

3 According to the writer, in what two ways does tourism harm local culture and economies?

4 Why, according to the writer, is it strange to accuse the tourist industry of creating misery?

5 Explain in your own words exactly what the writer means in this context when he says 'the claim ... does not square with the facts'. (lines 25-26)

6 What is the main argument the writer makes in support of the tourist industry?

7 What does 'it' refer to in line 31?

8 What is the writer implying with the phrase 'a quick, lead-free engine'? (line 31)

9 What does the writer mean by the phrase 'might well split the jury' (line 35) and what is he referring to?

10 Explain in your own words how the writer suggests that tourism might be similar to other major industries.

11 What reason does the writer give for feeling that tourism is actually different from other industries?

12 Who does the expression 'up-beat' (line 55) refer to, and what does it mean in this context?

13 What does the writer feel is needed to secure the future development of tourism?

14 Why does the writer feel that tourism in the third world is 'a metaphor for the unjust world in which we live'. (line 60)

15 In a paragraph of 60–80 words, summarise the ways in which the writer feels that tourism can be seen as a force for good.

For the summary, follow this procedure.

1 Look back through the whole text and find:
   - two reasons why the writer feels that tourism has been a good thing already
   - three reasons he gives for supporting its development in the future.

2 Note these reasons down briefly in your own words.

3 Use your notes to complete the task.

4 Check and edit your summary.

See Exam Focus Units 2 and 8 for help with general techniques.

3 Discuss these questions.

1 How far do you consider that tourism is or can be 'a place where cultures meet, a catalyst to international understanding and to the transfer of wealth from visitor to visited'? Give examples to support your opinion.

2 What regulations would you introduce to try to bring about a 'more just and sustainable form of tourism'?

Vocabulary: style

1 The text on page 169 uses the idea of a trial as a way of organising the arguments for and against tourism. Use legal expressions from the text to replace the words in italics in the sentences below. You may need to make other changes to the sentence.

1 *The list of complaints brought* against the tourist industry is long.

2 The tourist companies *are said to be* damaging eco-systems and helping to destroy the environment.

3 The industry should be treated like *an accused person in a court*.

4 Tour operators do not admit that they *have caused* social and environmental problems.

2 Rewrite the sentences below using idiomatic expressions and metaphors from the box to replace the phrases in italics. You may need to make other changes to the grammar of the sentence.

> thrown an economic lifeline
> cream off the lion's share of the profits
> has been fuelled by   billed itself as
> got a good track record   up-beat
> square with the facts   a freeloader

1 It is said that large companies *take most of the money made* from tourism before giving any to the poorer countries.

2 The apparent evidence *is not supported by the facts*.

3 The tourist is often seen as *someone who takes without giving in return*.

4 The industry has *provided essential financial support* to poorer countries.

5 The tourist industry has *promoted itself by saying it is* a force for improving international understanding.

6 Some people feel that tourism has not *done very well up to now* in the area of cultural understanding.

7 Many of its supporters are *optimistic* about the future.

8 Tourism *has grown quickly because of* the big difference between rich and poor countries.

Vocabulary: fixed phrases

1   Prepositional phrases

1   The following extract is from an article about a holiday disaster which appeared in the Travel section of a newspaper. Add the correct prepositions to complete the phrases.

Demand for adventure holidays in exotic places is (1) .... the increase and I was very taken by the idea of going on one. So (2) .... the very last minute, I decided to join a group on a walking holiday in the mountains of northern Spain. From reading the brochure, I was (3) .... the impression that it would be quite easy and not too tiring. It said that for each stage of the trip, your luggage was sent on (4) .... advance, so you weren't expected to carry it. It sounded ideal — but it all went horribly wrong. My backpack, containing everything I needed for the holiday, was put on a flight to Cairo (5) .... mistake. The tour guide wasn't (6) .... fault, and he was (7) .... hand to deal with the situation, but all his efforts to retrieve my luggage were (8) .... no avail. I had to start the trek with only the clothes I stood up (9) .... , and, worst of all, without my walking boots. After the first day's hike, wearing light canvas shoes, I was (10) .... agony. Everyone else in the group seemed much fitter than I was, and I got totally (11) .... (12) .... breath trying to keep up with them. Things went (13) .... bad (14) .... worse.

2   Add a suitable preposition to each of the phrases below.

1   make up .... lost time
2   walk .... a frantic pace
3   .... my horror
4   .... delay
5   .... the end

3   Now use the phrases to make up your own ending to the holiday story above.

---

2   Read the advertisement below. Write your own 150-word account of a good or bad journey or holiday experience for submission to the competition. Try to include some of the prepositional phrases from Exercise 1.

DO YOU HAVE A FUNNY TALE TO TELL ?

Or a horrendous ordeal to get off your chest?

Share your holiday nightmares by sending them to us!

Write an account of your disaster in no more than 150 words. Prizes for the best accounts include return flights to New York, Paris and Amsterdam. A collection of the best submissions will be published in a forthcoming book *Travellers Tales from Heaven and Hell.*

3   Sentence adverbials

The phrases in italics are all sentence adverbials. Match them to the list of functions below.

1   I would like to extend all our thanks to the person who has done more than anyone else to make this holiday a success – *namely*, Paula, our tour guide.
2   There were some problems but *on the whole* the facilities were satisfactory.
3   *In the first place* I don't like cut glass, *secondly* I don't need another vase, and *last but not least* I can't afford it.
4   *Hopefully*, we'll be able to return later this year – *in fact* we plan to book our next trip soon.

a)   signalling organisation of ideas
b)   reformulating what has been said
c)   indicating the attitude of the speaker
d)   summarising or generalising

4 Complete the passage below by adding a suitable sentence adverbial from the box. There is one word you do not need to use.

> all things considered   for a start   in addition
> in reality   naturally   not surprisingly
> rather the reverse   that is to say

Tourism may seem to assure those involved of untold riches, but (1) .... it can promise more than it delivers. (2) .... , it depends on a host of factors beyond our control — climate, economics, even politics. (3) .... , the success of a place as a tourist destination may lead to it losing the features that first attracted the tourists there — (4) .... , its unspoiled landscape and welcoming people. But this does not seem to have slowed down the expansion of tourism. (5) .... — more and more countries are opening up their doors to the tourists. (6) .... , no place can remain untouched by time. Tourism may be the way out of a life of grinding poverty for people who can see no other hope and they (7) .... welcome the chance to give their children a better life than they had. So (8) .... , it seems that tourism is here to stay — all over the planet.

5 Look at the question below and decide how you would answer it. List some points to support your answer.

'*Is tourism beneficial or harmful to the world and its people?*'

Then debate the question with the rest of your class.

6 Write a balanced composition on the topic you discussed in Exercise 5. (See Unit 7, page 104 for guidance.) Use some of the phrases you have practised in this section.

Exam Focus

Paper 3 Use of English (Section A, gapped sentences)

In Paper 3, Question 3 you have to complete six gapped sentences with an appropriate word or phrase. You usually need between two and five words. Typical items tested include phrases using modal verbs, conditionals, inversions and collocations. Some gaps may include more than one structure. You lose marks for incorrect spelling in the parts of the sentence that are assessed.

1

1 Read the following sentences and match them to the hints below. Don't fill the blanks yet.

(a) I .... the journey if I had been told about the possible environmental consequences.

(b) It's high time he .... whether he'll take the course or not.

(c) I really wish .... leave your room in such a mess!

(d) She .... better than to have told him the secret – he can't keep anything to himself!

(e) The girl told the dentist that she .... from toothache for several days.

(f) If you don't .... step, you can be misled by clever advertising techniques.

1 This is testing your knowledge of idioms.
2 Think about the verb form needed after *wish*.
3 You need to use a conditional structure and also to think about collocation.
4 You need to use a modal verb and a fixed phrase.
5 This involves the use of reported speech and a collocation.
6 A fixed phrase which affects the tense of the following verb.

2 Now fill each of the blanks with a suitable word or phrase.

2 Fill each of the blanks with a suitable word or phrase.

(a) I took the scratched CD back to the shop to ask if they .... for a new one.

(b) The trip was fun: you really .... stayed at home.

(c) He likes nothing .... sit in his chair and watch TV.

(d) Only when I saw her clearly .... who she was.

(e) Although I tried to persuade him to tell the truth, he paid .... me.

(f) I think you .... an effort to be nice to him, even if you didn't like him much.

> ### Exam Strategy
>
> When you do gapped sentences, always:
> - read the whole sentence before filling in the gap.
> - try to identify what is being tested — it may be a structure such as an infinitive or a gerund, or a verb or adjective with a dependent preposition.
> - check the form of the words which come before and after the gap — they may give you information about the structure you need to use.
> - make sure your spelling is accurate.

Writing: magazine article

For the task-directed question in Paper 2, you may be asked to write an article, either for a magazine or a newspaper. For this type of task, it is very important to think about:

- the target reader
- the purpose of writing
- an appropriate style.

In this unit you will write an article for a magazine. In Unit 13 you will write a newspaper article.

1   Read the following writing task and answer the questions below.

> You have been asked to write an article for a local English-language magazine about a newly-opened Tourist Information Centre in your town, giving your personal perspective and recommending it to both local residents and visitors. (About 300 words.)

Which two of the following are **not** generally features of a magazine article?

- detailed information about the topic
- the writer's personal opinion, supported by evidence
- reports of conversations, using direct speech
- summaries of information from conversations and interviews, using reported speech
- a dramatic style, to get the reader's attention
- a fairly formal style

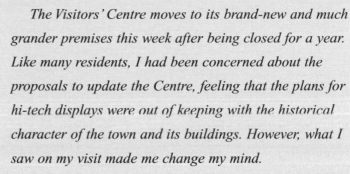

2   Now read the article, which was written in answer to the task. Check your answers to the question in Exercise 1.

The Visitors' Centre moves to its brand-new and much grander premises this week after being closed for a year. Like many residents, I had been concerned about the proposals to update the Centre, feeling that the plans for hi-tech displays were out of keeping with the historical character of the town and its buildings. However, what I saw on my visit made me change my mind.

The new Centre, located in the Main Square, has kept its original eighteenth-century façade, but inside it opens up into a large, airy reception area. Each room has a special focus. One has virtual-reality computer programmes, allowing visitors to explore historical sites in the area, such as the famous rock paintings. Another room has full details of accommodation, events, and guided tours, with computerised booking facilities. Upstairs there is a gallery with pictures by local artists depicting well-known beauty spots. The most impressive part, however, is the museum section, with its displays of historical artefacts and computer-animated models of street scenes from the past. Headsets are available with recorded commentaries in a number of languages.

The manager told me that the whole project has been designed to be attractive to both casual visitors and serious historians, and the overseas visitors I spoke to in the Centre were very impressed by the facilities offered and by the standard of the displays. Inevitably, there is a shop but I was pleasantly surprised by the quality of goods on sale, and it has an excellent selection of books on local history and the culture of the region.

So in spite of my initial reservations, I feel this is a real asset to the town – not just to visitors, but to all of us. Why not go and have a look? You might learn more about our town than you think!

3 The article is divided into four paragraphs. Match the following topics to the appropriate paragraphs.

a) author's initial attitude
b) description of visit
c) details of attraction
d) further detail
e) introduction of topic
f) reaction of others
g) recommendations
h) summary of changed attitude

Paragraph 1 ....
Paragraph 2 ....
Paragraph 3 ....
Paragraph 4 ....

4 Look at the phrases below, which were used in the article to express the writer's changing personal opinion.

*I had been concerned about the proposals ... **However**, what I saw on my visit made me change my mind.*
*... **in spite of** my initial reservations, I feel this is a real asset to the town.*

Complete the sentences below using your own ideas. Think about places you have visited or projects you have been involved in.

1 I had been very dubious about ... but now ...
2 I had my doubts about ... but I have since ...
3 At the outset I was enthusiastic about ... but then I began ...
4 My initial reaction to ... was ... but after a while ...
5 I was sceptical about ... at first, but now ...
6 Although I was unenthusiastic about ... at first, I soon ...

5 The statements below were made about the attraction described in the article in Exercise 2. Match the reporting verbs in the box to the quotes below, to indicate the attitude of the speaker. Then rewrite each sentence as reported speech, to make them appropriate for inclusion in a magazine article.

| admire | reject | propose | complain |
| recommend | praise | urge | |

1 'The whole centre was just wonderful!'
The tourists ....
2 'It's going to ruin the town.'
She ....
3 'I don't accept any of it!'
He ....
4 'I think it's ideal for families – everyone should go.'
They ....

5 'Why don't we discuss the possibility of extending the facilities?'
The manager ....
6 'I think they've done a terrific job.'
The mayor ....
7 'We should all be proud of it.'
The manager ....

6

1 Read the following writing task. What information do you have to include?

> You have been asked to write an article for a local magazine about a new cultural facility in your town, recommending it and saying how you think it will benefit the town in general. (About 300 words.)

2 Think about what kind of facility you will write about – an art gallery, a theatre, a computerised library – or an idea of your own.

3 Plan your answer using the structure given in Exercise 3.

The National Centre for Popular Music, Sheffield.

7 Now write your article. Make sure you include the features of a good article which were discussed in Exercise 1. When you have finished, check and edit your work carefully.

Exam Strategy

DO plan your time carefully in the exam.
- 10 minutes for thinking and planning
- 40-45 minutes for writing
- 5-10 minutes for checking
DON'T
- take longer than one hour for each composition.
- write more than the number of words required.
- include information that is not relevant to the question you are answering.
- use too many connecting words and phrases – they should not be used when necessary, not in every sentence.

1 Complete each of the following sentences with one of the words from the box below.

boosted	cramped	culmination	gradient
indigenous	intrepid	intractable	prospect
provisions	reputable	risky	target

1 The tourists showed little interest in the rich culture of the .... people, preferring to stay in their hotels.

2 Although the living areas are spacious, the sleeping quarters are .... and uncomfortable.

3 In the early days, we had to carry all the .... we needed in our rucksacks.

4 We had planned to travel by canoe, but accepted that it was too .... under the circumstances.

5 The walkers .... their energy levels by eating chocolate as they went along.

6 A few .... individuals even ventured into the local shops and bars.

7 We'd tackled most of the difficulties, but the issue of energy supplies remained an apparently .... problem.

8 The advertising company is aiming to .... young people looking for a new kind of adventure with this campaign.

9 There is little .... of persuading him to rest while there's still so much work to finish.

10 The launch of this spacecraft marks the .... of many years' research and experimentation.

11 No .... guide would take newly-arrived tourists to such a dangerous area.

12 The road out of the village, with a .... of 1 in 5, was often impassable in the winter.

2 Rewrite each sentence in reported speech using the correct form of a word from the box.

accept	assure	plead
promise	threaten	wonder

1 'I'm asking you to forgive me,' he said to his wife.

2 'Will I ever be able to trust you again?' she said.

3 'I'll never let you down again.'

4 'I'll leave if you don't keep your word.'

5 'Don't worry – everything will be different from now on.'

6 'Well, I suppose you mean what you say.'

3 For each of the sentences below, write a new sentence as similar as possible in meaning to the original sentence, but using the word given. This word must not be altered in any way.

1 The only employment opportunities left for students are temporary jobs in factories. **bar**

....

2 The new college building was not expected to be ready for the beginning of term. **feared**

....

3 Your explanation of the matter is incompatible with the facts. **square**

....

4 It was obviously his intention to cause serious trouble. **bent**

....

5 It is clear that his departure resulted from the publication of the report. **cause**

....

6 People are saying that several ministers have been implicated in the scandal. **alleged**

....

7 The young man was promoted because he had performed excellently in the past. **track**

....

8 They reckon that fewer than half the students took part in the protest. **estimated**

....

4 Read the passages below. Decide where they may have been taken from and how they link with the general theme of the unit. In what ways do you think people can benefit from foreign travel?

1. *Travel companies aren't accountable enough for what they do – they're damaging environments and diluting cultures wherever they get their foot in the door. It's not entirely their fault – consumers should insist on such companies taking a more responsible attitude. The trouble is that people are not prepared to pay over the odds – they just want a cheap deal. If people didn't go, then the companies would think again – and that's what I'm trying to make people aware of with this campaign.*

2. My quest began in an insignificant place on a tributary one thousand miles up the River Amazon and ended in a city of a million people. Between the fears with which my journey started and the new, saddened understanding of my return to civilisation lies an experience of wilderness that was for me both exhilarating and unsettling. I wanted to examine people's relationship with the natural world; I chose the Amazon because it remains the greatest single expression of untamed nature on this planet.

UNIT

13 The price of success

Reading: literary text

1 Interview a partner using these questions.

1 What ambitions did you have when you were a young child?

2 Are they the same as your ambitions now? If not, what made them change?

2 The following extract is from a novel by Amy Tan, a Chinese-American whose parents emigrated to the USA from China when she was a child. In the novel, she writes about a girl in a similar situation to herself. You will find some examples of non-standard English in some of the direct and reported speech, reflecting the influence of the mother's Chinese background.

Read the text, and decide which one of the following is the mother's ambition for her daughter.

- to run a restaurant
- to own a home
- to achieve financial security
- to be well-known
- to be the best in whatever she does
- to be happy in her old age

Does her daughter share this ambition?

My mother believed you could be anything you wanted to be in America. You could open a restaurant. You could work for the government and get good retirement. You could buy a house with almost no money down. You could become rich. You could become instantly famous.

"Of course, you can be prodigy, too," my mother told me when I was nine. "You can be best anything."

In the beginning I was just as excited as my mother, maybe even more so. I pictured this prodigy part of me as many different images, trying each one on for size. I was a dainty ballerina girl standing by the curtains, waiting to hear the night music that would send me floating on my tiptoes. I was Cinderella* stepping from her pumpkin carriage with sparkly cartoon music filling the air.

In all of my imaginings, I was filled with a sense that I would soon become *perfect*. My mother and father would adore me. I would be beyond reproach. I would never feel the need to sulk for anything. But sometimes the prodigy in me became impatient. "If you don't hurry up and get me out of here, I'm disappearing for good," it warned.

"And then you'll always be nothing."

Every night after dinner, my mother and I would sit at the kitchen table. She would present new tests, taking her examples from stories of amazing children she had read in the magazines she kept in a pile in our bathroom. My mother got these from people whose houses she cleaned. And since she cleaned many houses each week, we had a great assortment. She would look through them all, searching for stories about remarkable children.

The first night she brought out a story about a three-year-old boy who knew the capitals of all the states and even most of the European countries. A teacher was quoted as saying the little boy could also pronounce the names of the foreign cities correctly.

"What's the capital of Finland?" my mother asked me, looking at the magazine story.

All I knew was the capital of California, because Sacramento was the name of the street we lived on in Chinatown. "Nairobi!" I guessed,

*a reference to a famous children's fairy story about a poor girl involving a fairy godmother, a glass slipper and a handsome prince

3 Read the text again and choose the best option, **A, B, C** or **D** to answer the questions or finish the statements.

1 At first, the girl felt the same way as her mother in that
A she wanted to stay in America.
B they shared the idea of unlimited opportunity.
C she wanted to achieve something special in life.
D they had many different ideas of what success was.

saying the most foreign word I could think of. She checked to see if that was possibly one way to pronounce "Helsinki" before showing me the answer.

The tests got harder – multiplying numbers in my head, finding the queen of hearts in a deck of cards, trying to stand on my head without using my hands, predicting the daily temperatures in Los Angeles, New York, and London.

One night I had to look at a page from the Bible for three minutes and then report everything I could remember. "Now Jehoshaphat had riches and honor in abundance and ... that's all I remember, Ma," I said.

And after seeing my mother's disappointed face once again, something inside of me began to die. I hated the tests, the raised hopes and unfulfilled expectations. Before going to bed that night, I looked in the mirror above the bathroom sink and when I saw only my face staring back – and that it would always be this ordinary face – I began to cry. Such a sad, ugly girl! I made high-pitched noises like a crazed animal, trying to scratch out the face in the mirror.

And then I saw what seemed to be the prodigy side of me – because I had never seen that face before. I looked at my reflection, blinking so I could see more clearly. The girl staring back at me was angry, powerful. This girl and I were the same. I had new thoughts, wilful thoughts, or rather thoughts filled with lots of won'ts. I won't let her change me, I promised myself. I won't be what I'm not.

So now on nights when my mother presented her tests, I performed listlessly, my head propped on one arm. I pretended to be bored. And I was. I got so bored I started counting the bellows of the foghorns out on the bay while my mother drilled me in other areas. The sound was comforting and reminded me of the cow jumping over the moon**. And the next day, I played a game with myself, seeing if my mother would give up on me before eight bellows. After a while I usually counted only one, maybe two bellows at most. At last she was beginning to give up hope.

**a reference to a children's nursery rhyme

2 Why did the mother give her daughter tests every night?
   A She found material for the tests in magazines.
   B She thought that success could be achieved by factual knowledge.
   C She wanted to improve her daughter's pronunciation.
   D She wanted to improve her daughter's knowledge of the world.

3 In the story about Nairobi, which of the following techniques does the writer use to make the point?
   A sarcasm
   B contrast
   C exaggeration
   D humour

4 The girl's attitude to the tests changed when she realised that
   A she would never come to the end of them.
   B they were of no real educational value.
   C they did not reflect her true potential.
   D she would never be beautiful because of them.

5 The girl began to show her boredom during the tests in order to
   A assert her own identity.
   B disobey her mother.
   C be able to play games instead of working.
   D concentrate on other things.

4 In the extract, we see how the daughter's attitude changes during the period of time described.

1 In what order does she experience the following emotions? Find evidence from the text to support your answer.

☐	disappointment and frustration
☐	rebellion
☐	determination to be herself
☐	optimism and excitement

2 Match the following words and phrases to each stage above and say what they mean in the context.

wilful	unfulfilled expectations
listlessly	beyond reproach
powerful	try something on for size

3 Use the following framework to describe the changes in the daughter's attitude to her mother. Write a word or phrase in each space.

The writer describes how the daughter's attitude gradually changes. At first the daughter is (1) .... because (2) .... Then her feelings change to (3) .... when (4) .... Eventually she decides (5) .... and she (6) ....

5 How do you think the situation described at the end of the extract could have been avoided? Think of some advice you could give to a) the mother b) the daughter.

6 How what ways have your family encouraged you to achieve your potential? In what ways have they left you free to make your own choices?

Listening: three-way choice

1 Work in pairs. What is your definition of success? Write a short definition that you can both agree on.

2 You will hear three successful people, Jonathan Fisher, Robin Green and Kate Roberts, talking about their own experience of success and how it has affected their lives. Each of the statements below reflects the opinion of **one** of the speakers.

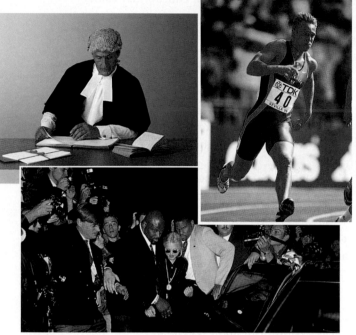

1 Before you listen, read through the statements to get an idea of the opinions given by the speakers. This is important as they will not be in the same order in the Listening.

1	I have mixed feelings about my success.	1
2	My parents gave me sympathetic support.	2
3	I feel my life is complicated.	3
4	I sometimes envy people who are not famous.	4
5	I would give up my success for personal happiness.	5
6	I feel my success carries great responsibility.	6
7	I regret my chosen career.	7
8	I like to be able to use my money to help others.	8
9	I need to maintain a good relationship with advertisers.	9
10	I have to deal with the negative side of fame.	10

 2 Now listen to the recording, and indicate which of the opinions are given by each speaker. You will hear the recording twice.

In each box write:

   J (Jonathan)
or **R** (Robin)
or **K** (Kate)

3 **Vocabulary:** idiomatic expressions
1 The idiomatic expressions in the box all come from the Listening text. Use them to rewrite the sentences below, making any other necessary changes.

> drum something into someone   eat away at
> rock the boat   a cut-throat world

1 I really don't want to upset the situation – everything's going so well.
2 The thought of the old man living there on his own was really worrying her.
3 International commerce and finance can be highly competitive and unfair.
4 I was always being told by my parents that I had to work hard.

2 The phrases in the box are all collocations from the Listening text. Use them to complete the sentences below, making any necessary changes.

> a lurid story   the down side   set for life
> a good cause   come at a price

1 I was shocked by the violent details of .... he told me.
2 I don't mind giving money to charity if it's for ....
3 Having problems with press intrusion is .... of being successful and famous.
4 Being wealthy and successful at an early age can mean that you are ....
5 Success isn't all positive – sometimes it ....

4 Discuss the following questions.

1 Look back at the definition of success you came up with in Exercise 1, and compare the speakers' ideas. Which speaker do you consider has actually been the most successful?
2 Which of the speakers do you feel most sympathetic towards? Why?
3 What do you think each of the speakers could do to improve their situation?

Grammar check: continuous and perfect aspect

1

1 Read the following conversation between two old friends who meet up at a wedding. Fill in the gaps using an appropriate form of the verb in brackets.

SARAH: Tony, hi!

TONY: Sarah – great to see you. I was hoping you'd be here.

SARAH: Yes. You (1) .... (look) really well.

TONY: Yes, you too. Anyway, what (2) .... (do) all this time? Are you still working with Red Lane Associates?

SARAH: No, I left them three years ago. I (3) .... (ask) them for a promotion for ages, and not getting anywhere, and then all of a sudden I got offered this job at Reever, and decided to go for it.

TONY: Oh, (4) .... (work) at Reever now? Do you like it?

SARAH: Yes, well I've got a lot more responsibility, and I certainly can't complain about the salary – but it doesn't leave much time for a life. And I (5) .... (do) a lot of travelling – I just got back from New York last night and I (6) .... (go) to Spain and Italy next week.

TONY: It (7) .... (sound) like a real jet-set life. I must say I (8) .... (envy) you.

SARAH: Oh, I don't know. Sometimes I (9) .... (think) it would be nice to settle down a bit. Anyway, how about you and Debbie? When I last saw you ...

TONY: ... goodness, it must be ten years ago. We'd just moved in – I remember Debbie and I (10) .... (decorate) the living room when you called in, and the heating (11) .... (not work) and the baby (12) .... (scream). It was chaos!

SARAH: Oh, yes, I remember – but it was a lovely house – do you still live there?

TONY: Yes, and I (13) .... (still work) for Debbie's father. In fact, if everything goes well I (14) .... (take over) the firm in the next few years when he retires.

SARAH: Well I'm glad it's all worked out so well for you ...

 2 Now listen to the conversation and compare your answers. Make a note of any differences between your answers and those on the recording. Remember that your answer may also be possible even if it's different.

3 Read through the conversation again. For each verb form 1–14, decide the following:

1 Is it possible **in this context** to use a different verb form, e.g. simple instead of continuous, or vice versa?
2 If so, what effect does the change of form have?
3 If not, why not?

For example, for gap 1 there are two correct possibilities. What's the difference, if any?
  You *look / are looking* really well.

For gap 2, why is it not possible in this context to say:
  So what *have you done* all this time?

4 Now match the tense forms and the definitions.

1 Simple tenses   a) describe events in relation to a later event or point in time.

2 Continuous forms   b) describe activities in progress and therefore suggest the activity is temporary and may not be complete.

3 Perfect forms   c) describe states, single events and habits.

5 Complete the following definitions with the correct terms, **event** verbs or **state** verbs.

1 .... refer to activities and situations that may not have a definite beginning or end, e.g. *be, have, know,* and are not commonly used in the continuous form.

2 .... refer to activities with a definite beginning and end, e.g. *ask, leave, offer,* and may be used in the simple or continuous form.

▶ Grammar reference pp. 214-215

2 Discuss these questions.

1 In what ways do you think Sarah and Tony's lives have been successful?
2 Whose life would you choose to have, Tony's or Sarah's?

3 Read the information in the box, then do the exercise below.

> Some **state verbs** may be used in the continuous form to refer to a **single action** or a **temporary event**, e.g.:
> *I feel nervous about flying.* (= in general)
> *I'm feeling nervous about flying to New York.* (= a specific occasion)
> In some cases, the use of the continuous form changes the meaning of the verb, e.g.:
> *I saw a lot of interesting places on my trip.* (see = with one's eyes)
> *John has been seeing a lot of Mary recently.* (see = meet, go out with)

Both sentences in the following pairs are possible. For each pair, decide whether the verb has the same or a different meaning. If the meaning of the verb is the same, what is the effect of using simple or continuous forms?

1 a) I have a lot of friends in Australia.
   b) I'm having some friends round for dinner at the weekend.
2 a) I think it would be nice to settle down.
   b) I'm thinking about settling down.
3 a) The bus driver was very patient.
   b) The tour guides were being very patient.
4 a) I'm feeling really hungry – let's stop and eat.
   b) I feel it's important to do your very best.
5 a) Did you want to see me?
   b) Were you wanting to see the manager?
6 a) John can't hear very well – you'll have to speak up.
   b) I hear you've been getting up to your old tricks again.
7 a) I'm hoping to get home by Sunday.
   b) I hope to arrive before dark.
8 a) Our tickets cost an arm and a leg.
   b) The whole holiday was costing an arm and a leg.
9 a) I imagine you must be tired.
   b) Thank goodness you're safe – I've been imagining all sorts of terrible things.
10 a) That food tastes a bit salty.
   b) I'm just tasting the pudding to see if it needs more sugar.

4 **Use of English:** gapped sentences
Fill each of the blanks with a suitable word or phrase.

1 That perfume .... a bit sickly to me – I'd prefer something lighter.

2 I don't know who this book .... – there's no name inside.
3 I wonder if anything's going on between Mark and Annie – they .... a lot of one another lately.
4 Fortunately, the stolen wallet .... much money, but he was still annoyed at himself for being so careless.
5 If you .... anything else tonight I wonder if you'd mind babysitting for us?
6 She says she .... about doing a course in computer technology.
7 Many people think it would be nice to be a successful public figure, but actually I .... with them – I'd not change places for the world.
8 What on earth can he .... of – he should have known it wouldn't work.

5 **Simulation**
1 It is the year 2012. To find out what has happened in your life in the last few years, follow the instructions below.

1 Write **one** letter of the alphabet in the circle.

2 Choose a number between 1–5 and write it in the box.

3 Think of two countries (not your own) and write their names on the lines.   ....
....

4 Circle **one** of these letters.

P
M E

2 Now work with a partner.

Student A should look at page 221.
Student B should look at page 223.
When you are ready, roleplay the conversation you have when you meet at a friend's wedding in 2012. Ask and answer questions to find out what you've both been doing over the last few years.

Vocabulary: phrasal verbs and idiomatic expressions

1 Phrasal verbs with get and go

1 Read through the following sentences. Then choose phrasal verbs from the box below to replace the phrases in italics. Be careful: you may need to change the form of the other words, or add a word.

1 Oscar studied law and *passed* the final exams with flying colours.
2 After he graduated, he *applied for* a variety of jobs and soon found one he liked.
3 After he found his feet, he *concentrated on* making as much money as possible.
4 His money-making schemes became so complex that he never *had enough time* to develop a social life.
5 Then he met a girl who persuaded him to *take part in* high-risk sports such as parachuting and mountain climbing.
6 Oscar became so keen to succeed in these activities that he didn't do his work properly, but he *wasn't found out* because he did enough to keep the business going.
7 He became so successful as a climber that he gave up his business and *managed to make enough of a living from* the money he earned writing about his exploits.
8 He was asked whether he was happier now than when he was making a lot of money. 'Of course,' he replied, 'there's more to life than just *being successful* financially.'

> get on   go ahead with   get through   go in for
> get away with something   get by   go for
> get down to   go into   get round to

2 Read the story again. Do you agree with Oscar's changed attitude to success?

3 Look at the phrasal verbs you didn't use. Write a sentence about your own ambitions using each one.

2 Idioms with get and go

1 Read the following text. Then replace the words in italics with an idiom from the box. You may need to make other changes.

> get up and go   get your act together
> getting nowhere/somewhere
> go one better than ...   go for it
> go all out for something/to do something
> go it alone   have a go at something

I've always believed there's only one way to achieve success: you've just got to (1) *put all your effort into* it. Even if you seem to be (2) *making no progress whatsoever*, you have to (3) *strive to get what you want*. You may find you've got no-one to lend a helping hand, you may have to (4) *struggle without help*, but if you can (5) *achieve more than* the rest, then you'll make it to the top.

2 What difference have these changes made to the style of the passage?

3 Look at the expressions you didn't use. What do they mean? Write a sentence including each of them.

4 Do you agree that it is always possible to achieve success by individual effort?

3 Use of English: key word transformations
For each of the sentences below, write a new sentence as similar as possible in meaning to the original sentence, but using the word given. This word must not be altered in any way.

1 The sports day was so well-organised that there were no problems at all.
hitch

....

2 This group of trainees is showing great promise and I'm sure they'll all be very successful.
far

....

3 Paul didn't let us down and managed to get us tickets for the show.
trumps

....

4 If you try this new software it should solve the problem.
trick

....

5 In the 1980s the pop music video industry really started to become successful.
off

....

6 Nina will never be good enough to be a professional tennis player.
grade

....

7 Against all expectations, the team won a great victory.
pulled

....

Use of English: cloze

1 Look at the picture and discuss these questions.

1 How is the man feeling?
2 What kind of sacrifices do you think he might have had to make to achieve his success?

2 The following passage is by Roger Black, a British athlete who won both team and individual Olympic medals. First, read the text through to get a general idea of its content, then fill in each of the numbered blanks with one suitable word. Finally, read it again to make sure your answers make sense.

The meaning of success

Success is a balancing act, but in the end it is very simple. It comes if you focus (1) .... what you can control and you don't put (2) .... under the pressure of worrying (3) .... what everybody else does. Another man (4) .... beat you in a race, but he cannot (5) .... away from you your own personal (6) .... of achievement. You can control that. Many people feel 'I've got to win, I've got to win. If I don't win it's not (7) .... doing.' But only one person is going to win. (8) .... winning is everything to you, then you are going to (9) .... disappointed. But you can always be a winner (10) .... saying, 'I ran my perfect race', because rules for your success are not (11) .... on a gold medal.

In March 1996 I was looking (12) .... Ana art gallery during one of my training visits to California. It had been at the (13) .... of my mind to see if I could chance upon any inspiration in (14) .... was an Olympic year, when I was drawn to a magnificent sculpture of a gymnast hanging on a point of sublime balance on a pommel horse*. (15) .... I read the notes on this sculpture I was thrilled to discover that (16) .... was a small-scale copy of the official Atlantic Olympic sculpture (17) .... had stood outside the city's Georgia Dome. The artist had (18) .... inspired by an Olympic motto I had never heard of until then: The essence lies not in the victory but in the struggle. The (19) .... I thought about it the better it got. This phrase summed up my entire career. To me the message is that there is no (20) .... in achieving any goal if you have not learned from, or enjoyed the journey. I bought the sculpture.

*a piece of gymnastic equipment with two handles on top which you hold on to and jump over

3 Discuss these questions.

1 Compare the writer's attitude towards success with others you have discussed in this unit.
2 The writer found inspiration in a sculpture. Discuss any objects, ideas, or people that have inspired you personally, and explain why they were important to you.

Grammar plus: clauses of concession

1 Read the information in the box, then do the exercises that follow.

Clauses of concession can be introduced by:

1 the conjunctions *although, even though, while, whilst* (formal), *whereas*, e.g.:
   *She carried on training, **even though** she had little hope of winning the race.*
   Note: *may* is often used in clauses of concession to express possibility, e.g.:
   *While some people **may** disagree, I feel the plan is basically sound.*

2 *whatever, whoever, however, whichever, wherever*, e.g.:
   ***However** hard I try, I just can't find the answer.*
   ***Whatever** I asked for, I was immediately given.*

3 *no matter what / who / how / which / where*, e.g.:
   ***No matter what** you do, you'll never manage on your own.*

4 *much as* (= *although*) + verb, e.g.:
   ***Much as I like him**, I don't feel he is the right person for this job.*

5 adverb / adjective + *as / though* + subject + verb, e.g. :
   ***Strange as it may seem**, I let him overtake me and win the race.*
   ***Hard though it was**, I struggled on.*
   ***Talented though he may be**, he does not have the determination to win.*

6 intensifying expressions with the linkers *and yet / but still*, e.g.:
   *It was a warm day, **and yet** she was shivering.*
   *He'd been warned many times, **but still** he continued to misbehave.*

7 *even so / all the same*, e.g.:
   *It was almost impossible. **Even so**, she decided to try.*

8 the prepositions *despite, in spite of*.
   Note that these must be followed by a noun or an *-ing* form, e.g.:
   ***In spite of the fact** that she knew the answer, she refused to reply.*
   ***Despite having** lost the last match, he rallied and went on to win the next three.*

2   Use of English: key word transformations

For each of the sentences below, write a new sentence as similar as possible in meaning to the original sentence, but using the word given. This word must not be altered in any way.

1   Another job may pay better, but it will not offer you the same satisfaction. **while**

....

2   It doesn't matter who you ask, you'll always get the same answer. **whoever**

....

3   You'll never find a better place to spend a holiday, wherever you go. **matter**

....

4   Although she'd met him several times before, she still couldn't remember his name. **yet**

....

5   There were reports of severe traffic jams, but in spite of this they decided to set out. **same**

....

6   She got the job even though she had no qualifications. **fact**

....

7   I like him a lot, but I don't want to marry him. **as**

....

8   In spite of all her efforts, she didn't manage to get there on time. **even**

....

3   Use of English: sentence transformations

Finish each of the following sentences so that it is as similar as possible in meaning to the sentence printed before it.

1   It doesn't make any difference which number you choose – you'll still win a prize.
    Whichever ....

2   He couldn't see a way of getting round the problem, however hard he tried.
    No ....

3   I don't think the article should be published, although I admit it's interesting.
    Interesting ....

4   He offered to make a speech, although he did not have much self-confidence.
    Despite his ....

5   It was a difficult choice, but I had to make it.
    Difficult ....

6   In spite of the tight deadline, they managed to complete the project on schedule.
    Even though ....

Listening: multiple-choice questions

1

1   Look at the situations below. In which situation do you think mental attitude might play the greatest part in succeeding or failing?

2   Discuss the following questions.

1   Have you ever been afraid of failing?
2   What caused this fear?
3   How did it affect you?
4   Did you overcome it? How?

2   You will hear a speech being made to a group of school-leavers by a businessman as part of a general careers programme. Listen and indicate the most appropriate response, **A, B, C** or **D**.

1   The speaker feels that being successful
    A   is a similar feeling for everyone.
    B   involves making money.
    C   is a great accomplishment.
    D   is less important to some people.

2   The speaker describes the fear of failure as
    A   the way to accept coming second.
    B   the way to get to school on time.
    C   an advantage and a disadvantage.
    D   very important in sporting situations.

3 The reason that people make excuses for not taking chances is
   A they don't have enough time.
   B they lack confidence in their own ability.
   C they have tried as hard as they could.
   D they need support from their family.

4 The speaker's advice for managing the fear of failure is to
   A face the problem.
   B plan for the worst.
   C ask your friends questions.
   D strengthen yourself physically.

5 The speaker feels that the fear of success is a bigger problem because
   A success is hard to handle.
   B you may fail.
   C you may be jealous.
   D success is unknown.

6 The speaker's advice for managing the fear of success is
   A to accept greater responsibility.
   B to make different friends.
   C to accept the benefits of success.
   D to think about the future carefully.

7 The speaker's attitude towards his own life is that he has
   A missed opportunities.
   B accepted extra responsibility.
   C been very lucky.
   D enjoyed his success.

3

1 Match the verbs and nouns to form phrases connected with achieving success.

1	play	a)	a chance
2	take	b)	in glory
3	set	c)	your mark
4	seize	d)	results
5	handle	e)	an aim
6	bask	f)	it safe
7	make	g)	something well
8	accomplish	h)	yourself a target
9	get	i)	an opportunity

2 Can you think of a time when you or someone you know did three of the things in the list above? Tell a partner what happened in each case.

Exam Focus
Paper 5 Speaking (complete interview)

The interview in Paper 5 lasts about 15 minutes for an individual candidate, about 20 minutes for paired candidates and about 25 minutes for a group of three. The test has three parts. All three parts are on the same general theme. You are assessed on your fluency, grammatical accuracy, range of vocabulary, pronunciation and interactive communication.

In **Part 1** you talk about one or more photographs.
In **Part 2** you talk about a short extract.
In **Part 3** you take part in a communicative activity.

In all three parts of the interview it is important that you take the lead in the conversation; don't just wait for the examiner to ask you questions. If you are taking the exam in a pair or a group, it is important to interact together, although you will be marked on your own performance.

Part 1

1 Work in pairs. Choose one of the photos opposite and take turns to talk about your photo for a couple of minutes. While **Student A** speaks, **Student B** should listen. B can prompt with a question if A seems to be running out of ideas! Follow the stages below. Then swap roles.

1 Briefly describe what you can see in the photo.

2 Link the photo to your own experience – maybe you know someone who has been successful in this area, or you have ambitions yourself.

3 Broaden the topic by talking about:
   a) what kind of success the photo illustrates.
   b) how easy this might be to achieve.
   c) what advantages and disadvantages this success might bring.
   d) which type of success you think would be:
   • the most difficult to achieve
   • the most satisfying
   • the least interesting
   • the one you would most like to achieve.

 2 Now listen to an English student talking about one of the photos.

1 Were her ideas the same as yours?

2 There are useful phrases you can use when discussing the photo. Listen again and note down the phrases the student uses:

1 when describing the photo.
2 when relating it to her own experience.
3 when moving on to a wider discussion of the theme.

3 For further practice, turn to the photos on page 221.

Photographs

1.

2.

Part 2

In the second part of the interview you have to read a short extract silently, then comment on its style, origin and content. You should read the text quickly for the main idea – remember that it relates to the theme of the photo. Don't worry if there are words you don't understand, as you only need to discuss the passage in general terms.

1 In the exam you have to make your decision about style and source quickly. Here is a checklist of questions to ask yourself.

1   Is it written or spoken?
2   Is it formal or informal in style?
3   Where might it come from?
4   What's it about?

Look at the following passage. In pairs, discuss the questions above.

1. David Hempleman-Adams became the first person to complete the so-called Grand Slam, eleven death-defying feats of strength, stamina and skill involving climbing the world's highest mountains on each continent and journeys to the four poles, magnetic and geographic. He doesn't like a fuss being made over his achievements: 'I've always been a believer that if you want to do something don't bitch about it, just go and do it! If you fail, well at least you tried.'

 2 Now listen to the English student talking about the same passage. Were her ideas the same as yours?

 3 Listen again and tick the phrases the student uses when discussing the passage. What reason does she give for her ideas in each case?

1   Well, I think this is probably written/spoken because ...
2   It could be written/spoken as there are ...
3   It's clearly written/spoken because ...
4   It must be formal/informal because of words like ...
5   It seems to be formal/informal because ...
6   It could be from ...
7   I think it's an extract from ... because ...
8   It looks like ... because ...
9   It's about ...
10 It talks about ...

4 Work in pairs.

1 **Student A**: You have a few seconds to read passage 2. When the examiner asks you about the passage, answer in as much detail as possible and try to use some of the phrases from Exercise 3.

Student B: You are the examiner. Give Student A a few seconds to read passage 2 and then ask the examiner's questions on page 221.

2 Now swap roles. **Student B** reads passage 3, **Student A** asks the examiner's questions.

Passages

2. *Richard Noble took the land-speed record after being obsessed with speed since childhood. He thrives under pressure. He explained: 'I was trying to carve my own identity. I guess it's an ego thing. The old land-speed record bug was emerging and there comes a point where you have to just go and do it. You see, life to me is all about competition, that's what breeds success.'*

3. We learn from our mistakes much more than our successes. They give us useful feedback, and we spend a lot more time thinking about them. We rarely get something right the first time, unless it is very simple, and even then there will be room for improvement. We learn by a series of successive approximations. We use this as feedback to act again and reduce the difference between what we want and what we are getting. Slowly we approach our goal.

Part 3

In the third part of the interview you have to discuss a topic with the examiner, or with the other candidate. You may be given statements to react to, or a situation to discuss, and the examiner may ask you additional questions. You need to have plenty to say about the topic and to maintain a good flow of language. If you run out of ideas, then try to relate the subject to your own experience.

1 Here are some useful phrases you can use in the discussion to keep up the conversation while you are thinking of ideas.

> Well, I'm not sure what I think about that ...
> What I really wanted to say was ...
> It seems to me that one of the important things here is ...
> Well that might be true, but ...
> That's an important point ...

Listen to the English student discussing the statement below. You will hear short extracts from the conversation. As you listen, mark which of the phrases above they use.

'Being successful isn't worth it – it's too much like hard work.'

2 Work in pairs.

1 **Student A**: You have a few seconds to read Task 1 below. When the examiner asks you to discuss the task, answer in as much detail as possible and try to use some of the phrases in the list above.

Student B: You are the examiner. Give Student A a few seconds to read the task and then ask the examiner's questions on page 221.

1. Discussion

Look at the two statements below.

> *'I don't care whether I make any money or not – I just want to be happy'.*

> *'I have to be number one – if I don't make it, then it just drives me on to try harder.'*

Discuss the two different attitudes to success.

2 Now swap roles. **Student B** reads Task 2, **Student A** asks the examiner's questions on page 222.

2. Ranking

Look at the list of qualities below. Which four do you think are most important for achieving success? Rank them in order from the most important to the least important.

- ambition
- ruthlessness
- enthusiasm
- energy

- sense of humour
- intelligence
- ability to work hard
- luck

Writing: newspaper article

In Unit 12 you practised writing a magazine article. In this section you will write an article for a newspaper.

1   Read the following writing task.

> Look at the newspaper headlines below. Choose any one as your main headline and write the newspaper article, using the information in the other headlines to guide you. (About 300 words.)
>
> **Businesswoman of the Year named**
>
> Woman succeeds in overcoming all the odds
>
> *Company is roaring success. 'I owe it all to family support' claims businesswoman*
>
> **Future looks rosy for company**

Discuss which headline you think would make the best main headline for the task.

2   What are the main features of a newspaper article? Choose from the following.

- gives the writer's own opinions
- may include direct speech
- makes recommendations
- concentrates on the facts

3

1   Read the newspaper article, which was written in answer to the task. Which headline would you give it?

2   Some of the sentences in the article give unnecessary information, or are written in an inappropriate style for a newspaper. Some sentences may be both irrelevant and in the wrong style. Find the inappropriate sentences and cross them out.

3   Compare your answers with other students. Which of the sentences you crossed out:

a)   gave unnecessary information?
b)   used informal vocabulary or was too personal in style?

Some sentences may do both a) and b).

Susan James was named Businesswoman of the Year at a dinner in the Commerce Union building last night. I had not expected her to win, but it was a really nice surprise. In winning the award, she had beaten long-established businessmen and well-known entrepreneurs. Her rise to the top has been meteoric, although she has worked hard for her success. She was born on a small farm in the heart of the country in 1960. She loved the farm and often helped her father with the cows. She attended the local school where she was a popular student. In fact I knew and liked her. Her academic record at school was exemplary, and she was awarded several prizes for outstanding achievement. She was dead smart, and she always got amazing grades. She went straight into business without going to university, as her parents could not afford to send her to college. After joining the company, she worked her way up through the ranks until she took over as Managing Director last year. Friends described her poor upbringing and her struggle against the odds. 'It has been a privilege to work with her,' one said. She has a lot of friends, and a lovely house in the south of the city which she has bought with her large salary. Susan herself was modest about her achievements. 'I couldn't have done it without my family behind me – they've been fantastic,' she declared. When asked about the future of the company, she was upbeat. 'The sky's the limit,' she said. She is obviously a good role model, and I strongly recommend that everyone should try to follow her good example.

4 News articles are usually divided into several quite short paragraphs.

1 Look back at the article on page 187. Mark with a slash where you think a new paragraph should start. The article should have five paragraphs altogether.

2 Each paragraph has one main idea, listed below. Number them in the order in which they appear.

- ☐ Background information on Susan
- ☐ Reason for the article
- ☐ The future
- ☐ Reactions of friends
- ☐ Reasons for her success

5

1 The notes below were made by a journalist researching an article. Compare them with the final article he then wrote (on the right), and answer the following questions.

1 What did the journalist leave out of the final article? Why?
2 What changes did he make to the language he used in the notes? Why?

> Sat 15th – Green Centre, Thorley – high-up Scouting award – Silver Acorn – "Not many people get it" (Joe)
> Joe Reynolds (75) – "I'm very pleased about it because it's quite a rare award in this area. I was quite overjoyed." Mrs Reynolds "I'm very proud." Married, 2 children, 3 grandchildren, ex-lift engineer, (retired at 60) – now mans Scout Shop/ badge secretary. Lives locally.
> Enjoys football, bowls, camping – great guy – bit of a practical joker – I liked him.

2 The article follows a typical pattern of organisation and structure. Number the parts in the order in which they appear.

- ☐ background information to key event
- ☐ key event/reason for article
- ☐ quote from key person
- ☐ summary of situation

Rare award for Scouting

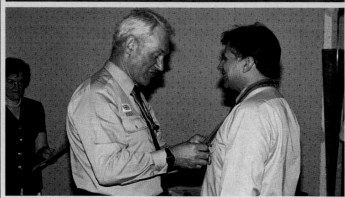

A PRESTIGIOUS scouting award was handed out to Joseph Reynolds on Saturday night at the Green Centre, Thorley.

Joe Reynolds (75), who is the district badge secretary, was given the Silver Acorn in recognition of his 34 years of service to scouting.

Mr Reynolds began his scouting career as Scout Leader and then became Assistant District Commissioner.

When he retired as a lift engineer at the age of 60, he moved into his present post of running the district Scout Shop and took over as badge secretary for the local district groups.

"I'm very pleased about it because it's quite a rare award in this area. Not many people get it. I was quite overjoyed," he said.

3 What other information do you think would have been appropriate for the article? Select from the list below and give your reasons.

- details about the presentation evening
- more information about Mr Reynold's scouting activities
- description of the scouting organisations

6 Read the following writing task.

> A local celebrity has announced his/her retirement and has been given an award in recognition of his/her achievements. Write the article that appeared in the local newspaper on this occasion. (About 300 words.)

1 Decide what type of celebrity you will write about, and make some notes on the background information you want to include.

2 Plan your article using the organisational structure you identified in Exercise 5.

7 Write the article in 300 words. When you have finished, check and edit your work carefully.

► Exam Maximiser

1 Complete the following sentences by writing **one** word in each of the spaces.

1 Jealousy of his sister's success .... away at him, destroying his peace of mind.
2 He plans to gatecrash the party but I doubt whether he'll get .... with it.
3 I have somewhat mixed .... about the proposed scheme as I'm unsure whether the benefits will outweigh the disadvantages.
4 The school .... success as passing exams, whereas my parents were more concerned with how much I might earn.
5 No-one protested when my mother explained her plan, for fear of .... the boat when the future of the family business was so uncertain.
6 The team were reminded that while representing their country abroad, their conduct should at all times be beyond ....
7 It's as much as I can do to finish my own work, ... doing yours every evening as well.
8 I'd never have wanted to be famous if I'd realised how much I'd have to .... up in my personal life.
9 We discovered Jane had changed from a little girl, eager to please, into a .... teenager, determined to have her own way.
10 Why are you always finding .... with everything I try to do?

2 Six of the following sentences contain an inappropriate verb form. Find the errors and correct them.

1 I had considered whether to apply for university until I heard about the new training scheme.
2 You are very stubborn about this – we'll all suffer if you don't change your mind!
3 They're always changing the timetable at the last moment – it shouldn't be allowed.
4 I've tried to contact you for days. Where have you been?
5 They were expecting to see her at the airport but she didn't turn up.
6 It was a dreadful hotel. The dining room was dirty and the bedrooms were stinking of smoke.
7 You can't be feeling hungry already. You've only just had lunch.
8 He was working all evening and just wasn't noticing how the time passed.
9 The girls are supposed to have revised for their exams this weekend, but judging by the giggling, I don't think they've done much yet.

3 Choose the word or phrase which best completes each sentence.

1 It's no good .... just because you haven't got your own way for once.
   A spoiling **B** scorning **C** sulking **D** spurning
2 Even when I thought it was hopeless, my trainer never gave up .... me.
   A over **B** with **C** for **D** on
3 The cinema audience emerged .... into the bright sunshine.
   A blinking **B** winking **C** peeping **D** peering
4 Zoe .... a great deal of responsibility for someone so young.
   A wears **B** carries **C** holds **D** wields
5 Marcus works so hard, everyone agrees he deserves to .... it to the top of his profession.
   A do **B** push **C** make **D** get
6 My grandmother had wanted to attend university, but her father had refused to .... such a move.
   A agree **B** consent **C** entertain **D** countenance

4 Talk about the photo.

1 Describe the photo and the situation. How are the people feeling?
2 How does the photo relate to the topic of the unit?
3 What do you think are the easiest and most difficult things about being successful? What advice would you give to those who did not come first?

UNIT
14 Is culture doomed?

Speaking: discussion

1 Read the following statement and discuss the question below.

'Books, art and music all contribute to the development of individual members of society'

What do you think individuals can gain from:

- reading books?
- looking at art?
- listening to music/playing music?

Think of three benefits of each.

2

1 Discuss how important the following are in your own life. Answer the questions below.

- music
- dancing
- film
- theatre
- poetry

Why are they important to you?
How are you involved in them?
Do you take an active part in any of them?

2 Choose two of the areas listed. Work out three arguments to persuade others to become involved in them.

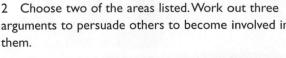

Use of English: comprehension and summary

1

1 Look at the title of the passage. What arguments do you think the writer might use to answer the question?

2 Now read the passage quickly to see if your ideas were included.

Will our children read books?

Before describing the hierarchy of the arts in the 21st century, it is sensible and sobering to recall the pundits' forecast for the 20th century. The headline stories were the rise of cinema and then television. And these successes, it was assumed, would
5 mean failure for older forms of entertainment and information. Since the 1950s, commentators have regularly predicted that these two new visual giants would eventually destroy theatre, radio, newspapers and books by taking over the functions of these earlier forms or eroding the time
10 available for enjoying them.

In fact, despite the advent of multi-channel, 24-hour TV and multi-screen movie theatres, it can be said that only two cultural forms have died in the past 100 years – music hall and the letter – and the second of these was killed, not by television
15 but by the telephone, before, in the strange way of these things, being somewhat restored by the inventions of the fax machine and email. So the cultural story of the 20th century – an epoch of electronic invention and mechanical radicalism – has unexpectedly been that of the durability of traditional and
20 particularly printed forms.

Looking forward then, we should be aware of pessimism's poor record. The book, for example, seems as obvious a candidate for redundancy now as it has since the middle of the 20th century. Where people previously assumed that tele-
25 literacy would finish reading, they now point to computer literacy as the executioner. Yet the book, to an extraordinary degree, has learned to coexist with its visual rivals.

Most Hollywood projects derive from novels: often trashy ones, it is true, but also the classics. And not only do movies
30 and television series descend from books, but, almost

35 routinely, they return to them as nearly every screen product has its tie-in book. It all suggests that the desire of the viewer to follow the visual experience with a print experience is even more tenacious than ever.
40 The threat to the conventional book in the 21st century is, though, subtly different. Where the first challengers were alternatives to reading, the current ones are alternative ways of reading: CD rom, computer disc, the Internet, recorded books. The smart money would bet that the standard home or
45 library reference book is going the way of D for Dodo, simply because the new technology can make information more visually appealing. But, with regard to fiction, it seems a reasonable assumption that the portability of the standard book and the aesthetic affection that established readers
50 still have for it as a product will confound pessimism in the future.

In fact, the arts most vulnerable to change, at least in Britain, are television and theatre. This is because both depend on state subsidy: a political idea which must be regarded as
55 highly unlikely to see out the next century. The effect of this will be the increased commercialism of both television and theatre. The casualties will be new theatre writing, the riskier classical repertoire and high-quality television journalism and drama for a general audience, although the last two of these
60 may survive on cable subscription to the middle classes. The rise of television in the 20th century may not, as feared, have killed the book, but the continuing rise of popular television through the 21st century will kill high quality television programming.
65 Clearly the twentieth century was startling both for the emergence of three new mass cultural pursuits – television, cinema and computers – and for the survival of the existing ones. This then is the big question for the 21st century. Do we now have our full cultural hand? Might it expand further? Or
70 will there be a showdown between the old and the new? And will our children no longer read books?

2 Read the passage on page 191 again and answer the questions which follow.

1 Explain in your own words what factors could bring about change to 'older forms of entertainment and information'? (line 5)

2 Explain the meaning of 'advent' in this context. (line 11)

3 What was the unexpected effect of the fax machine and e-mail?

4 What point is the writer making when he mentions the durability of printed forms of communication?

5 How have assumptions about what might discourage people from reading changed?

6 Explain in your own words the way in which films are actually encouraging people to read.

7 Explain the writer's use of 'tenacious' in line 39.

8 Explain in your own words how the threat to books in the 21st century is seen as different from the 20th century.

9 What is the writer's view about the future of books of fiction, and why?

10 How does their dependence on state subsidy affect the future of television and theatre in Britain?

11 What does 'this' refer to in line 55?

12 Explain what the writer feels is the big question for the 21st century.

13 In a paragraph of 70–90 words, explain why pessimists thought people would stop reading books, and why, according to the writer, books have survived.

For the summary, follow this procedure.

1 Look back through the whole text and find:
   • two reasons why pessimists thought that people might stop reading
   • three reasons the writer puts forward for why books have survived.

2 Note these reasons down briefly in your own words.

3 Use your notes to complete the task.

4 Check and edit your summary.

See Exam Focus Units 2 and 8 for help with general techniques in summary writing.

3 How would **you** answer the question 'Will our children read books?'

Grammar check: comparison

1 Read the information about ways of making comparisons and expressing preferences, then do the exercises that follow.

• We can use the following structures to say that things are **similar to** or **different from** each other.

1 *as* + adj/adv + *as* / *not as/so* + adj/adv + *as*
Books seem to be just **as popular** now **as** they were in the past.
The effect of TV has not been anything like **as/so** detrimental to reading habits **as** once feared.

2 *as* + adj + *a/an* + noun + *as*
The book seems **as obvious a candidate** for redundancy now **as** it has since the middle of the 20th century.

3 *such* + *a/an* + noun + *as*
This structure is mainly used in negative sentences.
Compare the position of the article *a/an* with the examples in Point 2 above.
The rise of cinema and TV has not had **such a** negative **effect** on the book **as** some people predicted.

4 *as* + clause
In comparisons, *as* is a conjunction introducing a clause.
Commentators believed that cinema and TV would destroy books, **as** many writers also feared.
Inversion can be used with an auxiliary verb, e.g.:
A good proportion of TV series are based on novels, **as are many films**.

• We can use the following structures to express preferences.
I much **prefer** playing music **to** doing sport.
I'd **much/far sooner** read a good book **than** go to the cinema.
TV producers should concentrate on quality **rather than** quantity.
Rather than watching sport on TV, I'd much prefer to go to a real game any day.

---

2 Rewrite the following sentences using an appropriate phrase from the box.

as ... a ... as	as did	such a ... as
a good deal	sooner	rather than
nowhere near as ... as		nothing like as ... an ... as

1 The original version of the film was superior in every way to the new version.
The new version of the film is ....

2 The first time I went I had a better time than I did on the second visit.
I didn't have ....

3 I always go to the theatre in preference to seeing a film.
I'd ....

4   The critics predicted the musical would be a big
     hit, but in fact it didn't do very well.
     The musical wasn't ....

5   I had the same high opinion of the book as many
     other critics.
     I thought the book ....

6   I prefer to read than watch television.
     My preference ....

7   I can find the solution much more easily if you
     help me.
     The solution will be ....

8   His father was a much better artist than him.
     He is ....

3   Using structures from Exercises 1 and 2, and other
comparative structures you know, compare the following:

1   letters/radio/TV/computers as media of
     communication today
2   the importance of reading to children and young
     people now with its importance before TV
3   the relative benefits to society of subsidising
     Information Technology versus the arts

Vocabulary: multiple-choice questions

1   The following sentences form a complete text
about recent research into the popularity of reading.
Choose the word or phrase which best completes each
sentence.

1   .... a recent research study, children nowadays
     are growing up in a youth culture that regards
     books as boring and old-fashioned.
     A Owing to   **B** Due to   **C** According to
     D Referring to

2   This study claims that children only .... fifteen
     minutes a day reading.
     A pass   **B** take   **C** use   **D** spend

3   Apparently, most children are .... to the
     television or computer screen during their leisure
     time.
     A glued   **B** fixed   **C** adhered   **D** attached

4   However, this particular study is totally ....
     other research.
     A in favour of   **B** in line with   **C** at odds with
     D by contrast to

5   All .... evidence indicates that in fact we are all
     reading more than ever before – and this is
     particularly true of children.
     A available   **B** present   **C** positive   **D** accessible

6   This increase in reading is partly .... the very
     technology that has been accused of destroying the
     desire to read.
     A because   **B** due to   **C** as to   **D** out of

7   Using the Internet stimulates children's desire to
     find out more about things they .... there, and
     the cheapest and quickest way for them to do this
     is by reading books.
     A come over   **B** come to   **C** come across
     D come through

8   This theory is backed up by solid, reliable
     research – .... the actual statistical evidence,
     which shows an ever-increasing number of
     children's books being sold each year.
     A not to say   **B** not to mention
     C not to account for   **D** not to include

9   .... it is certainly true that more children have
     televisions and computers in their bedrooms, the
     evidence proves that they are also reading more
     books than ever before.
     A While   **B** When   **C** Since   **D** Nevertheless

10 It therefore seems clear that .... than lowering
     standards of literacy, computers and television have
     actually contributed to raising them.
     A other   **B** sooner   **C** better   **D** rather

11 It is true that reading is not considered a
     fashionable pastime by children, who try to ....
     their enjoyment of books in case they are seen as
     'soft'.
     A bottle up   **B** cover up   **C** blot out   **D** put away

12 Nevertheless, the .... facts are that book sales
     are soaring and bookshops are going from strength
     to strength.
     A indiscernible   **B** indisputable   **C** uncertain
     D positive

2   In the light of what you have read and talked about
in this unit so far, discuss the two statements below and
decide which you agree with.

'The development of technology and mass media has
given young people today a far greater awareness and
understanding of culture than their parents.'

'People spend so much more time nowadays involved in
passive leisure pursuits such as watching television and
playing computer games that they have far less interest in
cultural activities than their parents and grandparents.'

Listening: sentence completion

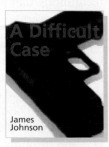

1 Look at the book covers and discuss the following questions.

1 What do you think each book might be about?
2 Which would you prefer to read? Why?

 2 You will hear two writers discussing what they think makes a good novel. Listen and complete the sentences with a word or short phrase. Make sure that the words you add are grammatically correct. You will hear the recording twice.

According to James, novels that are gripping tend to be less
....(1).

Susan feels that novels should contribute towards a
....(2) of life.

Susan's book is both ....(3).

When a person is reading a novel, their mind is
....(4) than when they are
watching a film.

Susan says that when you re-read a good book, you can
always ....(5).

According to James, writing a novel that will allow people to
escape from their everyday lives is ....(6)

James found that to get facts right, he had to do
....(7).

The plot of 'Horizons' develops through
....(8).

Both James and Susan are planning to
....(9).

3 Discuss these questions.

1 Which writer's ideas are closest to yours?
2 What makes a good book or story for you?
3 How do you choose a book to read or a film to see?

Reading: the set text

For the exam you may choose to study a set text. You can write about the set text in Paper 2 and you may also talk about it in the interview (Paper 5). You may be asked to:

- describe and analyse characters and discuss their importance to the story
- outline and explain the plot or describe important scenes
- discuss the structure, language and style of the book, including aspects such as suspense or atmosphere.

In this section you will study a short story in detail. The same principles of analysis can be applied to the longer set text that you choose to study.

1 You are going to read a short story called *Machete* by the Australian writer, Robert Drewe. The story is set in a newly built suburb on the outskirts of an Australian town. It tells how a man finds a machete on his front lawn one morning when he goes to collect his newspaper from the mail box at the end of his driveway.

Before you read the story, look at the illustration and read the definition of a machete below. Then discuss these questions.

> **machete** *n* [C] large knife with a broad heavy blade, used as a weapon or a tool

1 What do you associate a machete with? What can it be used to do?
2 If you found a machete on your front doorstep,
- how might you feel?
- what questions would you ask yourself about it?
- what would you do?

2 Read the story to find out what happened.

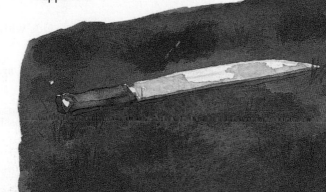

MACHETE

1 ▶ At eight this morning there was a machete lying on the lawn, flat in the middle of my front yard. It gave me a jolt. It's hard to describe the feeling of seeing a machete lying on your lawn when you're picking up the morning paper. I don't own a machete. It's not a common garden tool around here. In my mind a machete is a weapon of foreign guerrillas. Rural terrorists. I associate machetes with the random slaughter of innocent villagers, the massacre of peasant farmers who backed the wrong party.

2 ▶ Well, I picked it up – my heart beating faster – and hefted it in my hand. The blade was heavy and sharp; it was in good order. All the while I couldn't believe it was there in my yard, in my hand. I was peering around to see if the machete's owner was about to appear but there were only the usual sleepy-looking suburban houses coming to life. People were backing cars out of their driveways and leaving for work; children were setting off for school; a woman down the street watered her garden. In a moment I began to feel self-conscious standing there in my suit and tie all set for work, with the rolled newspaper in one hand and a machete in the other.

3 ▶ Belleview is a new suburb. Gillian and I moved here six months ago but we don't know anyone yet. These sandy, gravelly plains on the outskirts of the city were never thickly vegetated, and the developers bulldozed those trees and bushes, mainly spindly acacias, which had persevered. The residents are just starting to establish their lawns and gardens, but it's a battle in the sand. Everything blows away, and when it rains your topsoil washes half a kilometre down the road. What I'm saying is that it's not tropical rainforest or anything. A rake, a spade and a pair of secateurs will see you through. There is no need for slashing and hacking.

4 ▶ So I was standing in the front yard holding the machete and thinking all sorts of imaginative things. How a machete came to get there in the middle of the night, and so forth. It's a long drive to work, to the bank, and I knew the highway would be jammed already, but now I'd found the machete I couldn't just leave.

5 ▶ My mind was whirling. Gillian left work three weeks ago, in her seventh month of pregnancy, and she would be at home, alone, all day. It was our first baby and she was in a state just being pregnant, without me mentioning the machete.

6 ▶ So whose machete was it? I didn't know the neighbours, only that the other young couple on the right worked long hours and that the fellow on the left kept Rottweilers. His wife was Filipino and stayed indoors all the time. Her face peeping through the curtains looked wistful. We'd heard him shouting at night. My guess was that a Rottweiler owner was more likely to own a machete, and to care for it so well.

7 ▶ From where I was standing with the machete I lined up with the front door of the Rottweiler residence. There was only the low paling fence separating us. Someone could have thrown the machete from the front door to where I stood if they were impelled to do that. But it was hard to think of a reason why.

8 ▶ I couldn't see myself going next door past all the Rottweilers and asking "Excuse me, did you leave your machete in my yard? When you were trespassing last night?" By then, it was well after eight and my one clear thought was not to frighten Gillian with any quirkiness. Things were making her weepy and anxious lately: all those children on TV with rare diseases, the hole in the ozone layer, fluoride in the water. I wanted to keep her serene. I took the machete around to the back of the house. I pushed it hard into the sandy flowerbed until only the handle stuck up, and that was hidden by shadow. Then I got into the car, drove to work and forgot about it.

9 ▶ But tonight, as I was driving home past the Hardware Barn I remembered it. The strange feeling came back and I speeded up. These nights the sun sets well before five and our end of the street was in darkness when I pulled up. I left the headlights on and ran to the back of the garage.

10 ▶ There is something more alarming than the presence of a machete. The absence of a machete.

3

1   Answer the following comprehension questions about the story on page 195.

1   Why is the narrator shocked when he finds the machete? (para. 1)
2   Why does he feel self-conscious when he is holding it? (para. 2)
3   What does he suggest a machete could be used for in some areas and why would it not be needed here? (para. 3)
4   Why does he not want to upset his wife? (para. 5)
5   What makes him think that his neighbour might be the owner of the machete? (para. 6)
6   Why does he hide the machete? (para. 8)
7   What does he do when he returns home from work? (para. 9)

2   How do the last two lines make you feel? What do you think may have happened to the machete?

4   The writer uses the following techniques to build up suspense and a sense of unease and foreboding in the story.

*   revealing important information bit by bit so that it has maximum impact
*   implying that something is strange when it could be quite normal

The following exercises focus on those techniques.

1   Number the events below in the order that they are described in the story (not the order in which they actually happened). How does the sequence in which the information is revealed help to build up suspense?

1	The narrator finds the machete lying on the lawn.
	He can't find the machete.
	His wife leaves her job because she is going to have a baby.
	He goes to work.
	He hides the machete.
	He and his wife move to the suburb.
	People go to work as usual.

2   What is the effect of the first line? How does it contribute to the creation of suspense in the story?

3   Look at the following sentences and find how the same information is expressed in the text. What associations does the writer set up through his inclusion of these details? What are the possible implications?

1   A machete is used by people who fight.
2   This machete had been looked after well.
3   The neighbour owns dogs.

4   The neighbour's wife often looks out of the window.
5   The narrator felt worried driving home.

5   In the exam you may need to refer to the writer's use of language to explain how he creates an effect.

1   Answer the following questions, which focus on how the choice of language and use of stylistic devices contribute to creating a sense of unease.

1   Which two words in the first paragraph connect the machete with the idea of killing. What kind of killing is it? Who are the victims?
2   What is the effect of the word 'sleepy-looking' in the description of the suburb?
3   Paragraph 3 describes the new suburb. How do you know
   a) that there are no trees?
   b) that the soil is dry and dusty?
   What is the relevance of this information to the story?
4   Which two words in paragraph 3 emphasise the violent way a machete cuts?
5   What is the effect of the direct speech in paragraph 8?
6   Underline the verbs used in paragraph 9 to describe the man's actions. What idea do they share? What effect do they have?

2   Find examples in the story to support the following statement.

'The story is written in an informal and personal style, with colloquial expressions, and direct appeal to the reader'

3   How does the style emphasise the strangeness of the discovery of the machete?

6   In the exam you may need to describe how the writer conveys a character's personality, feelings and emotions.

1   Answer the following questions with reference to the writer's choice of language.

1   What does the phrase 'my heart beating faster' tell you about the narrator's state of mind when he finds the machete? (para. 2)
2   How do you know that the man is confused and uncertain? (paras. 4 and 5)
3   How do you know his wife is feeling emotional and upset? (para. 8)

2 Which of the words in the box below would you use to describe:

a) the narrator?   b) the neighbour?   c) Gillian?

Find evidence in the text to support your ideas.

> nervous anxious weird thoughtful secretive
> strange sensitive emotional quick-tempered

7 People react to this story in different ways. Do you think it is:

a) ironic – a parody of a horror story?
b) funny – a comedy not to be taken seriously?
c) menacing – a real horror story in which the writer is trying to scare you?

Find evidence in the text to support your answer.

8 What do you think happened when the man entered his house after the end of the story? Discuss different ways in which the story might continue.

Speaking: the set text

In Paper 5 you may choose to talk about the set text. If you do, your interview will include the following three parts.

In **Part 1** you discuss pictures in relation to the story.
In **Part 2** you identify a passage from the book and indicate its significance to the story.
In **Part 3** you discuss different aspects of the book, including:

● character and plot
● whether you think it is a good book or not, giving your reasons
● the main themes in the book and how the title relates to them.

There are no right or wrong answers to the questions in the interview. It doesn't matter if your opinion of the book is different from the examiner's, but you must give evidence from the text to support your ideas

1 Look at the picture. Discuss your own ideas about:

● how it relates to the story
● what aspects of the story it shows
● where it might come from in the plot
● whether it would/wouldn't make a good book cover and why.

2 Read this short extract from the story and discuss the questions that follow.

> But tonight, as I was driving home past the Hardware Barn I remembered it. The strange feeling came back and I speeded up. These nights the sun sets well before five and our end of the street was in darkness when I pulled up. I left the headlights on and ran to the back of the garage.

1   Where does the extract come from in the story?
2   What happened before and after it?
3   What is the 'strange feeling' referred to?
4   What does it tell you about the state of mind of the narrator?

3 In the third part of the interview, the examiner asks you general questions on the set text. The following are a selection of the type of questions you may be asked – you won't have to answer all of them.

Discuss the following questions based on *Machete*.

1   Did you enjoy the story? Why/Why not?
2   Did you like or dislike any of the characters?
3   What is the main theme of the story?
4   Are there any memorable lines or scenes?
5   Did you find anything frightening?
6   Do you think it is a good title?
7   Do you think the story would make a good film? Why/Why not? Who would you choose to play the main characters?
8   Would you recommend the story to your friends? Why/Why not?

Writing: the set text

In Paper 2 you can choose to answer a question on a set text. For part or all of your answer, you may have to write about:

- aspects of structure, style and plot
- the main characters
- the importance of a character to the story.

Depending on the question, your composition may be descriptive or argumentative. Remember that you should always support your ideas with evidence from the text.

Discussing structure and plot

1 Read the following writing task, which is based on the short story *Machete* on page 195.

> How does the writer build up suspense in the story?
> (About 350 words.)

This is a descriptive composition. Look back at the work you did in the Reading section and at the story itself. What ideas would you include in this composition?

2 Read this composition, which was written in answer to the question.

1 Answer these questions.

1 How many ways of creating suspense are mentioned? Find the main topic of each paragraph.
2 What examples from the text are used to support each idea? Underline them in the composition.
3 What is the main conclusion reached about the way the story-writer builds up suspense?

2 How far do you agree with the ideas in the composition? What details would you add?

3 Highlight phrases and expressions in the composition that you can use yourself to introduce evidence in support of a point.

There is only one real event in this story – the finding of the machete. Yet the writer manages to build up suspense and create the feeling in the reader that something terrible is going to happen. How is this effect achieved?

The writer builds up suspense through suggestion and by the sequencing of information, not through actual events. First, he links the machete to the idea of terrorists. The use of words like 'random slaughter' and 'massacre' of innocent people arouses the fear that something similar will happen, even though there is no immediate evidence for this. He also sets up a clear contrast between the negative associations of the machete and the 'sleepy-looking', very normal suburb in which he lives. This technique of contrasting the normal with the abnormal creates a sense of unease.

Half-way through the story, the narrator introduces the fact that his wife is pregnant, and therefore possibly physically weak and vulnerable. This immediately creates a mental picture of a potential victim, even though no motive is given.

Another obvious example of how the writer uses suggestion to create suspense is in the description of the neighbour with the Rottweilers, dogs which are well-known to be potentially vicious. The man's wife is seen 'peeping through the curtains' with a 'wistful' expression. Nothing is stated, but the implication is that this man is dangerous, though why is unclear.

Towards the end of the story the writer's choice of language again helps to create the expectation that something bad is going to happen. The way in which the narrator hides the machete, then forgets about it, is described quite naturally. When he remembers it, however, words like 'speeded up' and 'ran' suggest urgency and possible danger. The anxiety created by these associations, added to the vulnerability of the wife, allows the reader's imagination to run riot and to visualise terrible things – none of which are based on real evidence.

Even the last line leaves the reader in suspense, wondering what might have happened. The writer creates an association of ideas and then leaves everything to the reader's imagination. When you look back at the story there is actually nothing to be afraid of – it is all in the mind.

3   The following composition question is on the same topic as Exercise 1, but this time your answer should be in the form of an argument.

> There is no suspense in the story, because there is no actual murder. How far do you feel this is true? (About 350 words.)

The focus of this composition should be to evaluate 'how far'? You need to think of evidence that could support the given statement to a certain extent, even if you disagree with it.

1   Before you write:

- decide whether you agree with the statement or not
- find evidence from the story to back up the statement and your own ideas
- organise your evidence into clear, well supported points
- make sure that your conclusion forms an effective end to your argument, and has been prepared for.

2   Prepare a short outline for this composition using the points listed above to guide you. You can use the same evidence as in the composition in Exercise 2.

3   Using the introduction given below, write your answer to the question.

> *The story 'Machete' is a short but intense account of the effect on a man of finding a machete in his garden. Very little actually happens and yet the story still seems to be very detailed. The writer manages to include a great deal of description and information in a very short space – but does he also create suspense?*

Discussing character

1

1   Read the following description of the narrator of *Machete*. Notice how every aspect of character mentioned is supported by reference to the text.

> *The narrator is a fairly young man, with a regular job. He is obviously not a violent man, because his reaction to the machete suggests he does not like the idea of terrorists – he uses the words 'random slaughter of innocent villagers' and 'massacre', which are very strong. He was also a little frightened by the machete – his heart 'beat faster' when he picked it up. He seems to be a kind person. For example, he feels sorry for the woman next door, and describes her as 'wistful'. He is also reluctant to worry his wife by telling her about the machete.*

2   The following description of the neighbour was written by a student. It does not give any evidence from the text to justify the opinions expressed, and there are also two factual mistakes. Rewrite the description, adding evidence where indicated.

> *The strange neighbour is a man who lives on the right of the narrator. He is clearly <u>interested in dogs</u>* — How do you know?
> *although the type of dog he sells might indicate that he is worried about security or <u>has something to hide.</u>* — Why? How?
> *This <u>adds to the interest of the story</u>.*
> *We can also guess that he <u>does not take good care of his wife</u> and he may be quick-tempered.* — What evidence is there?

2

1   Read the following exam question.

> Describe the character of Gillian and say how she is important to the story. (About 350 words.)

Look back at the story on page 195.

1   Decide what kind of person you think Gillian is.
2   Decide what her importance is to the story.
3   Choose evidence from the text that you can cite to support your ideas.

Use your answers to Exercise 6 on page 196 to help you.

2 Using the introduction below, write your composition. You can use the description in Exercise 1 to help you with the descriptive part.

> *Although Gillian does not actually do anything in the story, we know a lot about her and what kind of person she is. In fact she also plays a central role in the development of the plot because of the type of person she is. She is ...*

3 Read the following composition titles. Both involve argument as well as description.

> 'Without the character of the neighbour there would be no story.' How far do you agree with this statement? (About 350 words.)

> 'Gillian is the most important character in the story.' How far do you think this is true?

In which composition should you:

a) describe the character mentioned in the title in detail, and then evaluate that character's importance to the plot?

b) include descriptions of several other characters and evaluate their importance to the story?

4 Choose one of the titles in Exercise 3.

1 Using your ideas from Exercises 1 and 2, plan the first part of the composition. Then look back at the story and plan the second part of the argument.

2 Now write your composition.

Exam Strategy

In the exam you won't have your book with you. To prepare, make notes in advance on character, plot and the other aspects you have worked on in this unit. Include in your notes any key evidence for your ideas, including quotations. (You aren't expected to quote the exact words from the text in the exam, however.) In the exam, remember to:

- read the question carefully and decide if it is an argument or a description
- plan your composition carefully before you start writing
- give evidence from the text for your ideas.

Exam Focus

Paper 3 Use of English, Section A

The aim of this section is to help you plan your revision work for Paper 3, Section A, by reminding you of the key areas tested in the exam. To revise for all questions in Section A, it's a good idea to:

- review complex structures. But don't neglect the basics – you need to know the basic structures well.
- review dependent prepositions and phrases followed by particular patterns
- check you know the rules of punctuation – punctuation will give you clues to the required word in Question 1, the cloze passage.

1 Decide if the following statements about Paper 3, Section A, are true or false. Correct the false statements.

1 You don't have to answer the questions in any particular order.

2 It doesn't matter if you make spelling mistakes in any part of the paper.

3 It helps if you think of answers in phrases rather than individual words in all questions.

4 The cloze passage (Question 1) only tests your knowledge of structural items such as auxiliary verbs, prepositions, pronouns or articles.

5 You can change the form of the word in the key word transformations. (Question 4).

6 The sentences in Questions 2, 3 and 4 are linked thematically.

2 **Question 2:** sentence transformations
Important grammatical structures that may be tested in Question 2 are:

- tenses
- conditionals
- inversion
- cleft sentences
- gerunds and infinitives
- passive
- reported speech
- clauses of concession
- modal verbs
- connectors or link words

1 Finish each of the following sentences in such a way that it is as similar as possible in meaning to the sentence printed before it. For each sentence, decide which of the structures above is being tested.

(a) Over the last ten years no fish have been caught in the area.
It is ....

(b) 'As you're being so difficult I won't help you,' Alan told Peter.
Alan refused ....

(c) While the accuracy of some details in the report is disputed, the underlying truth is not.
The underlying truth ....

(d) There will be no change to the policy before everyone has voted on the proposal.
Not until ....

(e) The whole project would have fallen through without his support and hard work.
Had it ....

(f) We were very impressed by his plans, but found them rather ambitious.
Impressed ....

(g) He must have spent a small fortune renovating that old house.
It must ....

(h) The special effects were the part of the film I liked best.
What I ....

2   Now check you haven't made any mistakes relating to these points.

* changes in prepositions
* effects of changing from a positive to a negative sentence
* change in form, for example noun to verb

3   Question 3: Gapped sentences
Question 3 may test the same grammatical structures as for sentence transformations, and in addition:

* phrasal verbs
* phrases with particular grammatical patterns, e.g. *He doesn't **stand a chance of -ing.***

1   Fill each of the blanks with a suitable word or phrase.

(a) You'll just have to put .... the inconvenience if you want your house painted.

(b) The film was so weak that it doesn't .... of winning the prize.

(c) Unfortunately, the new computer system turned out to be not .... help as a hindrance.

(d) Never .... the film, I can't say whether it's any good.

(e) All the best seats .... if we don't get to the stadium in good time.

(f) I think you .... an effort to be polite to him – he was only trying to help.

2   Now complete the following strategy notes. Look back at Unit 12, p. 172, if necessary.

* Read the whole sentence first – the context may give clues to the required phrase.
* Try to identify ....
* The form of the word after the gap may ....

4   Question 4: key word transformations
Question 4 tests phrases, not single words, and you need to be familiar with:

* grammatical and lexical patterns
* phrases with similar meanings and synonyms
* phrasal verbs and idioms.

When you rewrite the sentence using the key word, you may have to make other grammatical changes to the rest of the sentence. What change had to be made to the example below?

EXAMPLE: She was able to do the work.
capable

ANSWER: *She was capable of doing the work.*

1   For each of the sentences below, write a new sentence as similar as possible in meaning to the original sentence, but using the word given. This word must not be altered in any way.

(a) I remember little about living in Italy as I was very young at the time. **scarcely**
....

(b) The British sprinter almost broke the world record. **close**
....

(c) The teacher felt that the new student could achieve a good grade. **capable**
....

(d) I just can't get that song out of my head. **brain**
....

(e) I made an attempt to open the top window but I couldn't reach it. **go**
....

(f) She thought of a wonderful idea for the party. **came**
....

(g) The film was nothing like the novel it was supposed to be based on. **resemblance**
....

(h) She will probably pass the exam. **chances**
....

2   Write your own list of exam strategies for this task. Look back at Unit 4, page 52, if necessary.

1 Choose the word or phrase which best completes each sentence.

1 After three years in my brother's room, the old chair was an obvious .... for the rubbish dump.
A candidate B nominee C delegate
D applicant

2 The sick child sighed .... and pushed aside the plate of food.
A disinterestedly B listlessly C revoltingly
D sensibly

3 The exhibition of Russian art is a .... with the series of concerts by the orchestra from Moscow.
A set-up B run-in C tie-in D spin-off

4 In spite of the late hour, we .... on with our work in the hope of finishing before morning.
A pressed B stretched C ran D dragged

5 Mary .... expectations by winning a scholarship to music school.
A confounded B confined C condemned
D contrasted

6 I can understand the theory when I study, but I'm not very good at .... it.
A spending B practising C applying
D working

7 The leisure .... of many youngsters are sometimes incomprehensible to their parents.
A actions B games C pursuits D hobbies

8 The director .... up a sense of magic through the use of special lighting effects.
A made B brought C caught D built

9 At the end of the chapter, the reader is left .... suspense, wondering what will happen.
A in B under C on D with

10 This centre attempts to cater .... the needs of many different local groups.
A to B about C with D for

11 The company is heading for a .... between the managing director and his deputy.
A walkout B turnover C showdown
D breakthrough

12 After his illness, he took a(n) .... holiday in the mountains.
A stretched B elongated C lengthened
D extended

13 Although you do not wish to .... to traditional dress codes, remember that others may.
A adhere B respect C regard D accord

14 Over the holiday period, some traders charged ridiculously .... prices.
A boosted B inflated C exploding D towering

15 The stage designs were out of this .... but unfortunately the acting was not so impressive.
A moon B planet C world D earth

16 To discuss this matter with anyone else would .... our professional regulations.
A contradict B counteract C contrast
D contravene

17 I .... on the grapevine that George is in line for promotion.
A heard B collected C picked D caught

18 This monument is .... to the memory of distinguished former students.
A erected B dedicated C commissioned
D associated

19 To begin studying chemistry at this level, you must already have proved your ability in a related ....
A line B discipline C region D rule

20 This sad song movingly conveys the .... of the lovers' final parting.
A ache B argument C anxiety D anguish

21 After visiting Scotland regularly for several years, they finally settled there for .... in the 1990s.
A good B ever C all D life

22 The plot of this film, like many others, ... from a novel.
A descends B derives C departs D deduces

23 We had to stop the treatment because it was causing .... side-effects.
A converse B reverse C adverse D perverse

24 Released from the coach, the children .... riot in the playground.
A held B ran C went D played

25 This attractive old building is likely to go the .... of many other small theatres unless funds are available immediately.
A path B route C course D way

2 Finish each of the following sentences in such a way that it is as similar as possible in meaning to the sentence printed before it.

1 Julia soon calmed down and explained her problem.
Julia soon pulled ....

2 He warned them against using the mountain road.
'I wouldn't ....'

3 Edward eventually organised himself and started work.
Edward eventually got his ....

4 I can't imagine myself ever singing in public.
I would ....

5 There had been allegations of drug-taking by members of the team.
It ....

6 As I listened to the music on repeated occasions, my respect for the composer increased.
The more ....

7 This device has the capacity to detect potential engine failure.
It ....

8 If ever a student dared to ask a question, the professor would sigh wearily.
In the ....

9 In spite of her initial reluctance to take the job, she's got on very well.
Reluctant ....

10 Why not try hang-gliding – it's really great!
Why not have ....

3 For each of the sentences below, write a new sentence as similar as possible in meaning to the original sentence, but using the word given. This word must not be altered in any way.

1 What exactly am I supposed to have done wrong?
stand
....

2 Good colour sense is instinctive for some people.
comes
....

3 Don't ask him about the accident, he's upset already. **state**
....

4 Everyone's saying the government is about to resign. **rumoured**
....

5 The senior students believe that they are old enough to choose which classes to attend.
regard
....

6 In her new job, Alison determined to impress everyone from the start.
mark
....

7 I felt vaguely that something was wrong, but what was it?
back
....

8 Despite having flu, she insisted on going out. **yet**
....

9 From my position I could see quite clearly what was happening.
standing
....

10 When they broke the news, she stayed perfectly calm and controlled. **hair**
....

4 Fill each of the blanks with a suitable word or phrase.

1 It's .... if we shall have to leave the party early.

2 Now, don't start blaming .... something you couldn't have prevented.

3 They continued to complain, in spite .... awarded compensation.

4 I insist .... acccpting this small gift as a token of our respect and gratitude.

5 They advised .... going by car, because the roads were so bad.

6 This course is .... lines as the others, but is slightly shorter.

7 It's not far to the airport, but we'd better .... safe in case the traffic's heavy.

8 Strange .... seem to you, we quite enjoy this work.

9 After years of delays, the authorities have finally agreed to go .... building the new hospital.
I .... to that restaurant for years before I realised who owned it.

Grammar reference

UNIT 1

Past and perfect tenses (p. 10/11)

The main uses of the tense forms relating to the past are as follows.

1 Past simple
1 a completed action at a specified time in the past.
I was born in Scotland in 1980.
2 a state, or habitual or repeated action in the past
I went to school until I was eighteen.

Note: The time referred to is usually specified by a time marker e.g. *in 1990* unless already clear from the context.

2 Past continuous
1 an activity in progress when another past event happened
I was studying in my room one Saturday when a letter arrived.
2 a temporary habit or repeated action around a time in the past
I was still hoping that something exciting would happen.

3 Present perfect simple
1 a state or habit beginning in the past and continuing up to the present
Lee has enjoyed reading since he was very young.
2 a completed event occurring in the past but affecting the present
He has written a novel to be published shortly.
3 a completed event at an unspecified time in a period leading up to the present
He has read Shakespeare's complete works.

4 Present perfect continuous
This may be used in the same situations as the simple form, but may also convey:
1 the idea of continuation or non-completion.
Susie has been writing an essay.
2 the duration of the event.
She's been working all morning.

5 Past perfect simple
an activity completed before a specified past time
The previous month I had entered a competition.

6 Past perfect continuous
a continuing activity or series of activities occurring before a specified time in the past
Ever since then, I had been waiting eagerly for the result.

7 used to/would
to refer to past habits (often long ago rather than the recent past)
1 *used to* refers to states, habitual and repeated actions
I used to dream of a very different life from the one I was leading.
2 *would* refers to habitual and repeated actions but **not** states
I would walk slowly to school, composing imaginary stories in my head.

Note: Once the time referred to has been established, it is not necessary to continue using past perfect, *would* or *used to* with every verb.

as versus *like* (p. 16)

As and *like* can be:

1 prepositions
We use *as* to describe the role or function of a person or thing.
I worked as a waiter to pay my way through university.
We use *like* to compare two different things.
He's nothing like his brother. (= He is completely different from his brother.)
It is often used in the phrase *I don't feel (much) like -ing.*

2 conjunctions, introducing a clause
He spoke very well, as we expected.
The house looks exactly like it did when I lived there.
(*as* is also possible here, and would be more formal)

UNIT 2

Conditionals: basic patterns (p. 23)

1 Open conditions

Sentences referring to real or possible events in the present or future follow these patterns:

1 (*if*-clause) present/future + (main clause) present
*Children **don't learn** if they're **not exposed** to new ideas.* (general truth)

2 (*if*-clause) future + (main clause) present
*He **won't get** the job if he **doesn't have** the right qualifications.* (open condition referring to future)

2 Unreal conditions

Sentences referring to unlikely or hypothetical events in the past, present or future follow these patterns:

1 (*if*-clause) past + (main clause) *would* + bare infinitive
*If I **felt** it was justified, I **would make** a formal complaint.* (hypothetical future)

2 (*if*-clause) past perfect + (main clause) *would / could have* + past participle
*If my friends **had not helped** me, I **would never have finished** the course.* (hypothetical past)

Note: It is not necessary to use a future form in the *if*-clause if the main clause makes it clear we are talking about the future. However, modals such as *will* and *would* may be used in the following cases:

1 to express willingness or lack of willingness to do something (*will/won't*)
*If you **won't** help me, I'll do it on my own.*

2 to suggest that someone is insisting on doing something (*will* is emphasised)
*If you **will** tease him, of course he'll cry.*

3 in polite requests (*would/wouldn't/could/couldn't*)
*If you **wouldn't** mind waiting for a minute, I'll see if anyone can help you.*

► See also Unit 7, mixed conditionals.

3 Other link words introducing conditional clauses

• *unless*
*Don't do it **unless** you really want to.*

• *providing/provided (that)*
*I'm prepared to go **provided** that you pay my fare.*

• *as long as*
*She'll let us come **as long as** we don't talk too much.*

wish/if only (p. 24)

The verb *wish* can be used in the following situations:

1 to express regret that something is not the case

*I wish I **didn't have** to take the exam.* (referring to present or future)
*I wish **I'd done** the course earlier.* (referring to past)

2 when giving good wishes for particular events, festivals or dates
*I **wished** him a happy birthday.*

3 as a formal way of saying *want to*
*Do you **wish** to make a formal complaint?*

Notes:

1 *If only* can replace *I wish* with no change of form. It is generally more emphatic.

2 *I wish* is only followed by *would* when referring to activities done by someone else in the present or future.
*I wish **he** would go.* (expresses annoyance)
NOT *I wish I would go.*

3 *Wish + would* cannot be used to describe a state.
*His parents wish he **liked** sport.*
NOT *... wish he would like sport.*

Unreal versus real tenses (p. 25)

1 *as if/as though*

These expressions introduce a clause which explains something by comparing it to something else. The comparison may be seen as possible/likely or as unlikely/hypothetical and this is indicated by the choice of either a present or past tense verb form.
*She behaves as if she **has** lots of money.* (possible)
*She behaves as if she **had** lots of money.* (unlikely)

When the main verb is in the past, the verb in the subordinate clause is also in the past for both real and hypothetical comparisons.
*She **behaved** as if she **had** lots of money.*

2 *It's time/I'd rather/I'd prefer*

1 *It's (high) time* + clause: unreal past referring to present or future
*It's high time that child **was** in bed – it's midnight!*

2 *I'd rather*
+ clause: usually unreal verb forms referring to past, present or future – as in hypothetical conditions
*I'd rather you **didn't tell** him.* (referring to future)
*I'd rather you **hadn't told** him.* (referring to past)

+ bare infinitive (present or perfect)
*I'd rather **tell** him myself.* (referring to future)
*I like this hotel, but I'd rather **have been** nearer the beach.* (referring to present)

3 **I'd prefer**

+ *it* + *if* clause: usually unreal forms referring to past, present or future

*I'd prefer it if we **could** go on our own.* (future)

*I'd **have preferred** it if I **could have studied** maths.* (past)

+ *to*-infinitive (present or perfect): not followed by an unreal form

*I'd prefer **to go** on my own.*

Note: The infinitive is only possible if the subject of the infinitive is the same as that of the main clause.

UNIT 3

Inversion after negative adverbials (p. 38)

Starting a sentence with a negative adverbial and reversing the order of the subject and verb is a way of adding emphasis or creating a dramatic effect in English. It is a feature of more formal writing, but may also occur in speech for dramatic effect. Expressions that can be placed first in the sentence include:

on no account	*under no circumstances*
at no time	*nowhere*
not once	*not a word*
not for a moment	*not since*
not until	*not only ... but (also)*
never (before)	*rarely*
seldom	*only (now/recently)*
only by chance	*only when*
hardly/scarcely ... when	*no sooner ... than*

If there is no auxiliary verb, *do/does/did* has to be added.

He never once came to see her in hospital.

*Never once **did** he come to see her in hospital.*

Note:

In the expression *hardly/scarcely ... when*, *when* introduces a time clause.

We had scarcely sat down, when the alarm went off.

The expression *no sooner ... than* is a comparative.

No sooner had we got to the station than the train arrived.

Participle clauses (p. 42/43)

Participle clauses are used to avoid repetition and make a point more economically. They can describe:

1 events happening at the same time (present participle)

__Drinking his coffee slowly__, he thought about the problem.

2 events happening in rapid sequence (present participle)

__Looking up__, she saw someone approaching.

3 events happening with a longer time gap between them (perfect participle)

__Having retired__, he found himself with time on his hands.

4 other time relations, when used with an appropriate conjunction

__Before__ being shown round, we were welcomed by the Principal.

__After__ finishing his speech, he took a sip of water.

*Wear protective gloves **when** using this equipment.*

__On__ arriving, you will find someone waiting for you.

__While__ travelling to work, she usually reads a novel.

*She has been much happier **since** changing schools.*

5 reason and result

__Not having had any breakfast__, I was very hungry.

(= Because I had not had ...)

*She became a local celebrity **as a result of having appeared once on television**.*

Note: State verbs such as *be, have, know, live* can be used in participle clauses expressing reason/result.

__Being__ a kind man, he agreed to help.

6 concession

*We intend to go **despite** having been advised against it.*

7 condition (past participle)

__Left to follow his own inclinations__, he would do no work at all. (= If he was left ...)

Note: If the subject of a participle clause is unstated, we assume it is the same as the subject of the main clause. If the subject of the participle clause is different from that of the main clause, it must be stated.

*__The weather__ being perfect, **we** decided to go for a swim.*

Otherwise, the result is known as a 'dangling' participle, meaning that the participle clause has no subject.

~~Kicking with all his strength, the ball went straight into the goal.~~

UNIT 4

Preparatory *it* (p.55)

1 *it* as a 'preparatory' subject

The pronoun *it* is often used to enable the speaker/writer to move the subject to the end of the sentence. It can sound less clumsy than starting a sentence with a very long subject. Compare:

*It is vital **to enclose all the necessary documents**.*

__To enclose all the necessary documents__ is vital.

2 *it* **as 'preparatory' object**

It can be inserted as a 'preparatory' object in order to move a long object clause to the end of the sentence. Compare:

> *Many people find* **working on their own at home** *quite difficult.*
> *Many people find it quite difficult* **to work on their own at home.**

Notice the change of form from gerund to infinitive in the second example above.

Note: Preparatory *it* in object position is essential when the object is a *that* clause.

> *I appreciated* **it** *that he had taken the trouble to phone.*

Gerund or infinitive nominals (p.55)

Both gerunds and infinitives may be used as the subject of a sentence. However, introductory *It* is usually preferred to an infinitive as subject.

> **To bring up children** *is a rewarding experience.*
> **It is a rewarding experience** *to bring up children.*

A nominal infinitive usually refers to things that will happen in the future, e.g.:

> **To have a code of advertising practice** (in the future) *would be a good idea.*

A nominal gerund usually refers to things that have already happened.

> **Receiving the award** *made him feel very proud.*

But a *to*-infinitive is used after introductory *It*.

> *It made him feel very proud* **to have received the award.**

UNIT 5

Modal verbs (ability, obligation, advice) (p.66)

1 Obligation/necessity: *must / have to*
Present/future: *I* **must / have to / will have to** *finish now/soon.*
Past: *We* **had to** *finish the report in a week.*

Note: *must* usually expresses the authority of the speaker; *have to* expresses the authority of another person.

2 Prohibition: *mustn't*
Present/future: *You* **mustn't** *touch that, it's dangerous.*

3 Lack of necessity
1 *needn't*
  Present/future: *You* **needn't** *come if you don't want to.*
  Past:
  a) *He* **didn't need** *to take the car, so he left it at home.*
    (= it wasn't necessary to take the car, and he didn't)

  b) *He* **needn't have taken** *the car, as there was plenty of transport.* (= he took the car unnecessarily)
  Note: *Need* can function as a modal verb, followed by a bare infinitive, or as a main verb, followed by a *to*-infinitive.

2 *don't have to*
  Present: *You* **don't have to** *do it if you don't want to.*
  Past: *He* **didn't have to** *help – it was very kind of him.*

Note the difference between *mustn't* (= prohibition) and *not have to* (= lack of necessity).

4 Advice: *should / ought to*
Present/future: *You* **should / ought to** *ask for more money.*
Past: *You* **should / shouldn't** *have gone there on your own.* (expresses an opinion about right/wrong)

5 Opportunity/free choice: *can / could*
Present/future: *You* **can** *take whatever you want.*
Past: *You* **could** *go anywhere. He* **could have been** *a doctor if he'd wanted to.*

6 Permission: *can / may / will / would*
Present/future: '*Could I have a lift to the station?' 'Of course you can.'*
'*May / might I have a lift to the station?*' (formal and rather old-fashioned)
Past: *I* **could / was allowed** *to drive my father's car whenever I wanted.*
He **was allowed** *to go on his own.* (permission to do something specific: *could* is not possible here.)

7 Ability: *can / could / be able to*
Present/future: *Can you / Will you be able to* **manage** *on your own?*
Past: *I* **could** *speak English when I was ten.* (refers to general ability)
I **was able to** *help my parents in the restaurant.* (refers to a specific occasion: *could* is not possible here)

Other expressions

- **be supposed to / suppose**
  Compare:
  You're **supposed to** *be working.* (suggests criticism = You're meant to be working.)
  I **suppose** *I will have to go.* (expresses reluctance = I'm afraid I will have to go.)

- **be to + infinitive**
  expresses an order, instruction or prohibition
  We **are to wait** *until they arrive.*

Modal verbs (degrees of likelihood) (p.70)

1 Possibility: *could/may/might*

It could	conceivably	have happened. (past)
It might	well	be happening. (present)
It may	possibly	happen. (future)

2 Possibility – negative: *may/might not*

It may/might not have happened. (past)
It may/might not be true. (present)
It may/might never happen. (future)

3 Logical deduction/assumption: *must/will/should*

*It **must be** true.* (present)
*It **must have happened**.* (past)
*'The phone's ringing.' 'That **will be** for me.'* (present)
*We **should be able to** get there on time.* (used for positive assumptions)

4 Impossibility: *can't/couldn't*

*It **can't be** true.* (present)
*It **couldn't/can't** ever happen.* (future)
*It **couldn't/can't** possibly have happened.* (past)

5 Annoyance/criticism

When used as an exclamation, *could* and *might* often express annoyance or criticism.
*You **could/might** have told me!*

UNIT 6

Passive: special points (p. 81–83)

1 *make, see, hear, help*

These verbs are all followed by the infinitive without *to* when they are active, and the infinitive with *to* when they are passive.
*They **made** him **stand** at the front.*
*He was **made to stand** at the front.*

2 *let*

This is never used in the passive.
*They usually **let** him **stand** at the front.*
*He **is** usually **allowed to stand** at the front.*

3 *by, with* and *in*

Usually, the agent of a passive verb is introduced by *by*. However, in some cases *with* or *in* may be used instead.
*The drain was blocked **with** rubbish.*
*The roads were crowded **with** people.*
*Service is included **in** the price.*

4 Future with *be to*

This is often used in the passive for reporting news items. It is a fairly formal structure.

*The government **is to introduce** new taxes.*
*New taxes **are to be introduced** (by the government).*

5 *need doing*

This structure has a passive meaning.
The house needs painting. = The house needs to be painted.

Subjunctives (p. 82)

Subjunctive verb forms are not used very often in English. There are three main types of subjunctive.

1 After certain verbs and adjectives

The subjunctive is used in *that* clauses after the following verbs and adjectives in formal contexts.

| advise | demand | insist | propose |
| recommend | require | suggest | urge |

It is essential/important/necessary/urgent/vital …
It has only one verb form, which is the same as the bare infinitive; there is no third person *-s* or past form.
It is vital that every employee attend the meeting.
The law demands that he be granted bail.
In less formal contexts, *that* clauses with *should* + infinitive or *to*-infinitives are preferred.
It is vital that every employee should attend the meeting/for every employee to attend the meeting.

2 The *were*-subjunctive

This is used instead of the usual *was* in conditional clauses and after verbs like *wish*.
*If I **were** in charge, I would make some changes.*
*I wish I **were** rich.*
*He shouted at her as if she **were** deaf.*

Note: In sentences using inversion, *were* is obligatory.
Were he to refuse permission, … (*was* is not possible)

3 Formulaic phrases

The subjunctive form is used in a few fixed phrases:
***Come** what may, (we will achieve our goal).*
***Suffice** it to say that (I was disappointed).*
***Be** that as it may, (your behaviour was unacceptable).*

Relative clauses (p. 87/88)

1 Defining relative clauses

1 refer back to the preceding noun and give essential information about it. If this information is omitted, the sentence will not make sense. It is therefore not separated off by commas.
2 can be introduced by the relative pronouns *who* (subject), *whom* (object), *whose* (possessive), *which/that* (for things), *where* (place), *when* (time). The relative pronoun **replaces** the original subject or object of the clause.

3 The relative pronouns *who/which* can be replaced by *that* in less formal contexts.

4 We can omit the relative pronoun only if it is the object of the clause.
   *The man (**whom**) I met yesterday phoned me up.*
   (See also below, **Reduced relatives**)

2 Non-defining relative clauses

1 give additional information about the preceding noun. They can be omitted without making the sentence meaningless, and are separated off by commas.

2 can be introduced by the same relative pronouns as defining relative clauses, except for *that*, which is not normally used.
   My grandparents' house, which was very old, was surrounded by fruit trees.

3 The relative pronoun cannot be omitted from non-defining relative clauses. It **replaces** the original subject or object of the clause.

4 Non-defining clauses are more formal than defining clauses and are more common in written than spoken English.

3 Relative clauses with prepositions

If a preposition is required, this may be placed before the relative pronoun in formal English, or at the end of the clause in less formal English.
   *He's the man **to whom** the prize was awarded.* (formal)
   *He's the man the prize was awarded **to**.* (informal)
Note: *whom*, not *who*, must be used after a preposition.

4 Sentence relatives

A non-defining relative clause may refer back to the whole of the previous clause.
   *I had left my money at home, **which** meant I had to borrow from my friend.*
The following phrases are also used to refer back to the whole clause.
   in which case   as a result of which   by which time
   at which time/point   since when/which time

Participle clauses/reduced relatives (p.88)

1 With an *-ing* form

-ing participle clauses can replace both defining and non-defining relative clauses with an active verb.
   *A new road has been built, **which bypasses** the town.*
   *A new road has been built, **bypassing** the town.*

2 With an *-ed* form

If the relative clause contains a passive verb, both the relative pronoun and auxiliary *be* can be omitted.
   *The area (**which was**) **chosen** for development was near the river.*

3 Verbless

If a relative clause contains only a relative pronoun and the verb *be*, both may be omitted.
   *The townspeople, (**who were**) tired of traffic pollution, decided to take action.*
   *His daughter, (**who is**) now a famous actress, still visits him regularly.*

UNIT 7

Mixed conditionals (p. 98)

In mixed conditionals, the main clause and the *if*-clause may refer to a different time period. A variety of modal verbs may be used.

1 Hypothetical conditionals: mixed

1 (unreal condition) past + (main clause) present
   *If you **hadn't worked** so hard then, you **wouldn't be able to** take such long holidays now.*
   *If he **could have seen** the doctor, he **wouldn't be** in hospital now.*

2 (unreal condition: state or habit) present + (main clause) past
   *If I **wasn't/weren't** so busy all the time, I **could have done** something to help.*

3 (unreal condition) present/future + (main clause) present/future
   *If we **had** a garden, we **would be able to** grow our own vegetables.*
   *If we **could have** a garden, we **might be able to** grow our own vegetables.*

2 Open conditionals: mixed

1 (open condition) past + (main clause) past
   This is used to state a fact about the past.
   *If I **was** sad, my grandmother **comforted** me.*
   *If she **could find** a spare moment, she **would** often **tell** me a story.*

2 (open condition) past + (main clause) present/future
   This is used to draw a conclusion about what is happening now/will happen in the future from a past situation.
   *If he **cheated** then, he's probably **cheating** now and he'll probably **cheat** again.*

3 (open condition) past/present perfect + (main clause) present/future
   This is used to describe a possible situation around the present time.
   *If we've **run out of** bread, we **can buy** some more.*

4 (open condition) present + (main clause) present
   This is used to state a general truth.
   *If you **look** out of the window, you **can see** the sea in the distance.*

5 (open condition) present + (main clause) present perfect
This is used to draw a conclusion about what happened in the past from a present situation.
*If there's no hot water, someone **must have** just **had** a shower.*

6 (open condition) present + (main clause) future
This suggests one event typically follows another.
*If it **needs** mending, they'**ll** usually **do** it for nothing.*

7 (open condition) future + (main clause) present
This is used to make a recommendation.
*If we **are to** get there by evening, we **ought to** set off now.*

Inversion in conditional sentences (p.99)

Conditions may be expressed without using *if* by inverting the first auxiliary verb. This is a fairly formal structure.
***Had** I seen him, I would have told you. (= If I had …)*
***Were** you to go there, you would find it disappointing. (= If you were to …)*

If the first auxiliary verb in the conditional is a form of *be*, it is not possible to use inversion unless *be* is replaced by *should*.
***Should** this **be** true, there will be serious consequences. (= If this is true … / If this should be true …)*

Other ways of expressing conditions (p.99)

1 Other structures expressing condition
In the following structures, the condition is implied, but not stated.

1 Imperative + *and* (a fairly emphatic structure)
***Buy** our new washing powder, **and** you'll be amazed at the results! (= If you buy …)*

2 Negative imperative + *or* (emphatic)
***Don't touch** it or it will explode! (= If you touch it, it will explode!)*

3 Past participle or preposition + noun
***Deprived** of light and water, the plant will soon die. (= If it is deprived of …)*
***Without** your help, he won't be able to manage. (= If he doesn't have your help …)*

2 Other link words expressing condition

* *suppose / supposing*
  ***Suppose** it were to break! What would we do?*
* *imagine*
  ***Imagine** we lived on Mars. What would it be like?*
* *assuming (that)*
  *We're planning to fly, **assuming** it's not too expensive.*

* *but for (the fact that)*
  ***But for** your help, we'd never have managed.*
  *We'd have made it to the wedding in time **but for the fact that** we got a flat tyre.*
* *otherwise*
  *We need to set out soon, **otherwise** we'll miss the train.*

3 *in case*
In case is used to talk about things we do to prepare for a possible later situation. Notice that *will* is not used in the clause with *in case*.
*I've brought a towel in case we **decide** to go swimming.*
It often refers to things we do to prevent or prepare for something bad.
Make a note of your passport number in case it gets stolen.
Sentences with *in case* cannot usually be rewritten with *if* without changing the meaning.
Take an umbrella if it rains. (i.e. if it is raining when you leave)
Take an umbrella in case it rains. (to be prepared for the possibility of rain)

Compare the structure *in case* + noun:
In case of any problems, phone 0014 – 829020. (= If you have any problems …)

UNIT 8

So and *such* (p. 111)

The intensifier *so* is used with adjectives, and *such* with nouns. They can be used in the following ways.

1 For emphasis
*It's **so** hot! I can't stand it!*
*It's **such** an effort to do anything!*
Be careful. This is a fairly colloquial use. Ordinarily, you would use *very*:
*It's **very** hot. Let's go for a swim.*

2 In result clauses
*It was **such a hot day** that everyone stayed indoors.*
*It was **so hot that** everyone stayed indoors.*

Note: When an article + noun are used with *so* + adjective, the article must immediately precede the noun.
*It was so hot **a** day that …*

3 Inversion

Inversion may be used with result clauses for dramatic effect.

*The weather **was so hot** that no-one could work.*

→ ***So hot was** the weather that ...*

→ ***Such was the heat** that ...*

*It **was such a hot** day that ...*

→ ***So hot a day was it** that ...*

When there is no auxiliary verb, the auxiliary *do* is used.

***He made such a moving appeal** that ...*

→ ***Such a moving appeal did** he make that ...*

→ ***So moving an appeal did** he make that ...*

UNIT 9

Verb patterns (p. 122/123)

When one verb follows another, the second verb must be either an infinitive with *to*, an infinitive without *to* (bare infinitive) or an *-ing* form (either a gerund or an *-ing* participle). The form of the second verb depends on what patterns the first or main verb can take. Some verbs may take more than one pattern, with or without a change of meaning. Others can only take one pattern.

1 Verb + verb (no object)

1 Verb + *to*-infinitive
Verbs in this pattern include:

agree arrange* apply appear* decide* pretend
fail hope* intend long plan* promise**

I have applied to go to university.
He promised to help us.

2 Verb + *-ing* (gerund)
Verbs in this pattern include:

admit advise consider* deny
finish postpone suggest* recommend**

The doctor advised/suggested taking a holiday.
We postponed making any decision.

3 Verb + *to*-infinitive or *-ing* (gerund)
a) with little change in meaning:

*begin continue hate like
love prefer start*

Note: If the verb is in the conditional, an infinitive is used: *I would like **to go** there.*

b) with a change in meaning:

- **dread**
  I dread to think what he will do. (only used with *think*)
  I dread seeing him again.

- **forget*/remember*/stop**
  I forgot to phone him.
  I have forgotten ever saying I would do it.

- **go on**
  After school he went on to study at university.
  He went on talking, not having noticed her enter.

- **mean***
  I didn't mean to insult you.
  The new job meant leaving everything she knew.

- **regret***
  I regret to tell you that we've lost the contract.
  I regret saying what I said.

- **try**
  Please try to remember.
  I've tried being strict with him, but it has no effect.

2 Verb + optional object + verb

1 Verb (+ object) + *to*-infinitive
Verbs in this pattern include:

ask choose expect* intend
need want wish**

They want (him) to go.

2 Verb (+ object or genitive) + *-ing*

anticipate appreciate* describe dislike
enjoy insist on recall* risk*

We anticipated (them/their) arriving late.
I recall (him/his) having won first prize at school.
We appreciate being given extra time.
I appreciate you/your doing that for me.

Notes:

1 The use of a genitive (possessive) rather than an object is more formal. It is more common when the second verb applies to a person rather than an object.

2 The pronoun *it* in object position is necessary if *appreciate* is followed by a *that* clause.

*I appreciate **it** that you did that for me.*

3 Verb + *for* + object + *to*-infinitive
Verbs taking this pattern include:

agree* apply arrange* long wait

I have arranged for the neighbour to water the plants.

Note: These verbs cannot be followed by an object and infinitive alone.

3 Verb + compulsory object + verb

1 Verb + object + *to*-infinitive
Verbs in this pattern generally have the meaning of imposing one's will on someone else, either asking or forcing them to do something. They include:

*allow compel force invite
order tell* want*

I want him to take the job.

Other verbs in this pattern include verbs of opinion:

assume* believe* consider* imagine* know*
We knew him to be trustworthy.

2 Verb + object + bare infinitive
make   let   help
They made him do it.
Note: *help* can also be followed by a *to*-infinitive.
3 Verb + object + *-ing* participle or bare
infinitive. Verbs of perception – *hear*, listen to,
notice*, see*, observe*, watch* – can take either of
these patterns.
The *-ing* form implies action in progress.
*He observed them **entering** the building.*
The bare infinitive implies completed action.
*They listened to her **speak**, then conferred amongst
themselves.*

4 Alternative *that* clause
The verbs marked with an asterisk (*) above can also
take a *that* clause. They are generally reporting or
thinking verbs.
They said that he was clever.
I knew that he would come.

Cleft sentences (p.125)

There are two types of cleft (divided) structure, which
behave in slightly different ways.

1 *It + be*
This type of cleft structure can emphasise the subject
or object of a sentence, or an adverbial, by making it
the complement of *It + be*. It cannot be used to
emphasise the verb.
Jane saw Peter yesterday.
→ *It was Jane who saw Peter yesterday.* (subject)
→ *It was Peter (whom) Jane saw yesterday.* (object)
→ *It was yesterday that Jane saw Peter.* (adverbial)

If there is a modal verb in the sentence, it goes before
the verb *be*.
*Jane **must** have seen Peter.*
→ *It **must** have been Jane who saw him.*
NOT *It was Jane who must have seen him.*

2 Wh-/All
1 In this type of cleft structure a relative clause
beginning with a *wh-* word, and a form of *be* are
added to focus attention on the part of the sentence
the speaker wants to emphasise.
*I particularly enjoy **going to the theatre**.*
→ ***What I particularly enjoy** IS going to the theatre.*
→ *Going to the theatre IS **what I particularly enjoy**.*
2 The verb can be emphasised by using *do* in the *wh-*
clause.
*We're **searching** for the best solution.*
*What we're **doing** IS searching for ...*

3 To emphasise the whole sentence, you can use
happen.
These days people are making more demands.
→ ***What's happening** these days IS that people ....*
4 *All* can sometimes be used to replace the *wh-* word.
I wanted my own car.
→ ***What** I wanted WAS my own car.*
→ ***All** I (ever) wanted WAS my own car.*
5 To focus on an adverbial or prepositional phrase
using a *wh-* structure, an expression such as *The
place where/The (time) when* etc. is usually added.
The conference is scheduled to take place in June.
→ ***The month when** the conference is scheduled to take
place IS June.*
6 To avoid starting a cleft with the *wh-* words
who/whom/whose or *why*, we can say:
The person who ...   The reason why ...

Note: State verbs (*be, have, know*, etc.) can't be used
with this structure (See Unit 13, p. 214).

UNIT 10

Adjectives (p. 136/137)

1 Position of adjectives
1 Adjectives that occur only **before** the noun include
the following types:
a) indicating a relationship, e.g.: *former, latter, elder,
younger, inner, outer*
b) limiting, e.g. *lone, only, single, main*
c) intensifying, e.g. *utter, mere, very, downright*
d) related to nouns, e.g. *coast-coastal, atom-atomic,
earth-earthen*
e) with a related, non *-ly* adverb, e.g. *south-
southern, indoor-indoors, inside-outside*
*We drove **south**.* (adv.)
*We live in the **southern** part of the city.* (adj.)
*Please go **outside**.* (adv.)
*Most houses used to have **outside** toilets.* (adj.)
2 Adjectives that occur only **after** the noun include:
a) some adjectives beginning with unstressed 'a' e.g.
above, alive, aware
b) health adjectives e.g. *fine, ill, well, unwell*
c) adjectives followed by a preposition or
infinitive, e.g. *glad (about)/pleased to ...*

Note: Compound adjectives usually have a hyphen
when they occur before the noun. Compare:
*I bought a **hand-fired** clay pot.*
*The clay pot I bought was **hand fired**.*

2 Order of adjectives

It is rare to find long strings of adjectives except in texts such as advertisements and publicity materials. The rules for order are as follows:

number + judgement + participle + dimensions + colour + origin + material + noun modifier
six charming hand-made miniature blue Peruvian clay fridge magnets

However, in general you need to remember these main points:

- Personal judgements (often gradable adjectives – see below) come before factual information (often ungradable adjectives) (*a nice iced drink*).
- Dimensions and colour come before origin and material (*a big brown clay pot*).
- Noun modifiers (nouns acting as adjectives) come immediately before the noun (*hand luggage*).

Gradable / ungradable adjectives (p.139)

1 **Gradable** adjectives have comparative and superlative forms. There are two types: '**weak**', e.g. *good, small, young, happy* and '**strong**' e.g. *wonderful, marvellous, terrifying, exhausted*.
Weak gradable adjectives are modified by adverbs such as *quite, fairly, moderately, exceedingly, very*.
Strong gradable adjectives can be modified only by adverbs such as *absolutely (wonderful/marvellous), totally (exhausted), completely (absorbing)*.

2 **Ungradable** (or **classifying**) adjectives don't normally have comparative or superlative forms. They include e.g. *perfect, boiling, French*. To modify them, we use the same adverbs as for **strong** gradable adjectives.
*It's **absolutely** boiling today.*
*The fit was **absolutely** perfect.*

3 The adverb *quite* can have two meanings, depending on the adjective being modified.
The film was quite good. (weak gradable adjective: *quite = moderately*)
The film was quite marvellous. (strong gradable adjective: *quite = very/extremely*)

Future forms (p.142/143)

No future event is absolutely certain to happen. The form which the speaker chooses will reflect:

- how likely the speaker feels the future event is
- the duration in time of the future event
- the relation of the event to another point in time.

The most important forms and uses are as follows.

1 Likelihood

1 *will*
  a) a fairly certain general prediction; the speaker is often an authority.
     *Share prices **will** rise.*
  b) a spontaneous decision made at the moment of speaking, therefore fairly certain to happen.
     I'll make you a cup of coffee.

2 *going to*
  a) expresses certainty, based on present evidence or speaker's opinion.
     *You're **going to** miss the train if you don't hurry.*
     *Look at those clouds - it's **going to** rain.*
  b) expresses intentions
     I'm going to look for a new job.

3 *be to*
  suggests that something is fixed and inevitable.
  *The office **is to be** closed for a week.*

4 *be likely*
  for an action that is fairly certain to take place.
  He's quite likely to accept the job.
  It's highly likely that they will win.

5 *could/may/might*: indicate possibility
  I might be late, I'm not sure.

2 Point and duration

1 **Future continuous**: for ongoing or repeated activities around a point in the future. Used with time expressions such as: *in (ten years') time, for a few more years yet, quite soon*
  We won't be living here in two years' time.

2 **Future perfect**: for an action finished before a point in the future. Used with time expressions such as: *by (2050), by the time, by this time (next week)*
  The continuous form emphasises the duration of the activity.
  *By this time next month, **we will have been living** here for 10 years.*

Tenses in time clauses (p.143)

In time clauses introduced by *when, after, as soon as, by the time, while, once,* a present or perfect tense form is used, not the future. This is because a future tense form is used in the main clause, and thus there is no need to repeat the future reference.
*He'll phone **as soon as** he **arrives** in London.*

The present perfect is used to show that the action in the subordinate clause is completed before the action in the main clause.
*Once they've **received** their instructions, they'll lose no time in getting started.*

UNIT 11

► For future forms with modals, see Unit 10 above.

UNIT 12

Indirect speech (p. 167/168)

1 Indirect statements
Verbs that can be used to introduce indirect statements include:

acknowledge agree answer argue
describe explain order recommend
refuse reply say suggest tell

For common patterns following these verbs, see
► Unit 9, page 211: **Verb patterns**
► Unit 6, page 208: **Subjunctives**

2 Indirect questions
1 Verbs that introduce indirect questions include:
ask enquire wonder
2 The following patterns can follow these verbs:
   a) verb + object
      They asked my name.
   b) verb + preposition + object
      They enquired about our families.
   c) verb + *wh*-clause
      He asked if I would go with him.
      She enquired whether there were any spare tickets.
      I wonder when the party starts.
      I can't imagine why he did that.

Note: Remember that in indirect questions there is no inversion in the question form.

3 Sequence of tenses
When the situation being reported no longer applies, tenses, pronouns and other expressions may all change to make this clear, especially in written narrative.
- **Tenses** shift backwards.
- **Pronouns** change from first and second person to third person.
- **Time expressions** change so that they no longer refer to the present.
- **Expressions of place** change so that they no longer refer to the immediate setting.
  'I'm hoping to stay here until tomorrow,' she said.
→ *She said she **was hoping** to stay **there** until **the following day**.*

These changes may not be necessary or appropriate if the situation has not changed.
*She says she's **hoping** to stay **here** until **tomorrow**.*
*He told me he **isn't** very happy at school.*

4 Paraphrasing
When we report what someone said, we often report the general meaning rather than the exact words.
'You must be tired. Come inside and have some food,' they said. → *They **invited** us to come in.*

Impersonal passive constructions (p.168)

After the following reporting or thinking verbs, a passive construction may be used:

allege believe expect fear
hope know report rumour
say think

The following patterns are possible:
a) It + passive verb + *that* + subject
   It is rumoured that he plans to resign.
b) Subject + passive verb + present/perfect infinitive
   He is rumoured to be planning to resign.
These structures are often used in newspapers to avoid naming the source of the information.

Note: When the active sentence uses *will* future, the second pattern is only possible with *expect*.
Compare:
Active: *People don't expect **him to come**.*
Passive: a) *It is not expected that he will come.*
            b) *He is not expected to come.*
Active: *People hope **that fines will discourage littering**.*
Passive: a) ***It is hoped** that fines will discourage littering.*
            b) **Fines are hoped to discourage littering.*

UNIT 13

Continuous and perfect aspect (p. 179/180)

1 **Simple verb forms** are used for single events, states and habits. **Continuous verb forms** describe activities in progress. They suggest that the activity is temporary, and may not be complete. Compare:
   I live with my parents.
   I'm living with my parents. (temporary period only)
2 **Perfect verb forms** describe events in relation to a later event or point in time.
   I have lived here for five years. (up to the present)
   By the time I'm 26 I will have finished my studies. (to refer to the point in time when something has been completed)

The use of the continuous form focuses attention on the duration of the activity.

What have you been doing all this time?

It may also suggest the activity is incomplete.

I've been writing my report. (incomplete)

I've written my report. (implies a completed action)

3 **Dynamic (event) verbs** refer to activities with a definite beginning and end. They may be used in the simple or continuous form and may refer to:

momentary acts: *kick, jump, knock*

activities: *walk, study, work, eat, drive*

processes: *grow, change, develop, enlarge*

4 **State, or stative, verbs** refer to activities and situations that may not have a definite beginning or end. They are not usually used in the continuous form. They include:

perception: *hear, see, feel, smell, taste, notice*

mental states and feelings: *love, hate, hope, imagine, remember, forget, understand, want, wish, prefer, seem, appear*

relationships and states of being: *have, own, possess, belong to, consist of, cost, depend on, require*

5 Some state verbs are used in the continuous form:

a) to focus on the temporary aspect of the action or event. Compare:

He's a very patient person.

You're being very patient, thank you.

b) with a change of meaning, e.g.:

verb	stative meaning	dynamic meaning
appear	seem	act in a play
have	own	do something (*have a bath/party*)
imagine	have a mental picture	have a wrong idea about sth.
see	with one's eyes	meet, go out with
taste	have a taste	try sth. to see what it tastes like
think	have an opinion	be considering, thinking about sth.

*He **appeared** (to be) quite friendly.*

*She's **appearing** in a play on Broadway.*

*Close your eyes and **imagine** a tropical island.*

*She doesn't love him, he's just **imagining** it.*

Writing reference

Useful linking expressions

The lists below provide a selection of linking expressions that you will find useful in your writing.

1 **Time sequence**

- *When/As soon as/The moment* they arrived, the meeting began.
- *On hearing* the news, we immediately phoned to congratulate them.
- *From early childhood/an early age*, she showed great aptitude for music.
- *Throughout his adult life*, he has dedicated himself to helping others.
- *Up to that time*, she had never even been abroad.

2 **Listing**

- *First of all*, it must be stated that ...
- *Secondly*, it could be argued that ...
- *Last but not least*, it must be remembered that ...
- *Finally*, it is important to ...

3 **Adding information/emphasising a point**

- He left early – and *on top of that/to cap it all*, he didn't pay for his share of the meal. (*informal*)
- She didn't really want to see the film, and *besides/anyway/anyhow* she was too tired to go to the cinema now. (*informal*)
- The rent is reasonable and *moreover/furthermore/in addition* the location is perfect.
- *Not only* has he achieved a great deal, *but* he has *also* set an example for a generation.
- They want new regulations in the hostel; *above all*, they want to restrict the noise level in the evenings.
- These new medicines are perfectly safe. *Indeed*, they can be given to young children.

4 **Giving examples**

- Many things contributed to her success, *for instance/for example/such as* hard work, good fortune and the support of her friends.
- *To illustrate this point*, ...
- *Let's take the example of* ...

5 Explaining/reformulating

- Some cars are more environmentally friendly than others. *That is to say/In other words*, they cause less pollution.
- He read the newspaper to confirm what he knew already, *that is/namely* that his team had lost.
- You should treat your colleagues as friends, or, *better still/rather*, as close friends if you want to create a good working atmosphere.

6 Contrast

- She was very kind. *By/In contrast,* he seemed very callous.
- Some people learn languages easily. *Conversely,* others find it very difficult.
- It wasn't a good thing; *on the contrary*, it was a huge mistake.
- They decided not to take the car. *Instead*, they caught the next train.
- *On the one hand* I enjoyed their company, but *on the other hand* their strange lifestyle disturbed me.

7 Concession

- *Although/Even though* he was feeling unwell, he attended the meeting.
- *Despite* feeling unwell, he attended the meeting.
- He felt unwell; *however/nevertheless/nonetheless*, he attended the meeting.
- He was feeling unwell *but* he attended the meeting *all the same/even so. (informal)*
- My friends left the cinema before the end of the film *whilst/whereas/while* I stayed until it had finished.
- *No matter how many/However many* times I listen to that music, it still moves me to tears.
- *Whoever* comes, it will be a valuable opportunity to discuss the problem.

8 Giving opinions

- *In my opinion/view*, he is one of the most impressive writers of our generation.
- *It seems to me that* one of the biggest problems facing us today is ...
- *(Personally,)I feel that* more needs to be done to encourage young people to take responsibility for the environment.
- *I can honestly say* that ...

9 Commenting/expressing own attitude (sentence adverbials)

- *Surely* it must be obvious to anyone that this plan is doomed to failure.
- *Clearly*, more needs to be done to persuade people to use public transport.

- *Not surprisingly*, there has been considerable opposition to this plan.
- *Irritatingly/Annoyingly*, the authorities have decided to cut the funds available for the project.

10 Giving reasons

- *Seeing that/As* it was getting late, they decided to return home.
- Trains are being delayed *owing to/due to/because of* the inclement weather.
- They liked his idea, *in so far as/to the extent that* it made money for the company.

11 Purpose

- *In order for* her *to* live a comfortable life, she had to find a well-paid job.
- She spoke quietly *in order not to/so as not to* wake the sleeping child.

12 Results/consequences

- A lot of people voted for his entry and *thus/as a consequence/therefore/as a result/accordingly* he was awarded the prize.
- He became a citizen in 1999, *thereby* gaining the right to vote.
- Many areas have been modernised *in such a way as to* make the city more attractive to tourists.

13 Comparisons

- It's *a good deal/a great deal/very much* easier to watch sport than to take part.
- She looked *as if/as though* she'd seen a ghost.
- He was *nowhere near/nothing like as* good at tennis *as* (he was at) basketball.
- *The more* cities expand, *the less* access we have to the countryside.

14 Summing up

- Although the day was not a complete success, *all in all* it went as well as could be expected.
- *To sum up/In short,* it was a highly successful visit.
- *Overall*, what I most admire is their determination to succeed.
- *In conclusion/Finally/To conclude*, it seems clear that tourism is having an adverse effect on the area.
- The team played well, but *at the end of the day* they just weren't good enough to win. *(informal)*

Checklist for editing

- **Understanding the question**
  *Your composition will be assessed on relevance to the task set. You must answer the **exact** question set.*

  Have you identified the key words in the question and answered **all** parts?

- **Organisation of the material**
  Your composition will be assessed on organisation as a whole and in terms of individual paragraphs.

1 Does your introduction make it clear what ideas your composition will develop?
  ► *In **formal letters**, you should state your reason for writing in the first paragraph.*
  ► *In **arguments** and **reports**, your introduction should state the main topic areas you will be covering – this is the 'plan of development'.*
  ► *In **narratives** and **articles**, your introduction should capture the reader's interest, e.g. by referring to a specific incident.*

2 Have you started a new paragraph for each new topic (not each new point)?
  ► *Each paragraph should have **one** main idea only. The main idea should be stated in a sentence.*

3 Do the topics in your supporting paragraphs match the opening statement or plan of development in your introduction?
  ► *Make sure you haven't strayed from your main theme and included any unrelated points.*

4 Does each paragraph contain plenty of supporting evidence for the main idea?
  You should include enough details or examples to convince the reader of your main point, or create a picture in his/her mind.

5 Is your conclusion prepared for in your composition?
  ► *In an **argument**, your conclusion should summarise your answer to the question and state your own opinion or conclusion.*
  ► *In a **report**, your conclusion should summarise the points made or make final recommendations.*
  ► *In a **narrative**, your conclusion should bring the story to an interesting or dramatic end.*
  ► *You should round off an **article** with, for example, an interesting point of detail about the topic, a quotation from a person interviewed in the article, or a rhetorical question to the reader that echoes the introduction.*

6 Have you linked your paragraphs so they follow on from each other clearly?
  ► *Your supporting paragraphs should follow a sensible, logical sequence and you should use a transitional sentence to help link one paragraph to the next. This can come at the end of one paragraph or the beginning of the next.*

7 Have you used a clear method of development to organise the supporting details within each paragraph?
  ► *Common methods of development are:*
  chronological or time order (see Unit 1, p. 18)
  flashback: to add interest to narratives (see Unit 8, p. 116)
  emphatic order: listing points from the least important to the most important, or 'saving the best till last' (see Unit 7, model 1, p. 103)
  contrast/concession: making a point followed by an opposite point (see Unit 7, model 2, p. 104)

8 Have you used appropriate linking words to help link the sentences within each paragraph?
  ► *Linking words signal the method of organisation you have chosen, and help the reader follow the direction of your thought – but don't over-use them.*

- **Range and appropriacy of language**

9 Have you used a style and register appropriate to the task?
  ► *Check that you haven't used language that is too formal or too informal for the task, and that you have been consistent. For example, you shouldn't use features of informal language in a formal letter. (See Register table, Unit 4, page 57.)*

10 Have you used a variety of structures and vocabulary?
  ► *Try to vary the way you start your sentences by using participle clauses, inversion etc.*

- **Accuracy**

11 Have you made any basic mistakes in grammar, spelling and punctuation?
  ► *Basic mistakes such as 'he don't' can create a very bad impression.*

- **Overall impression**

12 Is the composition interesting to read?
  ► *You will have a better chance if the examiner enjoys reading your work!*

Communication activities

Unit 1, Grammar Ex. 3 (p. 10)

Student A: Annette's story.

My husband and I were working as cook and waiter at a hotel in the south of England, and living with our six-month-old baby in a cottage nearby. For once we (1) .... (manage) to get an evening off together, and one of the hotel staff had volunteered to babysit for us so that we could go out to the cinema together.

We caught the bus to the nearest town, about ten kilometres away, but we (2) .... (not watch) the film for more than a few minutes before I (3) .... (start) to feel terribly uneasy. I could distinctly smell burning. I told my husband, but he couldn't smell anything and told me I (4) .... (imagine) things. But the smell persisted, and eventually I told him I was leaving. He (5) .... (follow) me reluctantly, muttering something under his breath.

As we made the journey home on the bus I prayed for it to go faster. At each stop I almost died. At last we (6) .... (rush) down the lane leading to the cottage. The smell of burning was now very definite to me, though my husband still couldn't smell anything. We reached the door and burst in. As we did, dense smoke (7) .... (pour) out and a chair by the fire burst into flames. I rushed through to the bedroom and got the baby, while my husband dragged out the unconscious babysitter. She (8) .... (smoke) and had fallen asleep and (9) .... (drop) her lighted cigarette onto the chair. We later worked out that it must have happened just as I first (10) .... (smell) smoke in the cinema.

Unit 2, Vocabulary Ex. 2 (p. 27)

Extract from *Longman Dictionary of Contemporary English*

---

mind¹ /maɪnd/ *n*

① BRAIN/THINKING PROCESS	⑧ OPINION
② DECIDE	⑨ STRONG/ DETERMINED
② THINKING ABOUT STH	⑩ ATTENTION
③ WORRY/STOP WORRYING	⑪ IMAGINE
④ CRAZY/MENTALLY ILL	⑫ INTEND/WANT
⑤ FORGET	⑬ INTELLIGENCE
⑥ REMEMBER	⑭ OTHER MEANINGS

① BRAIN/THINKING PROCESS
1 [C,U] the part of a person, usually considered to be their brain, that they use to think and imagine things: *I have a picture of him in my mind – tall, blond and handsome.* | *I don't know what's going on in her mind.*
2 get sb/sth out of your mind to stop yourself thinking about someone or something: *I just can't seem to get her out of my mind.*
3 go over sth/turn sth over in your mind to keep thinking about something because you are trying to understand it or solve a problem: *I kept turning the conversation over in my mind.*

② DECIDE
4 make up your mind a) to decide which of two or more choices you want, especially after thinking for a long time: *I just couldn't make up my mind, so in the end I bought both.* | *I wish you'd make your mind up whether you're coming or not.* **b)** to become very determined to do something, so that you will not change your decision: *I'm sorry but my mind's made up – I'm leaving.* | **make up your mind to do sth** *He's made his mind up to resign, and that's final.* | **make up your mind that** *They made up their mind that they would buy a new house once Larry changed jobs.*
5 change your mind to change your opinion or decision about something: *I've changed my mind – I'll have a beer instead.* | [+ **about**] *Try and get her to change her mind about coming with us.*
6 be in two minds about *informal* to be unable to make a decision about something: *We're in two minds about whether to sell the house or not.*
7 set your mind on (doing) sth to decide that you want to do something very much: *Tom had set his mind on a trip to the Seychelles.*

③ THINKING ABOUT STH
8 be the last thing on sb's mind to be the thing that someone is least likely to be thinking about: *One thing was for sure, marriage was the last thing on Nick's mind.*
9 come/spring to mind [not in progressive] if something comes to mind or springs to mind you suddenly think of it: *We needed someone to look after the kids, and your name sprang to mind.*
10 cross/enter your mind (that) [not in progressive] if something crosses or enters your mind, you have a particular thought or idea, especially for a short time: *It never crossed my mind that Lisa might be lying.*
11 turn your mind to to begin to think about a subject after you have been thinking about something else: *Let's now turn our minds to tomorrow's meeting.*

Unit 5, Grammar check Ex. 3 (p. 71)

Agatha Christie was found nine days after her disappearance. She had been staying in a hotel in the town of Harrogate, in the North of England. She claimed to have lost her memory: 'For 24 hours I wandered in a dream and then found myself in Harrogate as a well-contented and perfectly happy woman who believed she had just come from South Africa.' The truth was only discovered half a century later, when secret documents were at last made available. Agatha Christie in fact staged her own disappearance, not as a publicity stunt, as many believed, but because she wanted to ruin a weekend that her husband was planning to spend with his mistress. She and her husband stuck to the story that a blow to her head had resulted in amnesia to avoid public disgrace, but it was the end of their marriage. However, the affair did make Christie the most famous crime writer in Britain.

Unit 6, Listening Ex. 2 (p. 79)

Extract 1

In the following extract from the tapescript, single underlining relates to the wrong answers (distractors) and double underlining indicates the section which gives the correct answer. Read Question 1 below and circle the words which have been changed.

Interviewer: So what was it like when you arrived?
Woman: Oh, for example, the airport, I remember arriving at the airport and in those days it seemed total chaos, the airport, and you went out and there you were right in the middle of the city, in this hot, hot weather ... And the city was a mixture of ... there were very old, narrow streets, with lots of sharp corners and high old buildings on either side – too narrow for cars at all, except somehow the cars managed to edge their way through. And then there would be children playing and things like cats and goats along the streets as well, even whole herds of cattle occasionally, and there was the odd new block of flats, up to six stories or so, but no big office blocks or things like international hotels.

1 When the speaker first arrived in Jeddah, there were no
   A tall buildings.
   B cars in the city centre.
   C modern buildings.
   D large commercial buildings.

Extract 2

Use underlining in the same way to highlight the distractors and the correct answer in the following extract from the tapescript. Match the options A–D to each section you have underlined and decide exactly why each of the distractors is wrong.

Interviewer: And it's a port, isn't it – did you feel you were living by the sea?
Woman: Well it was certainly a working port, but you weren't at all conscious of the sea, I mean you could see it from some places but not really get to it unless you actually went right out of the city and the road which led from the city boundary up north along the coast was really dangerous – it had a very bad surface and there were lots of accidents on it ...

2 The city
   A had an industrial area near the sea.
   B didn't have easy access to the sea.
   C was built to the north of the port.
   D had roads which were very unsafe.

Interviewer: And so how did things change? Did the roads change?
Woman: Oh everything was changing ... for a time it seemed as if all the history was going to be lost, because in the first few years I was there, a lot of the old houses, the old town, was pulled down, but then that stopped and a really ambitious programme of restoration was started up, and the old houses were tidied up and the ... things like the latticed wooden windows, – they were traditional in Arabic building – they were all restored and the streets were pedestrianised so you could walk around there without being mown down by traffic. But this wasn't done to attract tourists ... tourism doesn't exist at all. It was done for the people who live there, and out of civic pride.

3 According to the speaker, a positive side to the changes was that
   A old houses were pulled down.
   B old houses were restored.
   C buildings had traditional features.
   D there were no tourists.

Unit 9, Exam Focus Ex. 3 (p. 124)

Read the following extracts from the tapescript and the questions. In which questions do you:

a) have to infer someone's feelings?

b) hear the word you need to use repeated several times?

c) have to choose the correct adjective from two with similar meanings?

d) relate a pronoun to a person who has already been mentioned?

e) change the form of the word used in the original passage?

A few months after the accident I had an idea for a short film about a quadriplegic who lives in a dream. During the day, lying in his hospital bed, he can't move. But at night he dreams that he's whole again. This is someone who had been a life-long sailor, and he had a beautiful gaff-rigged sloop. Not like my boat, the *Sea Angel,* which was modern and made of fiberglass. In his dream he sails down the path of a full moon – the kind of romantic night sailing anyone can imagine.

In Reeve's film, a paralysed man [_____ 1] that he can go sailing.

But in the morning, he's back in his bed and everything is frozen again. The dream is very vivid. At first it's just a dream, and he recognises it as such. But one night he finds himself getting out of bed and walking down the corridor and out the door and then into the boat, which, magically, is anchored not far away. Soon these voyages become so real to him that when he wakes up in his bed, his hair is wet.

Gradually, his night-time sailing trips come to seem [_____ 2] to him.

And the nurse comes in and says, 'Oh, I'm sorry. I didn't dry your hair enough last night when I gave you a shampoo. You slept with wet hair.' He says nothing, but he's thinking that his hair is wet from the spray when he was out on the water. One time he comes back still wearing his foul-weather gear, and he has to hide it in the hospital room closet.

In the mornings, the nurse thinks [_____ 3] is her fault.

Now his wife and children have been very distressed because, since he became paralysed, he has not been able to pull out of a very serious depression. His children are afraid of him because he is not himself and they don't know how to be with him. But as he continues to go sailing in his dreams, his mood begins to improve. His wife notices the change. He thinks that he may be losing his mind, but his dreams are making their life together happier.

His wife notices that he is becoming less [_____ 4]

He sails in Tenants Harbor, or a similarly idyllic spot like that in Maine, and there's an older man there, who always turns on the light in his cabin down by the water when our man is sailing. He doesn't sleep very well, and he never misses a chance to see the boat sailing so beautifully in the moonlight.

[_____ 5] watches him sailing at night.

Unit 11, Exam Focus Ex. 3 (p. 158)

Student A

(a) Without the support of the technicians, we would never have managed to do it.
Had ....

(b) It wasn't easy for Susie to make the arrangements without a telephone.
Susie had ....

(c) A more careful analysis of the problems would have saved a lot of work.
If the ....

(d) They were determined to get to the top of the mountain.
They resolved that nothing ....

(e) Their house will take them three years to renovate.
In three ....

(f) She couldn't possibly have done it on her own.
It's absolutely ....

(g) They considered it was impossible to sink the *Titanic*.
It ....

(h) You should lose no time in getting this checked.
You should get ....

Unit 13, Grammar check Ex. 5 (p. 180)

Student A

1 The letter you wrote is the first letter of your husband's/wife's name. Decide how and when you met. Why isn't your husband/wife with you today?

2 The number you chose tells you how many children you have in the year 2012. Decide on their names and ages. What are they all doing at present?

3 Country A is a place you've been visiting regularly over the past few years. Why? You'll be going to country B soon. Why?

4 If you circled **P**, you've been preparing for something recently. What have you been preparing for and why?

If you circled **E**, you had a narrow escape from a dangerous situation recently. What were you doing and what happened?

If you circled **M**, you moved to a new house recently. Where were you living before that and why did you move?

Now roleplay the conversation with your partner. Remember that this is a social occasion and that at the same time as giving information about yourself, you should find out what your partner has been doing. At the end, decide which of you has been having the best time.

Unit 13, Exam Focus (p. 184–186)

Part 1 Ex. 3

Choose one of the photos and take turns to talk about your photo for a couple of minutes.

Part 2 Ex. 4: Examiner's questions

1 Where do you think this passage is taken from?
2 What is the main point the passage is making?
3 How does it link to the theme of the picture(s) you looked at?
4 How far do you agree with the opinion expressed in the passage?

1.

2.

Part 3 Ex. 2 (Task 1): Examiner's questions
(These questions are to help your partner keep talking. You don't need to ask all of them, and you can ask them in any order.)

• How can you measure success? What are your criteria?
• What kind of people do you think each attitude represents?
• What type of responsibility does being successful bring?
• What problems can success bring?
• What advantages can success bring?
• Which attitude do you agree with?
• How do you personally define 'being successful'?

Unit 13, Exam Focus (p. 186)

Part 3 Ex. 2 (Task 2): Examiner's questions
(These questions are to help your partner keep talking.
You don't need to ask all of them, and you can ask them in
any order.)

- Why did you choose the four qualities?
- Why did you put them in that order?
- What kind of people do you think are often successful?
- Do you think that luck is at all important in achieving success?
- What price do you think successful people might pay in their private lives?

Unit 4, Writing Ex. 3 (p. 60)

Student B

UNITED COLORS
OF BENETTON.

Unit 1, Grammar Ex. 3 (p. 10)

Student B: Judi's story

It was in May 1989, about two weeks before the end of the school year. My son Corey, along with many of his classmates, had decided to skip school that day to have a party at the country home of a friend who (1) .... (graduate) the previous year. Corey had borrowed a motorbike from his older brother for the day. I (2) .... (know) nothing about any of this and just assumed that he was at school as usual.

Around noon as I (3) .... (stand) in my kitchen looking out of the window, I (4) .... (suddenly fill) with intense fear and immediately thought of Corey. I (5) .... (tell) myself that this was ridiculous because I knew Corey was in school and was just fine. But the feeling grew stronger and I started shaking and crying uncontrollably – all I could do was to think of Corey and to pray that he was alright. When I was able to calm myself I went and sat on the sofa, trying to understand what (6) .... (happen) to me.

Ten minutes later the telephone rang. It was Corey's best friend.

'Mrs Gradey, it's about Corey. He (7)........................ (involve) in an accident. You mustn't worry, he's OK. But he's been taken to hospital.'

I rushed to the hospital and found Corey had miraculously escaped with only a few scratches. Later I found that as he (8) .... (go) round a curve in the highway, he (9) .... (lose) control of the motorbike and been thrown off into a small ditch at the side of the road. He had skidded along the ditch on his stomach, passing directly between a cement post and a pile of rocks. If he had gone a couple of inches in either direction, he would have been killed.

As far as I can work out, I (10) .... (have) my experience just as Corey was involved in the accident.

Unit 4, Writing Ex. 2 (p. 60)

British Nuclear Fuels plc

Adjudication:

1. Complaint not upheld.

The advertisers said they had decommissioned the sites of old nuclear reactors and made this land available for general commercial use. [...] The Nuclear Installations Inspectorate had declared there was no longer any danger from ionising radiation on a site they had decommissioned. They also said they had the expertise to transform former commercial sites into reusable land, and cited an example of an old nuclear site that would be re-used in Colorado, USA. The ASA considered that, because of the context of the advertisement – it was addressed to the nuclear industry in the trade press – it was unlikely to mislead.

2. Complaint upheld.

The advertisers believed the claim was justified because they were the most experienced company in the industry. They said they had perfected their knowledge and expertise to solve customers' waste problems in ways that complied with international regulations and were unsurpassed in the industry. They believed that in the context of a trade magazine most readers would understand what they meant by the claim. The ASA was satisfied that the advertisers dealt with waste to within UK standards but was concerned that the readers would interpret the claim to mean the advertisers had advanced their methods significantly beyond those standards. The Authority asked the advertisers not to repeat the claim.

Unit 11, Exam Focus Ex. 3 (p. 158)

Student B

(a) Had we not had the support of the technicians, we would never have managed to do it.
Without ....

(b) Susie had trouble making the arrangements without a telephone.
It wasn't ....

(c) If the problems had been analysed more carefully, a lot of work would have been saved.
A more ....

(d) They resolved that nothing would stop them from getting to the top of the mountain.
They were determined ....

(e) In three years' time they will have renovated their house.
Their house ....

(f) It's absolutely impossible for her to have done it on her own.
She ....

(g) It was considered impossible to sink the Titanic.
They

....

(h) You should get this checked straightaway.
You should lose ....

Unit 13, Grammar check Ex. 5 (p. 180)

Student B

1 The letter you wrote is the first letter of your present job. (For example, if you wrote X, you could say that you install X-ray equipment in hospitals.)

2 The number you wrote tells you how many years you've been working in your present job. Decide what you did before this.

3 You have been visiting country A regularly on business. What have you been doing there? You'll be going to country B soon. Why?

4 If you circled **P**, you have recently been promoted at work. What are you doing now?

If you circled **E**, you will be earning a lot of money soon, as you've just heard you've got a new job. Tell your partner what you'll be doing.

If you circled **M**, you got married three years ago to someone from a different country. Tell your partner how you met him/her.

Now roleplay the conversation with your partner. Remember that this is a social occasion and that at the same time as giving information about yourself you should find out what your partner has been doing. At the end, decide which of you has been having the best time.

Pearson Education Limited
Edinburgh Gate
Harlow
Essex CM20 2JE
England
and Associated Companies throughout the world.

www.longman-elt.com

© Pearson Education Limited 2000

Set in 10/12.75 Gill sans and 10/12.75 Admark
Printed in Spain by Graficas Estella
First published 2000
Second Impression 2001
ISBN 0 582 32573 0

The authors would like to thank the following people: Nigel, Neil,
Ralph, Ken and Marjorie for their patience and support; the staff and
students of the Bell Language School, Saffron Walden; all the Longman
team, our editors (Andrew Jurascheck and Frances Cook) and, in
particular, Heather Jones (Senior Exams Publisher) for her exceptional
guidance and help.

The authors and publisher wish to express thanks and appreciation to all
the teachers who helped in the development of the course, in particular
Christine Barton, Frederika Beet, Raphaelle Collins, Patrick Dare, Bob
Davis, Elizabeth Heliotis, Sarah Hellawell, Philip Kerr, Richard Mann,
Nick Shaw, Elsa Silivestra, Mark Skipper, Tasia Vasilatou, Georgia
Zographou.

Special thanks are due to Louise Hashemi for writing the Unit reviews
and progress checks.

We are grateful to the following for permission to reproduce copyright
material:

Andre Deutsch for an extract from HOW LONG IS THE COURSE by
Roger Black; The Fourth Estate for an extract from HARE BRAIN,
TORTOISE MIND by Guy Claxton. Copyright © 1997 Guy Claxton;
Friends of the Earth for an extract from the article 'Take Action' by Tony
Juniper in EARTHMATTERS Winter 98; the author Peter Gillman for
an extract from 'Mount Everest' in DAILY TELEGRAPH; Gruner &
Jahr Ltd for an extract from the article 'Windsurfing the Edge' by Roger
Turner in FOCUS MAGAZINE Sep 95; Guardian News Service
Limited for adapted extracts from the articles 'One thousand days' by
Paul Brown and Robin Pellen in THE GUARDIAN, 'Peer Pressure' by
Christopher Reed in THE GUARDIAN 4.3.97, 'Countdown to the New
Millenium' by Ted Wragg in GUARDIAN EDUCATION 8.3.97, 'Big
Sell Tiny Targets' by Sarah Boseley in THE GUARDIAN 25.6.97,
'Plight of the Outsider' by Ann Robinson in THE GUARDIAN 2.12.97
and 'America's Big Bird is Back' by Martin Kettle in THE GUARDIAN
7.5.98; extracts from the articles 'Biodiversity: tearing up the map...' by
Tim Radford in THE GUARDIAN 11.8.98 and 'Cod is Dead' by Bill
McKibben in THE OBSERVER 14.6.98; HarperCollins Publishers for
an extract from THE GOD OF SMALL THINGS by Arundhati Roy;
HHL Publishing for an extract from the article 'Future Shock' by Simon
Reeve in HOTLINE MAGAZINE Autumn/Winter 1998; Hutchinson &
Co for an extract from THE HUNGRY SPIRIT by Charles Handy;
Impact Books for an extract from THE ISLANDS IN BETWEEN by
Annabel Sutton, Impact Books, 1989; Independent Newspapers (UK)
Ltd for an adapted extract from the article 'Will our Children Read
Books?' by Mark Lawson in THE INDEPENDENT ON SUNDAY
9.4.95. an extract from the article 'A winning formula' by
Waddington/Coe THE INDEPENDENT 10.10.98; Sir Alexander Macara
Chairman BMA, 1993-98 for an extract from the article 'Spare-part
surgery success' from TOMORROW'S WORLD MAGAZINE April
1998; Macmillan General Books for an adapted extract from AN
ANTHROPOLOGIST ON MARS by Oliver Sacks published by Picador
1995 and the short story 'Machette' in collection THE BAY OF
CONTENTED MEN by Robert Drewe, pub. Pan/Picador 1989; The
McGraw-Hill Companies for an adapted extract from SOCIAL
PSYCHOLOGY by Wiggins, Wiggins & Vander Zanden 1994; New
Scientist for an extract from the article 'All God's Children got ...' by
Margaret Wertheim in NEW SCIENTIST 20.12.97; News International
Syndication for adapted extracts from the article 'Maybe I'm Amazed/A
Hard Day's Nightie' by Lesley White in SUNDAY TIMES MAGAZINE
8.3.98 © Times Newspapers Ltd, extracts from the articles 'Robonurse
takes care of elderly' by Sean Hargrave in THE SUNDAY TIMES 4.1.98
and 'Trip of a Lifetime' in THE TIMES MAGAZINE 22.8.98 © Times

Newspapers Ltd 1998; Orbit Magazine for an extract from the article
'Issues for the 90s vol 33' edited by Craig Donnellen in ORBIT
March/April 1996; Orion Publishing Group Ltd for an adapted extract
from THE DEATH OF DISTANCE by Frances Cairncross published by
Orion Business Books, an extract from REMAKING EDEN -
CLONING AND BEYOND by Lee M Silver published by Weidenfelf &
Nicolson London 1998; Oxfam Activities Ltd for extracts from OXFAM
CATAGLOGUE Spring/Summer 99; Pan Macmillan Ltd for an extract
from THE GREENWAY by Jane Adams published by Pan Books 1995;
Pearson Education for an adapted extract from SOCIOLOGY IN
FOCUS - CRIME by Ian Marsh, © Longman Group Ltd 1986; Random
House Inc for text and recorded extracts from STILL ME by
Christopher Reeve. Copyright © 1998 by Cambria Productions, Inc; The
Random House Group Ltd for extracts from IN THE MIND OF THE
MACHINE by Kevin Warwick published by Arrow, THIS GAME OF
GHOSTS by Joe Simpson published by Jonathan Cape, STILL ME by
Christopher Reeve published by Century and GOODNESS by Tim Parks
published by William Heinemann; Robinson Publishing for extracts
abridged from MOTHER LOVE by Cassandra Eason; Solo Syndication
for an adapted extract from 'Back for the future' by Danusia Hutson in
EVENING STANDARD 5.10.98, an extract from the article 'Taking a
Liberty with Our Cities' by Rowan Moore in EVENING STANDARD
23.2.99; Taylor & Francis for an extract from THE BRAIN BOOK by
Peter Russell published by Routledge 1979; UK Confederation of
Futebol de Salao on behalf of Simon Clifford for information from
articles in INDEPENDENT ON SUNDAY and FOUR FOUR TWO;
Understanding Global Issues Ltd for an extract from the article 'The
Curitiba Experience/Healthy Cities' in UNDERSTANDING GLOBAL
ISSUES 96/4; Virgin Publishing for extracts adapted from 'Film Review
1992/3, 95/6 and 93/4' by F Maurice Speed and James Cameron-Wilson;
the author Sara Wheeler for an extract from the article 'Welcome to the
World's Loneliest Tourist Spot' in WATERSTONE'S QUARTERLY
GUIDE Summer/Autumn 1997 © Sara Wheeler.

We have been unable to trace the copyright holders of THE ANATOMY
OF RELATIONSHIPS by Michael Argyle and Monika Henderson, the
articles 'Robber stitched up by jeans' by Trent Edwards and 'Frontiers' by
Richard Noble and THE JOY LUCK CLUB by Amy Tan and would
appreciate any information which would enable us to do so.

We are grateful to the following for permission to use copyright
photographs:

Advertising Standards Authority for 59; AllSport for 106 (L; C; R), 111,
114, 117, 178 (TR), 182, 183 (BL), 34 (TL), (TR), 35 (TL); Ann Ronan
Collection for 142; Brian & Cherry Alexander for 164; Britstock-IFA
for 54 (R); Bubbles for132; CFCL for 108; Gamma Presse Paris for 39,
46, 47(R), 61, 78 (BR); Green Peace for (BR); Greg Evans for 83;
Hulton Getty for 162(L), 31; Image Bank for 47 (C), 63, 78 (CR), 133
(BL), 183 (TL), 176 (BR), 49; Image Select for 26, 90 (R), 183 (C), 176
(T); Impact for 58; Independent On Sunday for 166; John Walmsley: 22
(BR), 24, (T, CR & CL), 69, 145; Kobal collection for 150 (CL);
London features for 6 (all), 185 (T); Mary Evans for 84 (R); Pearson
Education/Gareth Boden for 11, 34(B), 53, 54 (L), 128, 161, 163, 191;
Photofusion: 47 (L), 68 (B), Panos for 112; Pictor for 24 (B), 78 (TR),
101 (all), 176 (C); Redferns for 190 (TR); Rex for 9, 17, 64, 68 (T),
126, 124 (TR), 124 (CR), 138 (R), 178 (C), 190 (CL), 191, 162(R),
133(TR), 221(TR), 183(TR); Ronald Grant Archive: 42 (all), 124 (CL),
150 (L), (CR), (R), 150/151 (C), 151 (R);Science Photo Library for 92
(BR), 148 (CL& CT); Spectrum Colour Library for 48 (TR, CR, BR &
CL), 78 (CL), 97 (BR), 133 (BC), 221(BR); Still Pictures for 22 (BL),
60, 74 (L), 90 (R) ,92 (L), (CT), (CB) & (TR), 97 (T), 129, 133(TL),
(CR) 105, 35(TR); Stock Market for 176 (BL), (TR); Sunday Times for
152; Tony Stone Worldwide for 19, 40, 72, 78 (C&L), 84 (L), 95, 102,
107, 138 (L),148 (L, CB, CR, TR & R), 178 (TL), 185 (B), 189, 190
(BR & CR), 183 (BR), 176(TL)

The Publisher wishes to express their special appreciation to the
following:

Berkshire Constabulary and County Archives for 70/71; Cadogan
Publishing for 48, 163; Coca cola for 48; Columbia Tri-Star Pictures for
150/151 (C); Flamingo Press for 34 (B); Gucci for 48; John Johnson
(Author's Agent) Ltd for 10; Macdonalds for 48; Microsoft Corporation
for 48; Modus for Benetton: 222; National Centre For popular Music
Sheffield for 174; Nescafe for 48; New English Library/Hodder &
Stoughton for 11; Oxfam for 136/137, (all) 134/135, 133 (BR); Puma
for 48; Sony Corporation for 48; United Kingdom Scouts Association
for 188; Warner Brothers for 6

Photo Research By: Nathan Grainger & Jo Roberts /Image Select
International; London

Illustrated by Graham Cox, Clare Deaville, Sarah Gibb,
Alex Green, Stephanie Hawken (The Organisation), Pantelios Palios,
Katherine Walker.

Project managed by Andrew Juraschek